Praise for previous editions:

"*The State of the World Atlas* is something else – an occasion of wit and an act of subversion...These are the bad dreams of the modern world, given color and shape and submitted to a grid that can be grasped instantaneously."
*New York Times*

"Unique and uniquely beautiful...a discerning eye for data and a flair for the most sophisticated techniques of stylized graphic design; the atlas succeeds in displaying the geopolitical subtleties of global affairs in a series of dazzling color plates...tells us more about the world today than a dozen statistical abstracts or scholarly tomes."
*Los Angeles Times*

"Coupled with an unusual non-distorting map projection and a series of brilliant cartographic devices, this gives a positively dazzling set of maps. It deserves to be widely used."
*New Society*

"A super book that will not only sit on your shelf begging to be used, but will also be a good read. To call this book an atlas is like calling Calvados, applejack – it may be roughly accurate but it conveys nothing of the richness and flavour of the thing. Its inventive brilliance deserves enormous rewards."
*New Scientist*

"A striking new approach to cartography...no-one wishing to keep a grip on the reality of the world should be without these books."
*International Herald Tribune*

"Outspoken cataloguing of global oppressions and inequities, painstakingly sourced."
*Independent on Sunday*

"Packed with fascinating facts and figures on everything from the international drugs industry to climate change."
*Evening Standard*

"A political reference book which manages to translate hard, boring statistics into often shocking visual statements... required reading."
*NME*

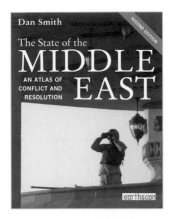

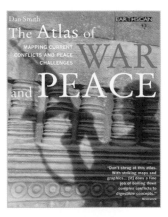

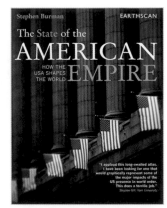

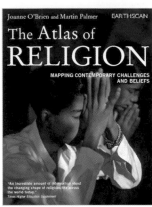

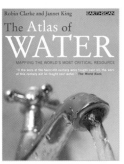

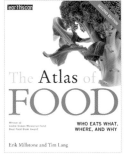

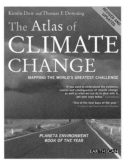

# The
# STATE OF THE WORLD
## Atlas

Produced for Earthscan by
Myriad Editions,
59 Lansdowne Place,
Brighton BN3 1FL, UK
www.MyriadEditions.com

Edited and co-ordinated by Jannet King and Candida Lacey
Designed by Isabelle Lewis and Corinne Pearlman
Maps and graphics by Isabelle Lewis


Printed on paper produced from sustainable sources.
Printed and bound in Hong Kong through Lion Production
under the supervision of Bob Cassels, The Hanway Press, London

For a full list of publications please contact:

Earthscan Ltd
Dunstan House
14a St Cross Street
London EC1N 8XA
UK
Tel: +44 (0)20 7841 1930
Fax: +44 (0)20 7242 1474
Email: earthinfo@earthscan.co.uk
Web: www.earthscan.co.uk

Earthscan publishes in association with
the International Institute for Environment and Development

# Contents

# Part Three: War and Peace

# Part Four: Rights and Respect

# Part Five: Health of the People

# Part Six: Health of the Planet

# Part Seven: Vital Statistics

# Author

**Dan Smith** is Secretary General of the London-based
international peacebuilding organization International Alert and
former Director of the International Peace Research Institute, Oslo (PRIO).
He is the author of *The State of the Middle East*, as well as successive editions of
*The State of the World Atlas* and *The Atlas of War and Peace*.
In 2002 he was awarded an OBE.

# Credits

Myriad is pleased to have been able to select all of the Part Title images as well as many of the smaller
photographs from **Panos Pictures**, an independent photo agency representing photojournalists worldwide.
Their photographers document issues and geographical areas that are under-reported, misrepresented or
ignored. In a media climate dominated by celebrity and lifestyle Panos aims to provide fresh perspectives
on the world. Half of the profits from the agency are given to the Panos Institute to further its work on
issues around media and communications, globalization, HIV/AIDS and environment and conflict.

In addition to the Panos photographers named below, we are grateful to the following for permission to
reproduce their photographs on the following pages: 16 Mark Henley / Panos Pictures; 20 World Bank /
Curt Carnemark; 24 Jennifer Trenchard / iStockphoto; 25 William Holtby / Circa Religion Photo Library;
26 World Bank / Trevor Sansom; 28 World Bank / Ray Witlin; 30 Los Angeles: Simon Horton / Panos
Pictures; Cairo, London, Mumbai and New York: Candida Lacey; Mexico City: Milan Klusacek /
iStockphoto; São Paulo: AM29 / iStockphoto; Paris: J B Russell / Panos Pictures; Lagos: George Osodi /
Panos Pictures; Istanbul: George Georgiou / Panos Pictures; Karachi: Giacomo Pirozzi / Panos Pictures;
Tokyo: Wikimedia Commons / Chris 73; 31 Jakarta: Martin Adler / Panos Pictures; Shanghai: Manfred
Leiter; 32 iStockphoto / Glenn Frank; 34 Ian Teh / Panos Pictures; 36 World Bank / Yosef Hadar;
40 World Bank / Anatoliy Rakhimbayev; 42 iStockphoto / Joseph Luoman; 46 iStockphoto / Pamela Moore;
49 iStockphoto / Cliff Parnell; 50 iStockphoto / Jan Will; 52 top: iStockphoto / Izabela Habur; bottom:
iStockphoto / Juergen Sack; 54 UNICEF India / Ami Vitale; 56 Iva Zimova / Panos Pictures; 60 George
Georgiou / Panos Pictures; 61 Tomas van Houtryve / Panos Pictures; 63–64 Elio Colavolpe / Panos Pictures;
68 Lutfallah Daher / Associated Press; 72 top: Ash Sweeting / Panos Pictures; bottom: Jenny Matthews /
Panos Pictures; 73 Andrew Testa / Panos Pictures; 76 Philippe Lissac / Panos Pictures; 79 Panos Pictures /
Jacob Silberberg; 81 Erik Millstone; 86 Eric Gevaert / iStockphoto; 89 top: Sadashivan; bottom: American
Cancer Society Inc; 91 UK Parliament; 93 iStockphoto / Ericsphotography; 94 Teun Voeten / Panos Pictures;
96 left: George Gerster / Panos Picture; right: World Food Programme / Sabrina Quezada; 100 World
Health Organization / Harry Anenden; 102 American Cancer Society Inc / Chris Hamilton; 106 Alvaro Leiva
/ Panos Pictures; 108 Panamanian golden frog: www.messiah.edu; 111 iStockphoto / kshishtof; 113 top:
Algalita Marine Research Foundation www.algalita.org; bottom: Greenpeace / Natalie Behring;
117 A Ishokon / UNEP / Still Pictures; 122 Dieter Telemans / Panos Pictures.

We would also like to thank Peter H Dana, The Geographer's Craft Project, University of Colorado at
Boulder for use of map projections (p.14), ODT maps / www.odtmaps.com for permission to adapt the
population cartogram (pp.18–19), the International Institute for Strategic Studies and Taylor & Francis for
use of data from *The Military Balance 2008* (pp.64–69, 130–37) and the Institute for Economics and Peace
for use of their 2008 Global Peace Index / www.visionofhumanity.org (pp.74–75). We have made every
effort to obtain permission for the use of copyright material. If there are any omissions, we apologise and
shall be pleased to make appropriate acknowledgement in any future edition.

# Introduction

The world faces some formidable challenges. If it were possible to make progress on five key ones – poverty, power, war, health and the natural environment – there would be grounds for real optimism about the prospects of moving towards a world of greater fairness and justice. The catalogue of problems is grim but they are all, in principle, open to solution.

**Poverty**

Today, more people are being lifted out of poverty than ever before, but a long-term problem of economic development persists. Not only are the gains of development unevenly distributed, but they have come at the price of eroding long-established social and cultural ties that have been of great benefit to people, and the old ways are not always replaced with equally viable new ones.

At the same time, despite progress on poverty reduction, inequality persists and the gap between the richest and the poorest in the world shows little sign of narrowing. The issue is not only injustice but also whether billions can be lifted out of poverty if the condition of people in the world remains so deeply marked by inequality. For, without a redistribution of existing wealth the poor can only get a little wealthier – unless substantially more wealth is generated. But can economic growth and development continue at today's pace, and for how long? Natural resources are not infinite, nor is the world's capacity to absorb waste, and keeping up "business as usual" means more emissions of greenhouse gases, thus accelerating global warming. If the world's population keeps growing, and without redistributing wealth, it seems as if there must be limits to poverty reduction.

And there is a further sustainability issue. The world's population is aging. On current projections, while the total population will increase by over 35 percent by 2050, the economically active part of the population will hardly grow at all. What quality of life will the working population enjoy in view of the extra burden they will have to carry?

In other words, pursuing the current model of economic development offers us a view of the future that is unsustainable for society and the natural environment.

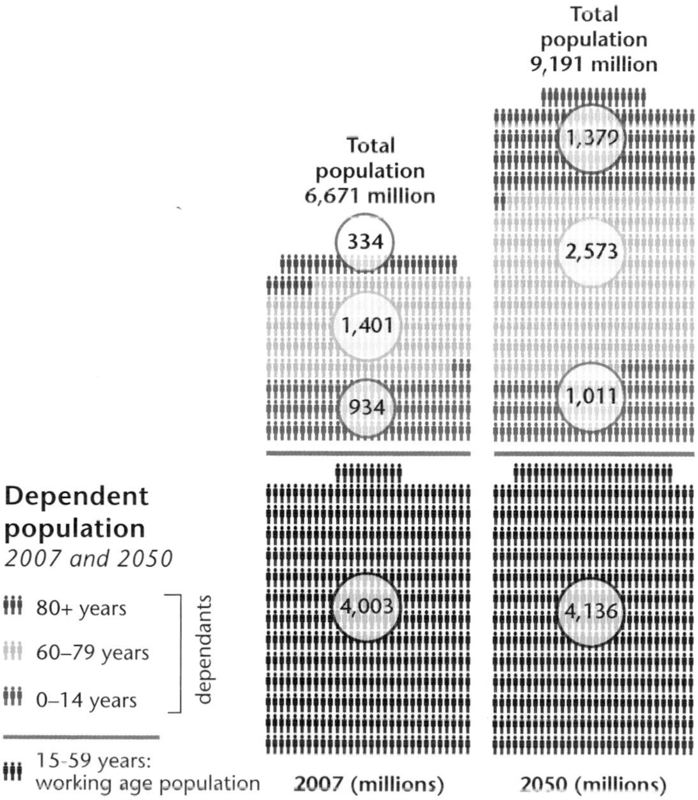

Dependent population
2007 and 2050
80+ years
60–79 years
0–14 years
dependants
15-59 years: working age population
Total population 6,671 million
334
1,401
934
4,003
2007 (millions)
Total population 9,191 million
1,379
2,573
1,011
4,136
2050 (millions)

## Power, participation and exclusion

The 19th and 20th centuries, despite wars and colonialism, experienced significant expansion of political rights and freedoms. The process frequently hit obstacles, when there seemed a risk of progress being blocked or even reversed. Yet, despite sham democracies in some countries and local reverses, there is more real freedom of political choice worldwide and more legal recognition of a fuller ranger of human rights than ever.

But are we now hitting a new period of obstacles and risks of reversals, in some countries at least? Some of the opportunities for extending democracy that arose in the former Soviet bloc countries after the end of the Cold War appear to have been spurned. And the real threat of terrorism in the first decade of this century has been used by some western governments to justify restricting rights and freedoms. What makes this more worrying is that in some countries, perhaps because long familiarity with political freedoms has dulled awareness of their fundamental importance, there has been a marked decline in public confidence in politicians and in the political process, and therefore in political participation.

## War and peace

Conditions of injustice feed violent conflict. Yet the surprisingly good news in today's world is that there are fewer wars now than 20 years ago, and that they are, in general, less lethal. The number of peace agreements to end civil wars in the years since the end of the Cold War in 1989–91 exceeds the number reached during the previous 200 years. The proportion of peace agreements that fail within the first five to 10 years also appears to be dropping. Horrors persist, and some conflicts have been suppressed rather than settled, but the overall trend is positive.

There is, however, a new question to which we should also attend. Is the nature of violent conflict changing? Wars between states have become relatively rare. The predominant kind of warfare since the end of World War II, and especially in the last two decades, has been *within* states rather than *between* them. Relatively

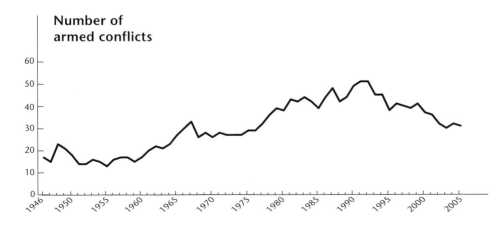

Number of armed conflicts

recently, the phenomenon of non-state wars has become visible – wars in which neither party is a state. It has also long been clear that in civil wars the business of fighting shades into criminal activity such as smuggling diamonds or cocaine, robbing banks, kidnapping or running protection rackets, to raise funds for the cause. And in some cases, the idea of a cause has rather slipped into the background. In conflicts of the future, in the mega-cities, for example, political and criminal conflict may be pretty much indistinguishable.

### The health of the people ...

It is not only the risk of social conflict that stands out when we look at marginalization and poverty. It is the basic question of health. At least 1 billion people worldwide lack access to clean water, 1.5 billion do not have enough water, and 3 billion do not have sanitation. These are conditions in which health suffers and disease flourishes. On top of this, the HIV/AIDS pandemic has devastated parts of Africa. The ill-health of the people lead to further doubts about the viability of current models of economic development.

In the rich world, health problems also persist. The largest single preventable cause of death is tobacco smoking. Obesity is an increasing problem and is associated with numerous diseases. The result will be to put increasing pressure on health services that also have to cope with an increasing proportion of the population that is getting to an age when reasonable health is maintained only by increasing medical attention.

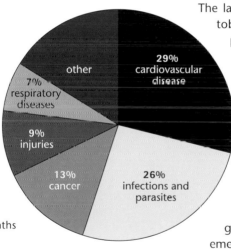

**Major causes of death**
as percentage of all deaths
2008

29% cardiovascular disease

other

7% respiratory diseases

9% injuries

13% cancer

26% infections and parasites

### ... and of the planet

The natural environment is under threat from consumption, production, waste and greenhouse gases. The global food crisis that emerged in the first half of 2008, as this atlas was being prepared, is the product of many factors, including short-term price speculation, but it is partly driven by changes in climate. These changes are broadly consistent with the predictions of climate models exploring the consequences of global warming. If we do not start to learn how to treat the natural environment with more care, there will be parts of the world where human habitats will become less habitable, with consequences including conflicts, migration and further instability in neighbouring areas.

### Problems with solutions

Solutions to these issues are not easy, but nor are they impossible. Progress on democracy and human rights can resume if we use the rights and freedoms that we have. There are fewer wars now than only a few years ago. Progress has been made on

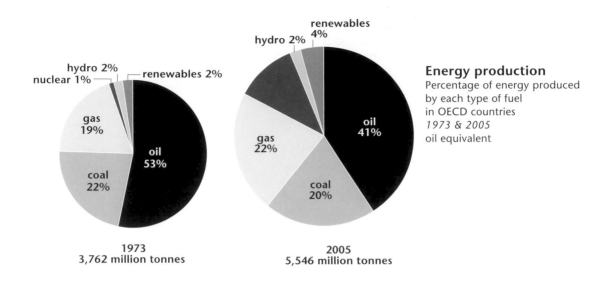

**Energy production**
Percentage of energy produced
by each type of fuel
in OECD countries
*1973 & 2005*
oil equivalent

hydro 2%
nuclear 1%
renewables 2%
gas 19%
coal 22%
oil 53%

1973
3,762 million tonnes

renewables 4%
hydro 2%
oil 41%
gas 22%
coal 20%

2005
5,546 million tonnes

poverty reduction and there can be more if political parties and leaders start to recognize that inequality is ultimately as much of the problem for those on top of the pile as for those at the bottom. While climate change throws down an enormous challenge, measures to reduce greenhouse gas emissions are technically feasible, but they come at a price and so far in most countries politicians have not found a way both to let the price be paid and to get re-elected. While the benefits of reducing emissions feed through the natural system, it will also be necessary for the countries that are vulnerable to climate change consequences in the short term to adapt to face the problems. Most of them are poor, and large-scale international assistance will be needed. It will be expensive but affordable for the rich world that caused the problem. And if the basic problems of power, peace, poverty and climate change are resolved, the scale of some of the issues of human health will be reduced to manageable proportions. In short, these are serious problems but solutions are, in principle, available.

**Knowing the world**
No single government can take on these big challenges and solve them. They will be addressed by agreement among governments or not at all. Elected governments need to be pressed to act by public opinion. Even non-democratic governments can often be influenced by international opinion. To generate that pressure, we need to know the issues and understand them.

But watch out for the trap of over-reliance on facts. Take the example of climate change. To insist on getting the facts about climate change before deciding whether and how to act means waiting, and, if the climate projections and scientists' estimates are right, that means waiting until it is too late. This was the posture of the US government under George W. Bush. If we accept the clear majority scientific view about the risks of inactivity on climate change, then we have to learn how to act before all the facts are in, and adjust as we go along if necessary. We have to act even when knowledge and understanding are always provisional. In a deep sense, we need to make it up as we go along.

That said, while knowing and understanding the facts may not be enough, it is essential. Projections and estimates about many issues, not just the consequences of climate change, build on known facts about the past and present to construct a picture of the future. But the knowledge and understanding that must be called on to help shape a world of justice and fairness are not only scientific. Local communities, for example, often know much more about the conditions in which they live than experts and scientists do. We need to learn how to combine abstract knowledge with the wisdom derived from experience and tradition, enriching both, in order to find peaceful solutions to difficult conflicts, to include marginalized groups in key decisions, to understand what is happening in the natural environment.

There is, in fact, a global storehouse of knowledge and understanding that is every bit as impressive as the problems and challenges we face. The issue is how to deploy it. Knowledge is very often the possession of a relatively small group of experts. Yet decisions on these issues affect everybody and should not be the purview only of a small group, however well qualified. They have extremely broad implications and need to be shaped not by narrow expertise but with reference to the bigger picture.

## Statistics ...

This series of *State of the World* atlases, which was initiated in 1982, and of which this is the eighth edition, has endeavoured to present the provisional facts about key world issues in a way that is reliable, digestible for the non-expert, and oriented towards revealing the larger picture. These books do not offer – and do not claim to offer – the only definitive worldview. They simply offer to help you see the broad outlines, the context for deeper knowledge on specific issues.

Running through the series' treatment of world issues over the years, one common thread has been the difficulty of knowing the world. The series – and likewise the related atlases on the state of women, war and peace, the Middle East, China, the environment, health, water, food, endangered species and others – grew from a choice to offer broad, global perspectives, drawing on world-level statistics, expressed visually as far as possible, with the main visual technique being world maps.

That choice has been fruitful but it does raise a couple of tricky issues. The closer one gets to statistics and the more one works with them, the more the words of 19th-century British prime minister Benjamin Disraeli are borne out. There are three kinds of lies, he said: lies, damned lies, and statistics. Statistics and the yearbooks in which they are published are indispensable, tricky, less reliable than they seem, and often consist of a quicksand of mutable assumptions, varying minutely and without notice from case to case and year to year. The world as seen through the statistical lens is often blurred, and individual countries can sometimes look quite strange.

### ... and maps

Choosing an atlas format means facing up to the problem of maps. Because the world is virtually round, it cannot be accurately depicted on a flat, rectangular piece of paper. Peel an orange and flatten out the skin and the problem is immediately understandable. Choices and compromises must accordingly be made – choices, essentially, about how to be inaccurate. These choices are packaged into the *projection* of the world that is utilized in drawing the map. The most widely seen world maps use projections that retain the shapes of the continents and islands, and therefore wildly distort their size. The most famous of these projections is the one developed by the 16th-century Flemish cartographer, Gerardus Mercator. Using that projection, the sizes of regions far from the equator are exaggerated. Thus, Europe looks bigger than it is, while China and India look smaller. The most notorious distortion of area in Mercator is that Africa looks smaller than Greenland but is actually 14 times bigger. Mercator's choice of projection was determined in part by his wish, as the sub-title of the original atlas put it, to produce an aid for navigators. Navigation was at the forefront of Europe's advance into the world between the 15th and the 18th centuries. Accurate cartography was the scientific precondition for sailing to far-flung destinations for trade and conquest.

There have been numerous attempts over succeeding centuries to correct the illustrative weakness in the Mercator projection. The best-known today is the one proposed in 1973 by Arno Peters, drawing on work in the 19th century by a Scottish clergyman, James Gall. The Peters, or Gall-Peters, projection is more accurate on the size of different regions but distorts the world's appearance in other ways. There are geographers who believe the depiction of the world on rectangular pieces of paper should be stopped.

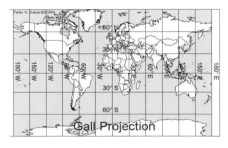

This atlas uses the 1913 Winkel Tripel; the "Tripel" refers to the three elements of area, direction and distance, between which Oswald Winkel compromised. The distortions are not eliminated but – check Greenland against Africa – they are minimized, and are mostly visible at the poles. This projection's curved lines of latitude and longitude make it useless for navigators, but the result is fairer and has become reasonably familiar, especially since it was adopted by the US National Geographic Society in 1998. Familiarity with approximate size and location of countries makes possible one of this atlas's ways of presenting information – the cartogram, which re-sizes countries to correspond to their relative scale when compared by size of population, for example, or number of armed forces.

## Acknowledgements

The atlas is the product of a team. Jannet King was responsible for most of the basic data research and has made a major editorial input. Isabelle Lewis kept thinking up innovative ways of graphically and cartographically presenting the information and, together with Corinne Pearlman, provided the creative oversight that gives the book its distinctive feel. Karina Kristiansen provided some life-saving research assistance late in the day. Candida Lacey ran and coordinated the Myriad team and me, and was, as with earlier editions and other atlases, a joy to work with. I thank them all unreservedly.

Dan Smith
London, June 2008

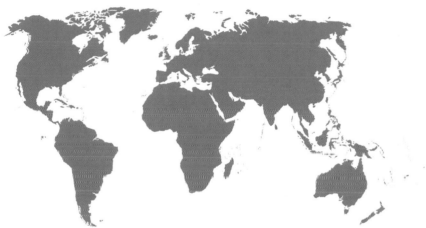

Myriad's world map based on the Winkel Tripel projection

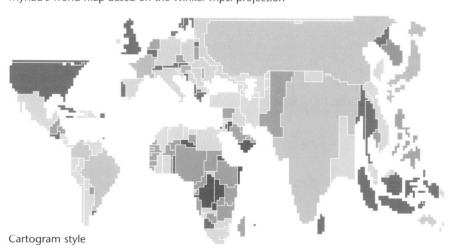

Cartogram style

There are over 6 billion of us and by mid-century there will be 9 billion.

# Part One: Who We Are

As countries get richer, the population grows more slowly. The world's population doubled in the second half of the 20th century, passing 6 billion at the start of the 21st. The rate of growth has slowed, especially in the two most populous countries – China and India – but on current trends the total will exceed 9 billion by 2050, with Africa and parts of the Middle East growing fastest.

SWEDEN FINLAND
NORWAY
RUSSIA
143m
DENMARK
ESTONIA
IRELAND
LATVIA
LITHUANIA
UNITED
KINGDOM
60m
16m
NETHERLANDS
GERMANY
82m
POLAND
39m
10m
BELGIUM
10m
BELARUS
10m
CZECH
REPUBLIC
SLOVAKIA
UKRAINE
47m
FRANCE
61m
AUSTRIA
SWITZERLAND
SLOVENIA
HUNGARY
10m
ROMANIA
22m
MOLDOVA
ITALY
58m
11m
SERBIA &
MONTENEGRO
CROATIA
BOSNIA-
HERZEGOVINA
PORTUGAL
11m
SPAIN
40m
ALBANIA
MACEDONIA
BULGARIA
GREECE
11m

CANADA   33m

USA
296m

MEXICO
106m

CUBA  11m
PUERTO RICO
JAMAICA   HAITI
DOMINICAN
REPUBLIC

15m
HONDURAS
GUATEMALA
NICARAGUA
EL SALVADOR
TRINIDAD & TOBAGO
COSTA RICA
PANAMA
VENEZUELA
25m
COLOMBIA
43m

ECUADOR
13m

BRAZIL
186m

PERU
28m

BOLIVIA
CHILE
16m
PARAGUAY

ARGENTINA
40m

URUGUAY

TUNISIA
10m   LIBYA
MOROCCO
33m
ALGERIA
33m
CHAD
10m
EGYPT
78m
MAURITANIA
MALI
12m
NIGER
12m
GAMBIA
SENEGAL
14m
11m
BURKINA
FASO
GUINEA-BISSAU
GUINEA
SIERRA
LEONE
GHANA
21m
NIGERIA
141m
SUDAN
40m
LIBERIA
COTE
D'IVOIRE
18m
CAR
BENIN
TOGO
CAMEROON
16m
GABON
CONGO
ANGOLA
11m
ZAMBIA
11m
MALAWI
12m
NAMIBIA
BOTSWANA
ZIMBABWE
13m
SOUT
AFRIC
43r

1820 1 billion
1930 2 billion
1960 3 billion
1974 4 billion
1988 5 billion
2000 6 billion

2050 9 billion

**Population growth**
*1820–2050 projected*

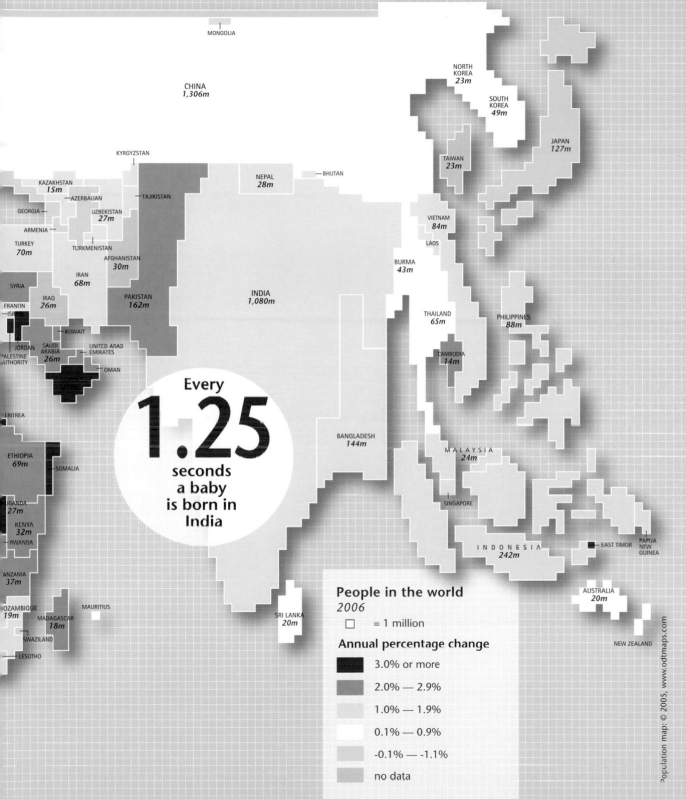

MONGOLIA

CHINA
1,306m

NORTH KOREA
23m

SOUTH KOREA
49m

JAPAN
127m

KYRGYZSTAN

KAZAKHSTAN
15m

AZERBAIJAN

TAJIKISTAN

NEPAL
28m

BHUTAN

TAIWAN
23m

GEORGIA

ARMENIA

UZBEKISTAN
27m

VIETNAM
84m

LAOS

TURKEY
70m

TURKMENISTAN

AFGHANISTAN
30m

BURMA
43m

IRAN
68m

SYRIA

IRAQ
26m

PAKISTAN
162m

INDIA
1,080m

THAILAND
65m

PHILIPPINES
88m

LEBANON

ISRAEL

KUWAIT

JORDAN

SAUDI ARABIA
26m

UNITED ARAB EMIRATES

CAMBODIA
14m

PALESTINE AUTHORITY

OMAN

ERITREA

ETHIOPIA
69m

SOMALIA

Every
## 1.25
seconds
a baby
is born in
India

BANGLADESH
144m

MALAYSIA
24m

UGANDA
27m

KENYA
32m

RWANDA

SINGAPORE

INDONESIA
242m

EAST TIMOR

PAPUA NEW GUINEA

TANZANIA
37m

AUSTRALIA
20m

MOZAMBIQUE
19m

MAURITIUS

MADAGASCAR
18m

SRI LANKA
20m

NEW ZEALAND

SWAZILAND

LESOTHO

## People in the world
*2006*

☐ = 1 million

### Annual percentage change

| | |
|---|---|
| ■ | 3.0% or more |
| ▨ | 2.0% — 2.9% |
| ▢ | 1.0% — 1.9% |
| □ | 0.1% — 0.9% |
| ▧ | -0.1% — -1.1% |
| ▨ | no data |

Population map: © 2005, www.odtmaps.com

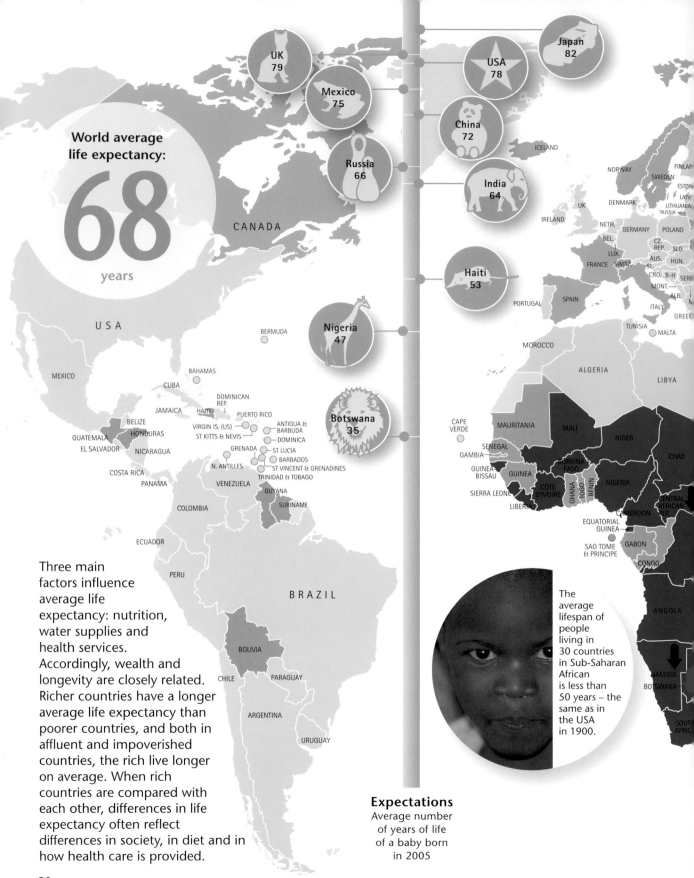

**World average life expectancy:**

# 68
years

UK
79

Mexico
75

Russia
66

Japan
82

USA
78

China
72

India
64

Haiti
53

Nigeria
47

Botswana
35

CANADA

USA

MEXICO

BERMUDA

BAHAMAS

CUBA

JAMAICA

HAITI

DOMINICAN REP.

PUERTO RICO

VIRGIN IS. (US)

ST KITTS & NEVIS

ANTIGUA & BARBUDA

DOMINICA

GRENADA

ST LUCIA

N. ANTILLES

BARBADOS

ST VINCENT & GRENADINES

TRINIDAD & TOBAGO

BELIZE

GUATEMALA

HONDURAS

EL SALVADOR

NICARAGUA

COSTA RICA

PANAMA

VENEZUELA

GUYANA

SURINAME

COLOMBIA

ECUADOR

PERU

BRAZIL

BOLIVIA

CHILE

PARAGUAY

ARGENTINA

URUGUAY

ICELAND

NORWAY

SWEDEN

FINLAND

ESTON

LATV

UK

DENMARK

LITHUANIA

RUSSIA

IRELAND

NETH.

GERMANY

POLAND

BEL.

CZ. REP.

SLO.

LUX.

AUS.

HUN.

FRANCE

SWITZ.

CRO.

B-H

SERI

MONT.

ALB.

PORTUGAL

SPAIN

ITALY

GREECE

TUNISIA

MALTA

MOROCCO

ALGERIA

LIBYA

CAPE VERDE

MAURITANIA

MALI

NIGER

CHAD

SENEGAL

GAMBIA

GUINEA BISSAU

GUINEA

BURKINA FASO

SIERRA LEONE

CÔTE D'IVOIRE

GHANA

TOGO

BENIN

NIGERIA

CENTRAL AFRICAN REP.

LIBERIA

CAMEROON

EQUATORIAL GUINEA

SAO TOME & PRINCIPE

GABON

CONGO

ANGOLA

NAMIBIA

BOTSWANA

SOUTH AFRICA

Three main factors influence average life expectancy: nutrition, water supplies and health services. Accordingly, wealth and longevity are closely related. Richer countries have a longer average life expectancy than poorer countries, and both in affluent and impoverished countries, the rich live longer on average. When rich countries are compared with each other, differences in life expectancy often reflect differences in society, in diet and in how health care is provided.

The average lifespan of people living in 30 countries in Sub-Saharan African is less than 50 years – the same as in the USA in 1900.

**Expectations**
Average number of years of life of a baby born in 2005

# Life Expectancy

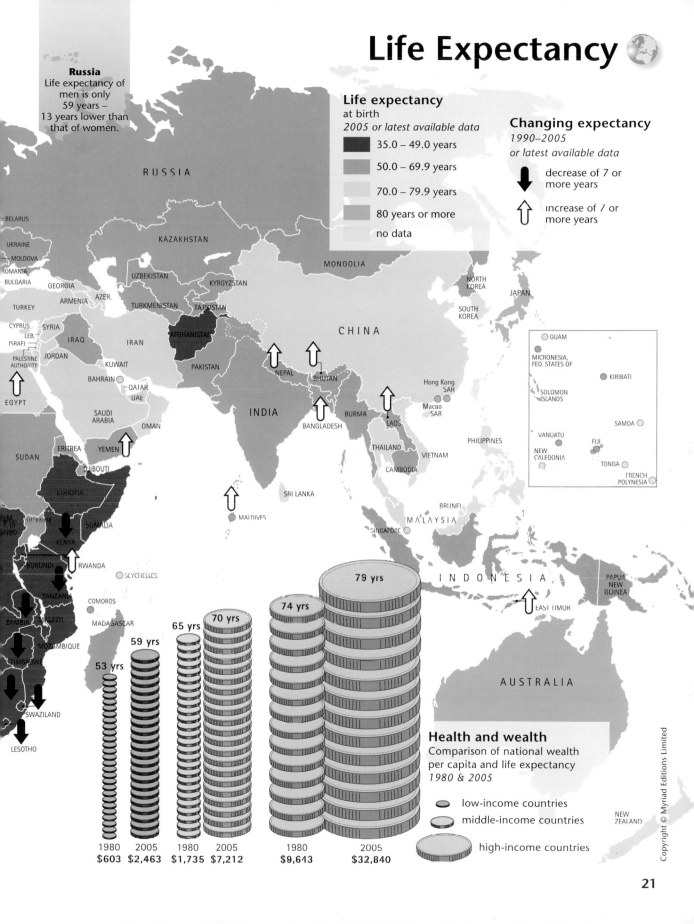

**Russia**
Life expectancy of men is only 59 years – 13 years lower than that of women.

**Life expectancy**
at birth
*2005 or latest available data*

- 35.0 – 49.0 years
- 50.0 – 69.9 years
- 70.0 – 79.9 years
- 80 years or more
- no data

**Changing expectancy**
*1990–2005*
*or latest available data*

↓ decrease of 7 or more years

↑ increase of 7 or more years

## Health and wealth
Comparison of national wealth per capita and life expectancy
*1980 & 2005*

- low-income countries
- middle-income countries
- high-income countries

| 1980 | 2005 | 1980 | 2005 | 1980 | 2005 |
|------|------|------|------|------|------|
| 53 yrs | 59 yrs | 65 yrs | 70 yrs | 74 yrs | 79 yrs |
| $603 | $2,463 | $1,735 | $7,212 | $9,643 | $32,840 |

21

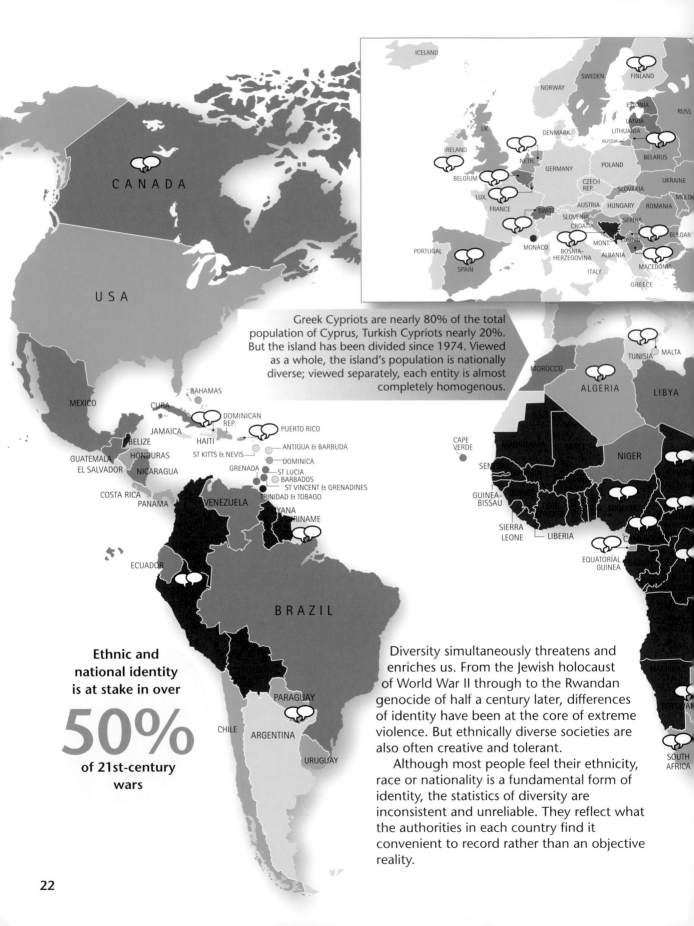

Greek Cypriots are nearly 80% of the total population of Cyprus, Turkish Cypriots nearly 20%. But the island has been divided since 1974. Viewed as a whole, the island's population is nationally diverse; viewed separately, each entity is almost completely homogenous.

**Ethnic and national identity is at stake in over**

# 50%

**of 21st-century wars**

Diversity simultaneously threatens and enriches us. From the Jewish holocaust of World War II through to the Rwandan genocide of half a century later, differences of identity have been at the core of extreme violence. But ethnically diverse societies are also often creative and tolerant.

Although most people feel their ethnicity, race or nationality is a fundamental form of identity, the statistics of diversity are inconsistent and unreliable. They reflect what the authorities in each country find it convenient to record rather than an objective reality.

# Ethnicity and Diversity

RUSSIA

KAZAKHSTAN

UZBEKISTAN

KYRGYZSTAN

MONGOLIA

GEORGIA

ARMENIA

AZERBAIJAN

TURKMENISTAN

TAJIKISTAN

TURKEY

CYPRUS
LEB.

SYRIA

JORDAN

IRAQ

IRAN

AFGHANISTAN

CHINA

NORTH
KOREA

JAPAN

SOUTH
KOREA

PALESTINE
AUTHORITY

ISRAEL

KUWAIT

BAHRAIN

PAKISTAN

NEPAL

BHUTAN

EGYPT

SAUDI
ARABIA

QATAR
UAE

OMAN

INDIA

BANGLADESH

BURMA

TAIWAN

SUDAN

ERITREA

YEMEN

LAOS

THAILAND

VIETNAM

DJIBOUTI

ETHIOPIA

SRI LANKA

CAMBODIA

PHILIPPINES

UGANDA

SOMALIA

MALDIVES

KENYA

RWANDA

SEYCHELLES

BRUNEI

MALAYSIA

BURUNDI TANZANIA

SINGAPORE

COMOROS

ZAMBIA

MALAWI

INDONESIA

ZIMBABWE

MADAGASCAR

MAURITIUS

MOZAMBIQUE

AUSTRALIA

SWAZILAND

LESOTHO

MICRONESIA,
FED. STATES OF

MARSHALL ISLANDS

NAURU

KIRIBATI

SOLOMON
ISLANDS

TUVALU

SAMOA

VANUATU

FIJI

NEW
CALEDONIA

FRENCH
POLYNESIA

**Indonesia**
The government
identifies over
300 ethnic groups,
speaking over
700 languages.

## Ethnic, national
and racial diversity
Minority group(s) as a proportion
of the population
*2007 or latest census*

- under 10%
- 10% – 29%
- 30% – 49%
- 50% or more:
  no single ethnic, national or
  racial group forms more than half
  of the population
- data unavailable or inadequate

## Language of government

more than one
official language

NEW
ZEALAND

## Schools and Schisms
Most popular religion by group and sub-group

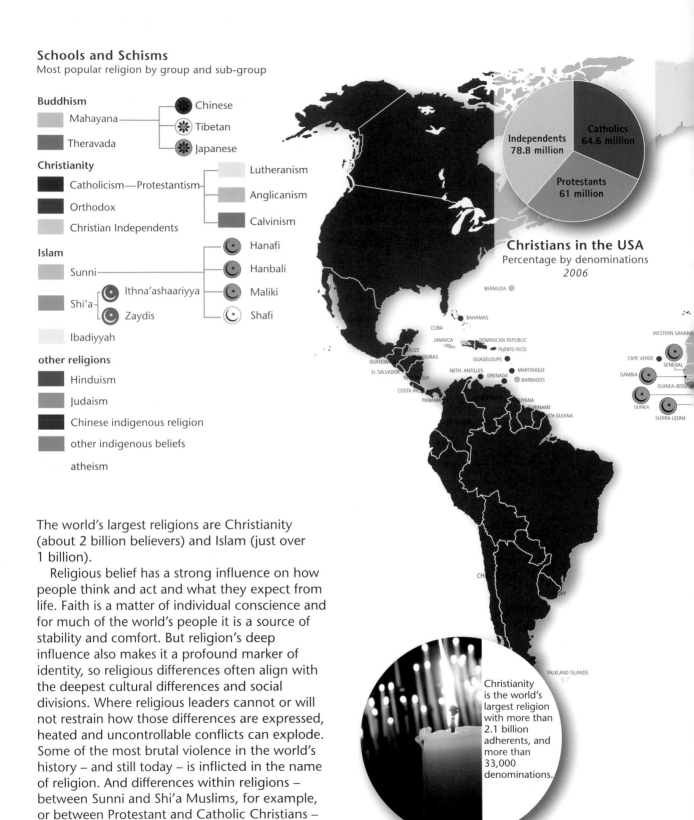

**Buddhism**
- Mahayana
  - Chinese
  - Tibetan
  - Japanese
- Theravada

**Christianity**
- Catholicism—Protestantism
  - Lutheranism
  - Anglicanism
  - Calvinism
- Orthodox
- Christian Independents

**Islam**
- Sunni
  - Hanafi
  - Hanbali
  - Maliki
  - Shafi
- Shi'a
  - Ithna'ashaariyya
  - Zaydis
- Ibadiyyah

**other religions**
- Hinduism
- Judaism
- Chinese indigenous religion
- other indigenous beliefs
- atheism

### Christians in the USA
Percentage by denominations
*2006*

- Independents 78.8 million
- Catholics 64.6 million
- Protestants 61 million

BERMUDA

BAHAMAS
CUBA
JAMAICA  HAITI  DOMINICAN REPUBLIC
MEXICO  PUERTO RICO
BELIZE  GUADELOUPE
HONDURAS  MARTINIQUE
GUATEMALA  NETH. ANTILLES
EL SALVADOR  GRENADA  BARBADOS
NICARAGUA  VENEZUELA
COSTA RICA  GUYANA
PANAMA  SURINAME
COLOMBIA  FRENCH GUIANA

WESTERN SAHARA
CAPE VERDE  SENEGAL
GAMBIA
GUINEA-BISSAU
GUINEA
SIERRA LEONE

FALKLAND ISLANDS

Christianity is the world's largest religion with more than 2.1 billion adherents, and more than 33,000 denominations.

The world's largest religions are Christianity (about 2 billion believers) and Islam (just over 1 billion).

Religious belief has a strong influence on how people think and act and what they expect from life. Faith is a matter of individual conscience and for much of the world's people it is a source of stability and comfort. But religion's deep influence also makes it a profound marker of identity, so religious differences often align with the deepest cultural differences and social divisions. Where religious leaders cannot or will not restrain how those differences are expressed, heated and uncontrollable conflicts can explode. Some of the most brutal violence in the world's history – and still today – is inflicted in the name of religion. And differences within religions – between Sunni and Shi'a Muslims, for example, or between Protestant and Catholic Christians – are often as intense as differences between them.

# Religious Beliefs

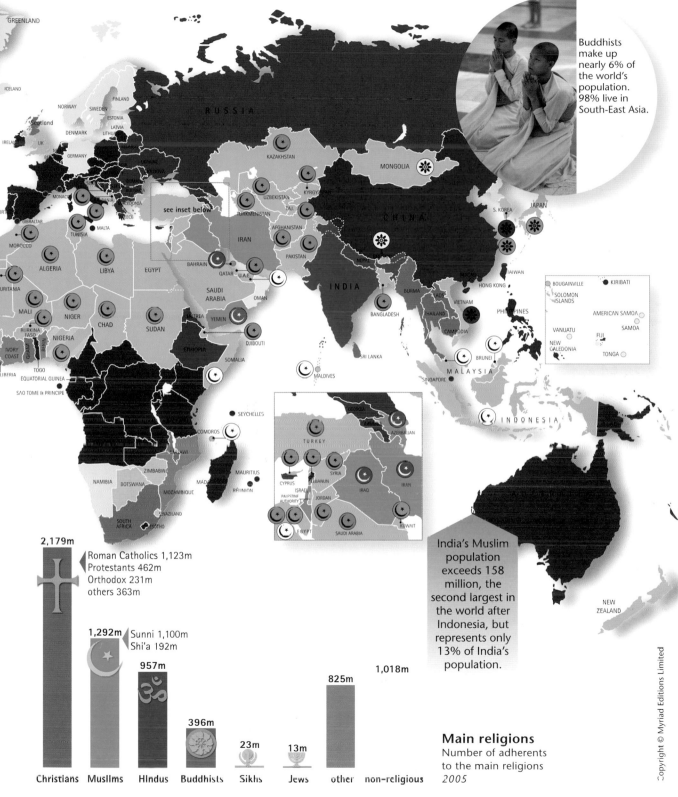

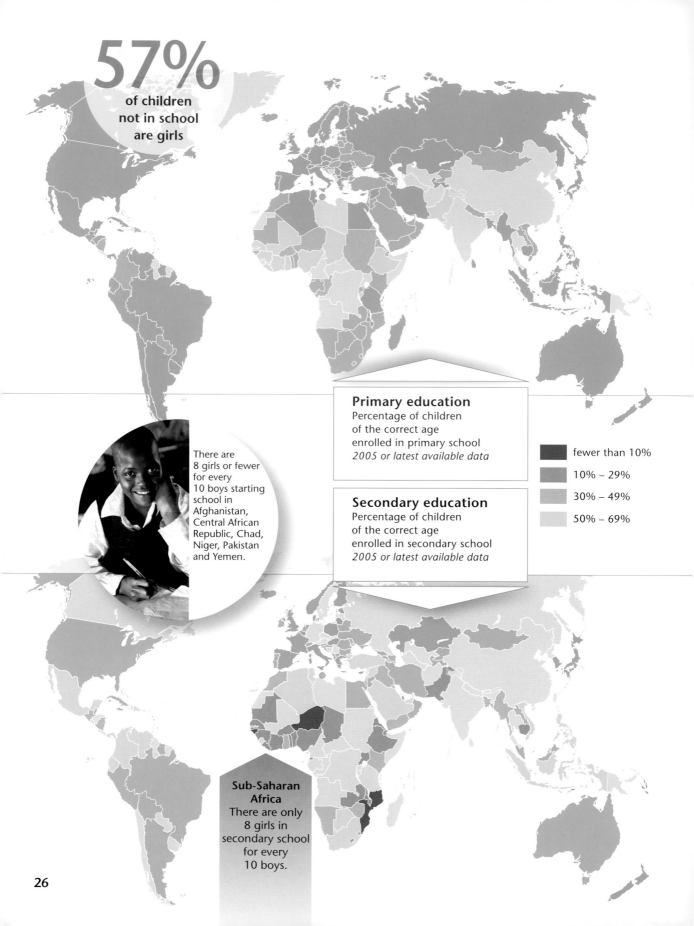

# 57%
of children not in school are girls

There are 8 girls or fewer for every 10 boys starting school in Afghanistan, Central African Republic, Chad, Niger, Pakistan and Yemen.

## Primary education
Percentage of children of the correct age enrolled in primary school
*2005 or latest available data*

## Secondary education
Percentage of children of the correct age enrolled in secondary school
*2005 or latest available data*

- fewer than 10%
- 10% – 29%
- 30% – 49%
- 50% – 69%

**Sub-Saharan Africa**
There are only 8 girls in secondary school for every 10 boys.

26

# Education

**Sub-Saharan Africa**
There are only 6 girls in tertiary education for every 10 boys.

**Tertiary education**
Percentage of young people enrolled in tertiary college
*2005 or latest available data*

70% – 90%

90% or more

no data

**Adult literacy**
Literate adults as percentage of adult population
*2005*

Literacy is simultaneously a functional need for modern societies, a basic tool for individual advancement, and a rich benefit in everybody's personal life. As modern trade and industry have spread, so have general literacy levels. In most countries, discrimination at school and at home means that more women than men are illiterate and girls still lag behind boys in worldwide school enrolment statistics.

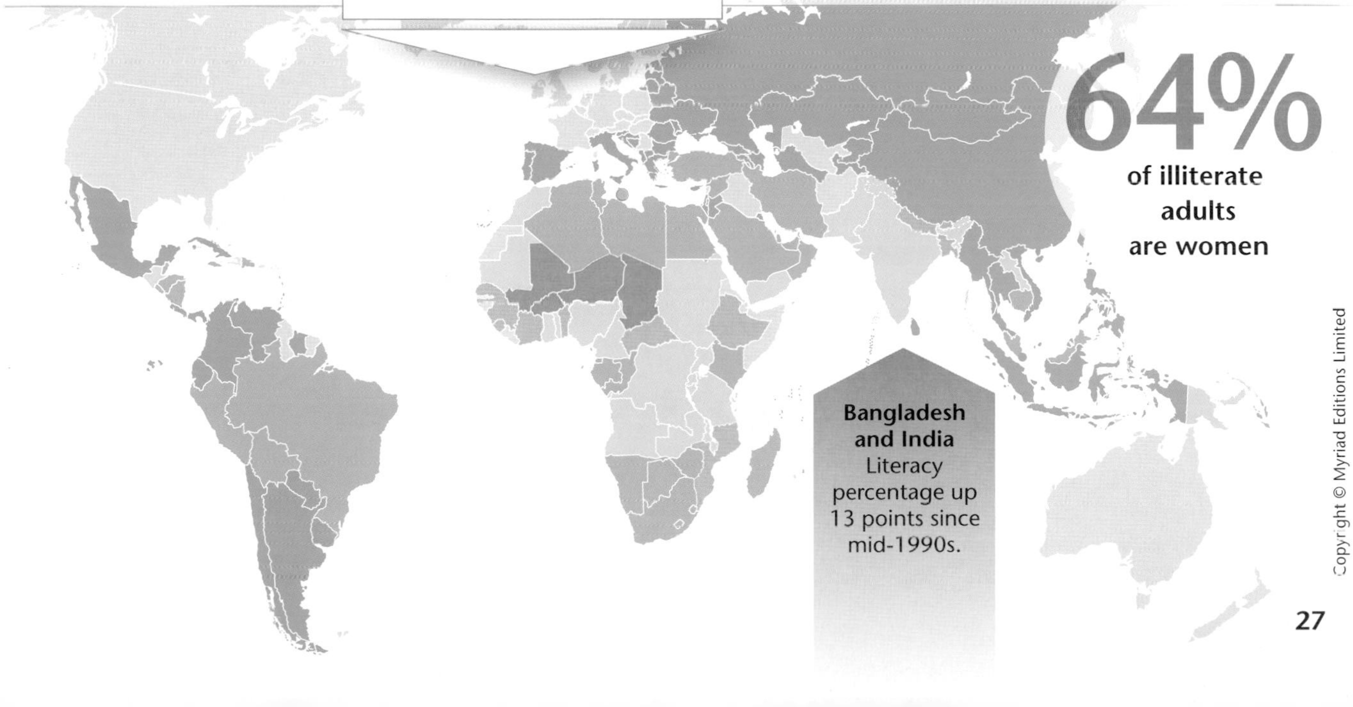

**64%**
of illiterate adults are women

**Bangladesh and India**
Literacy percentage up 13 points since mid-1990s.

Copyright © Myriad Editions Limited

27

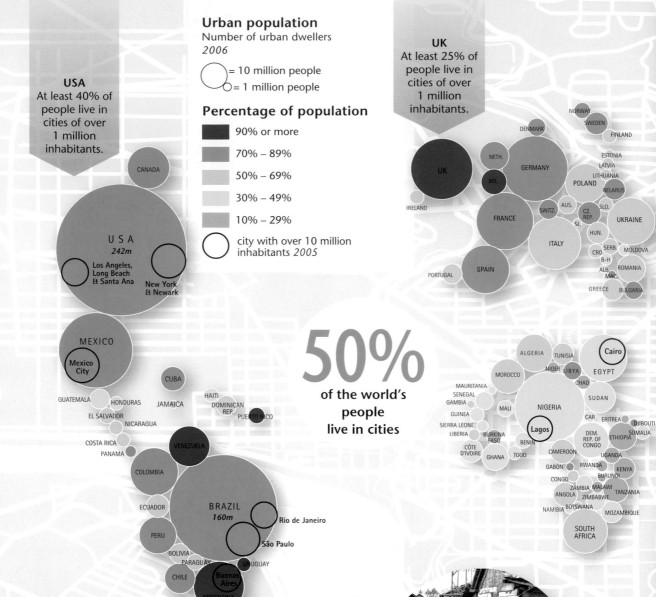

## Urban population
Number of urban dwellers
*2006*

◯ = 10 million people
○ = 1 million people

## Percentage of population

■ 90% or more
■ 70% – 89%
■ 50% – 69%
■ 30% – 49%
■ 10% – 29%
◯ city with over 10 million inhabitants 2005

**USA**
At least 40% of people live in cities of over 1 million inhabitants.

CANADA

U S A
*242m*

Los Angeles, Long Beach & Santa Ana

New York & Newark

MEXICO

Mexico City

GUATEMALA    HONDURAS    JAMAICA
EL SALVADOR
NICARAGUA
COSTA RICA
PANAMA

CUBA

HAITI
DOMINICAN REP.
PUERTO RICO

VENEZUELA

COLOMBIA

ECUADOR

PERU

BRAZIL
*160m*

Rio de Janeiro

São Paulo

BOLIVIA
PARAGUAY
URUGUAY

CHILE    Buenos Aires

ARGENTINA

**UK**
At least 25% of people live in cities of over 1 million inhabitants.

NORWAY    SWEDEN
DENMARK    FINLAND

NETH.    ESTONIA
UK    GERMANY    LATVIA
LITHUANIA
BEL.    POLAND    BELARUS

IRELAND
FRANCE    SWITZ.    AUS.    CZ. REP.    SLO.    UKRAINE
SI.    HUN.
ITALY    CRO.    SERB.    MOLDOVA
B-H
PORTUGAL    SPAIN    ALB.    ROMANIA
MAC.
GREECE    BULGARIA

ALGERIA    TUNISIA    Cairo
NIGER    LIBYA    EGYPT
MOROCCO    CHAD    SUDAN

MAURITANIA
SENEGAL
GAMBIA    MALI    NIGERIA
GUINEA
SIERRA LEONE    CAR    ERITREA    DJIBOUTI
LIBERIA    BURKINA    Lagos    SOMALIA
FASO    BENIN    DEM.    ETHIOPIA
CÔTE    REP. OF
D'IVOIRE    GHANA    TOGO    CAMEROON    CONGO    UGANDA
GABON    RWANDA    KENYA
CONGO    BURUNDI
ZAMBIA    MALAWI    TANZANIA
ANGOLA    ZIMBABWE
NAMIBIA    BOTSWANA    MOZAMBIQUE
SOUTH
AFRICA

# 50%
**of the world's people live in cities**

The world's population is growing rapidly, but the urban population is growing even faster. The proportion of people living in cities is on the way from an estimated 40 percent in 1980 to 60 percent in 2020, and 70 percent in 2030.

New urbanization is largely concentrated in the developing countries. Most major cities in Europe are static or declining in size, partly because improved transport and communications are reducing the economic benefits of concentrating large numbers of people in a few places. In developing countries, however, the big cities remain magnets for people seeking livelihoods when they can no longer sustain themselves in the countryside.

Many cities are ringed by houses built by the urban poor, leading to tensions between the authorities and desperate people with nowhere else to go.

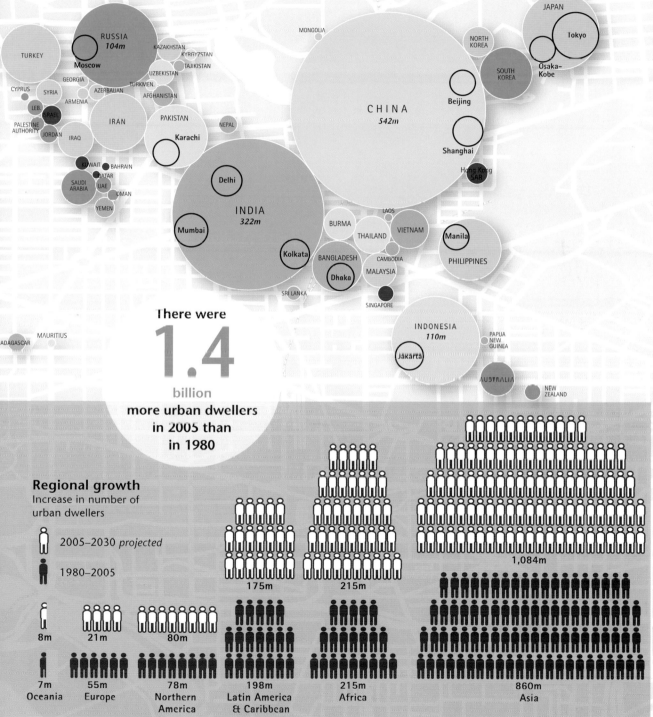

MONGOLIA

RUSSIA
*104m*
Moscow

TURKEY

KAZAKHSTAN

KYRGYZSTAN

TAJIKISTAN

UZBEKISTAN

GEORGIA

CYPRUS

SYRIA

AZERBAIJAN

TURKMEN.

ARMENIA

AFGHANISTAN

LEB.

ISRAEL

PALESTINE
AUTHORITY

JORDAN

IRAQ

IRAN

PAKISTAN

NEPAL

Karachi

KUWAIT

BAHRAIN

QATAR

SAUDI
ARABIA

UAE

OMAN

YEMEN

Delhi

INDIA
*322m*

Mumbai

Kolkata

BURMA

THAILAND

LAOS

VIETNAM

BANGLADESH

Dhaka

CAMBODIA

MALAYSIA

SRI LANKA

SINGAPORE

NORTH
KOREA

SOUTH
KOREA

Beijing

CHINA
*542m*

Shanghai

Hong Kong
SAR

JAPAN

Tokyo

Osaka-
Kobe

Manila

PHILIPPINES

INDONESIA
*110m*

Jakarta

PAPUA
NEW
GUINEA

AUSTRALIA

NEW
ZEALAND

MADAGASCAR

MAURITIUS

## There were

# 1.4

billion

**more urban dwellers
in 2005 than
in 1980**

## Regional growth
Increase in number of
urban dwellers

2005–2030 *projected*

1980–2005

1,084m

8m

21m

80m

175m

215m

7m
Oceania

55m
Europe

78m
Northern
America

198m
Latin America
& Caribbean

215m
Africa

860m
Asia

1 Tokyo  2 New York  3 Los Angeles  5 Paris  6 London  8 Mexico City  19 São Paulo  32 Shanghai  34 Istanbul  37 Mumbai  45 Cairo  46 Jakarta

## City wealth
Comparative rank of selected cities
*2008 or latest available data*

**London, UK**
Population **8m**
Area (sq km) **1,623**
Density (pop/sq km) **5,100**

50% of residents are Latinos • 30% are Anglophone • 10% of Asian descent • 40% were born outside the USA • 20% live in poverty.

30% of London residents are non-white • 95% of people moving to London since 1995 were born outside the UK.

**New York City, USA**
Population **18m**
Area (sq km) **8,683**
Density (pop/sq km) **2,050**

Paris is the most visited city in the world – with 30 million annual visitors. Few visit its suburbs – except Disneyland and Parc Asterix • 20% of population of Greater Paris were born outside France.

**Los Angeles**
Population **12m**
Area (sq km) **4,320**
Density (pop/sq km) **2,750**

48% of New Yorkers speak a language other than English at home.

70% of new jobs in Mexico City are in the "informal" sector (unregulated, unprotected by law) • its metro system is the world's cheapest and the fourth most used (4.5 million people a day).

**Paris, France**
Population **10m**
Area (sq km) **2,723**
Density (pop/sq km) **3,550**

**Mexico City, Mexico**
Population **17m**
Area (sq km) **2,072**
Density (pop/sq km) **8,400**

São Paulo is the largest Japanese city outside Japan; the largest Lebanese city outside Lebanon; the largest Spanish city outside Spain • 66% of population is under 20 years old.

**São Paulo, Brazil**
Population **18m**
Area (sq km) **1,968**
Density (pop/sq km) **9,000**

Annual population growth of 5% equals 74 new residents per hour • Over 50% of Nigeria's industry is located in Lagos's suburbs.

## City income
US$ per capita
in selected cities
*2008 or latest available data*

**Lagos, Nigeria**
Population **13m**
Area (sq km) **738**
Density (pop/sq km) **18,150**

| City | Income |
|------|--------|
| New York | $62,900 |
| London | $56,500 |
| Los Angeles | $53,300 |
| Paris | $46,000 |
| Tokyo | $36,000 |
| Mexico City | $18,500 |
| Istanbul | $14,800 |

# Diversity of Cities

**Worldwide 3 billion people live in cities; 1 billion in urban slums. In Sub-Saharan Africa, over 70% of city-dwellers live in slums; in South and Central Asia, nearly 60%.**

Istanbul has 19 new residents per hour • 50% of residents estimated to live in *gecekondus*, illegal constructions "built overnight" • over half of Turkey's international trade passes through Istanbul.

**Istanbul, Turkey**
Population 9m–12m
Area (sq km) **1,166**
Density (pop/sq km) **7,700**

99% of Tokyo's population is Japanese by birth • 40% of the city is built on landfill.

**Tokyo, Japan**
Population **33m**
Area (sq km) **6,993**
Density (pop/sq km) **4,750**

49% of Karachi's population are Urdu speakers, 19% Sindhi, 11% Punjabi, 9% Pashtun and 4% Balochi; the remaining 8% speak at least 14 other languages • Karachi's annual population growth of 5% equals 57 new residents per hour.

**Karachi, Pakistan**
Population **10m**
Area (sq km) **518**
Density (pop/sq km) **18,900**

99% of Shanghai's residents were born and raised in China • 29 new residents added per hour • Shanghai had 1 skyscraper in 1988 and 300 less than 20 years later.

**Shanghai, China**
Population **10m**
Area (sq km) **746**
Density (pop/sq km) **13,400**

60% of Cairo's inhabitants live in unlicensed housing • air pollution kills 10,000-25,000 each year.

**Cairo, Egypt**
Population **12m–18m**
Area (sq km) **1,295**
Density (pop/sq km) **9,400**

**Mumbai, India**
Population **14m**
Area (sq km) **484**
Density (pop/sq km) **30,000**

50% of Mumbai's population has no sanitation • with 1% of India's population, Mumbai pays 40% of national tax revenues.

Over 50% of Jakarta's buildings are temporary or semi-permanent • 25% of Jakartans have daily access to clean water • only 2% use public transport

**Jakarta, Indonesia**
Population **14m**
Area (sq km) **1,360**
Density (pop/sq km) **10,500**

| $13,900 | $12,500 | $10,500 | $8,200 | $7,000 | $5,500 | $2,300 |
|---|---|---|---|---|---|---|
| Shanghai | São Paulo | Mumbai | Cairo | Jakarta | Karachi | Lagos |

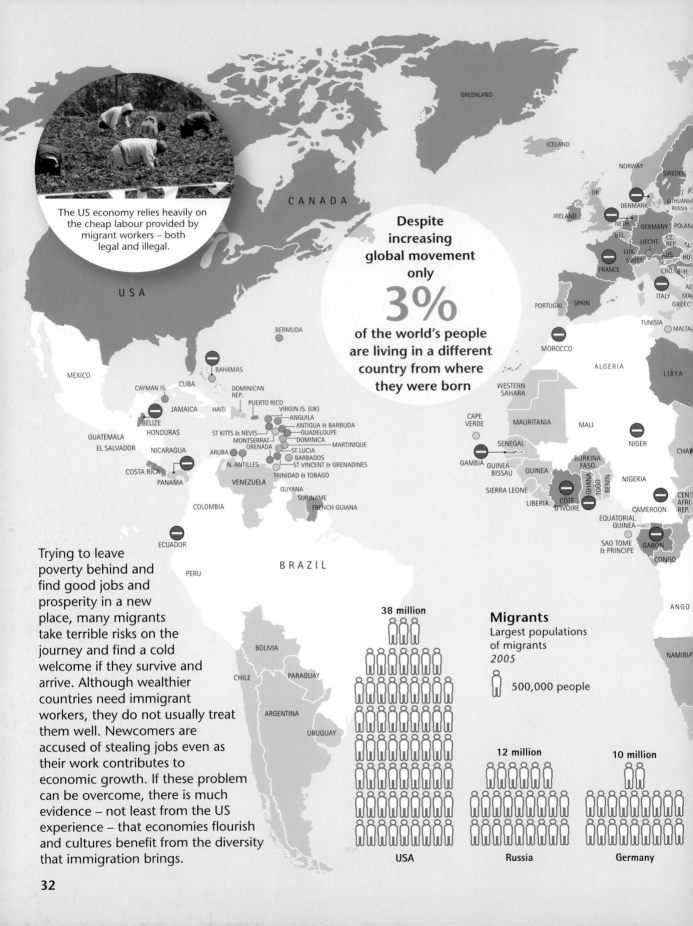

The US economy relies heavily on the cheap labour provided by migrant workers – both legal and illegal.

**Despite increasing global movement only**

# 3%

**of the world's people are living in a different country from where they were born**

Trying to leave poverty behind and find good jobs and prosperity in a new place, many migrants take terrible risks on the journey and find a cold welcome if they survive and arrive. Although wealthier countries need immigrant workers, they do not usually treat them well. Newcomers are accused of stealing jobs even as their work contributes to economic growth. If these problem can be overcome, there is much evidence – not least from the US experience – that economies flourish and cultures benefit from the diversity that immigration brings.

**Migrants**
Largest populations of migrants
*2005*

👤 500,000 people

**38 million**
USA

**12 million**
Russia

**10 million**
Germany

GREENLAND
ICELAND
NORWAY
SWEDEN
UK
IRELAND
DENMARK
LITHUANIA
RUSSIA
NETH.
GERMANY
POLAN
BEL.
CZ.
REP.
SL
LUX.
LIECHT.
AUS
HU
SWITZ.
SL
CRO.
B-H
FRANCE
PORTUGAL
SPAIN
ITALY
MA
GREEC
TUNISIA
MALTA
MOROCCO
ALGERIA
LIBYA
WESTERN SAHARA
CAPE VERDE
MAURITANIA
MALI
NIGER
CHA
SENEGAL
GAMBIA
GUINEA-BISSAU
GUINEA
BURKINA FASO
GHANA
TOGO
BENIN
NIGERIA
SIERRA LEONE
LIBERIA
CÔTE D'IVOIRE
CAMEROON
CENT AFRI REP.
EQUATORIAL GUINEA
SAO TOME & PRINCIPE
GABON
CONGO
ANGO

CANADA
USA
MEXICO
BERMUDA
BAHAMAS
CUBA
CAYMAN IS.
DOMINICAN REP.
JAMAICA
HAITI
PUERTO RICO
VIRGIN IS. (UK)
ANGUILA
BELIZE
HONDURAS
ANTIGUA & BARBUDA
ST KITTS & NEVIS
GUADELOUPE
MONTSERRAT
DOMINICA
GUATEMALA
GRENADA
MARTINIQUE
EL SALVADOR
ARUBA
ST LUCIA
NICARAGUA
N. ANTILLES
BARBADOS
ST VINCENT & GRENADINES
COSTA RICA
TRINIDAD & TOBAGO
PANAMA
VENEZUELA
GUYANA
COLOMBIA
SURINAME
FRENCH GUIANA
ECUADOR
BRAZIL
PERU
BOLIVIA
CHILE
PARAGUAY
ARGENTINA
URUGUAY

NAMIBIA

# Global Movement

**Gulf States**
These countries rely heavily on migrant workers, in particular those from Pakistan, to work in their oil and construction industries.

**Living abroad**
People born outside country, excluding refugees, as percentage of population *2005*

- 50.0% or more
- 25.0% – 49.9%
- 10.0% – 24.9%
- 5.0% – 9.9%
- 1.0% – 4.9%
- fewer than 1.0%

**Immigration policy**
⊖ to lower immigration

RUSSIA
KAZAKHSTAN
MONGOLIA
CHINA
INDIA
INDONESIA
AUSTRALIA

FINLAND
ESTONIA
LATVIA
BELARUS
UKRAINE
MOLDOVA
ROMANIA
BULGARIA
GEORGIA
TURKEY
ARMENIA
CYPRUS
AZER.
SYRIA
LEB.
ISRAEL
IRAQ
JORDAN
PALESTINE AUTHORITY
EGYPT
KUWAIT
BAHRAIN
QATAR
SAUDI ARABIA
UAE
OMAN
YEMEN
SUDAN
ERITREA
DJIBOUTI
ETHIOPIA
UGANDA
KENYA
SOMALIA
DEM. REP. OF CONGO
RWANDA
BURUNDI
TANZANIA
ZAMBIA
MALAWI
ZIMBABWE
BOTSWANA
MOZAMBIQUE
SOUTH AFRICA
SWAZILAND
LESOTHO
MADAGASCAR
SEYCHELLES
COMOROS
MAURITIUS
RÉUNION

UZBEKISTAN
KYRGYZSTAN
TURKMENISTAN
TAJIKISTAN
AFGHANISTAN
IRAN
PAKISTAN
NEPAL
BHUTAN
BANGLADESH
BURMA
LAOS
THAILAND
VIETNAM
CAMBODIA
SRI LANKA
MALDIVES

NORTH KOREA
SOUTH KOREA
JAPAN
Hong Kong SAR
Macao SAR
PHILIPPINES
MALAYSIA
SINGAPORE
BRUNEI

GUAM
NORTHERN MARIANA IS.
MARSHALL ISLANDS
MICRONESIA, FED. STATES OF
NAURU
KIRIBATI
SOLOMON ISLANDS
TUVALU
AMERICAN SAMOA
SAMOA
VANUATU
NEW CALEDONIA
FIJI
COOK ISLANDS
TONGA
NIUE
FRENCH POLYNESIA
PALAU

PAPUA NEW GUINEA
EAST TIMOR
NEW ZEALAND

## 2.6 million
people migrated from poorer to richer countries in 2005

| 6.8 million | 6.5 million | 6.4 million | 6.1 million | 5.7 million | 5.4 million |
|---|---|---|---|---|---|
| Ukraine | France | Saudi Arabia | Canada | India | UK |

33

The graffiti on the wall testifies to the power of the local Commando Vermelho (Red Command) drug cartel over the inhabitants of Cantagalo, a favela on the hillside above the wealthy resort of Ipanema, Rio de Janeiro, Brazil.

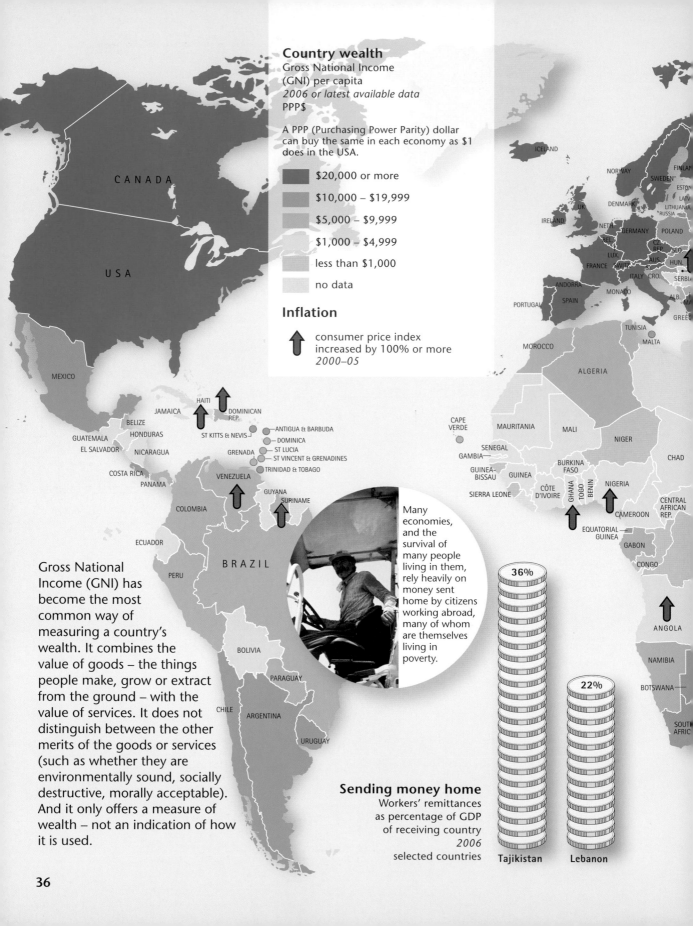

## Country wealth

Gross National Income
(GNI) per capita
*2006 or latest available data*
PPP$

A PPP (Purchasing Power Parity) dollar
can buy the same in each economy as $1
does in the USA.

- $20,000 or more
- $10,000 – $19,999
- $5,000 – $9,999
- $1,000 – $4,999
- less than $1,000
- no data

## Inflation

↑ consumer price index
increased by 100% or more
*2000–05*

Gross National
Income (GNI) has
become the most
common way of
measuring a country's
wealth. It combines the
value of goods – the things
people make, grow or extract
from the ground – with the
value of services. It does not
distinguish between the other
merits of the goods or services
(such as whether they are
environmentally sound, socially
destructive, morally acceptable).
And it only offers a measure of
wealth – not an indication of how
it is used.

Many
economies,
and the
survival of
many people
living in them,
rely heavily on
money sent
home by citizens
working abroad,
many of whom
are themselves
living in
poverty.

## Sending money home

Workers' remittances
as percentage of GDP
of receiving country
*2006*
selected countries

36% — Tajikistan

22% — Lebanon

CANADA
USA
MEXICO
GUATEMALA
BELIZE
HONDURAS
EL SALVADOR
NICARAGUA
COSTA RICA
PANAMA
JAMAICA
HAITI
DOMINICAN REP.
ST KITTS & NEVIS
ANTIGUA & BARBUDA
DOMINICA
ST LUCIA
GRENADA
ST VINCENT & GRENADINES
TRINIDAD & TOBAGO
VENEZUELA
COLOMBIA
GUYANA
SURINAME
ECUADOR
PERU
BRAZIL
BOLIVIA
PARAGUAY
CHILE
ARGENTINA
URUGUAY

ICELAND
NORWAY
SWEDEN
FINLAND
ESTON
DENMARK
LITHUANIA
RUSSIA
UK
IRELAND
NETH
GERMANY
POLAND
BEL
LUX
CZ
SLO
FRANCE
SWITZ
AUS
HUN.
ANDORRA
ITALY
CRO.
SERBIA
MONACO
ALB
PORTUGAL
SPAIN
GREE
TUNISIA
MALTA
MOROCCO
ALGERIA

CAPE VERDE
MAURITANIA
MALI
NIGER
CHAD
SENEGAL
GAMBIA
BURKINA FASO
GUINEA-BISSAU
GUINEA
SIERRA LEONE
CÔTE D'IVOIRE
GHANA
TOGO
BENIN
NIGERIA
CENTRAL AFRICAN REP.
CAMEROON
EQUATORIAL GUINEA
GABON
CONGO
ANGOLA
NAMIBIA
BOTSWANA
SOUTH AFRIC

36

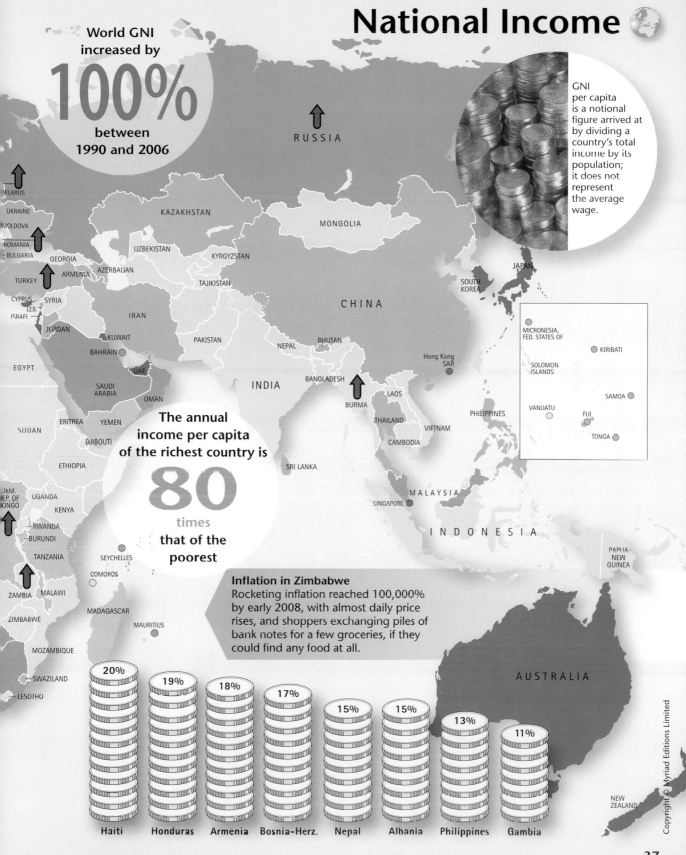

**World GNI increased by**

# 100%

**between 1990 and 2006**

GNI per capita is a notional figure arrived at by dividing a country's total income by its population; it does not represent the average wage.

RUSSIA

BELARUS
UKRAINE
MOLDOVA
ROMANIA
BULGARIA
GEORGIA
TURKEY
ARMENIA
AZERBAIJAN
CYPRUS
LEB.
SYRIA
ISRAEL
JORDAN
KUWAIT
BAHRAIN
UAE
SAUDI ARABIA
OMAN
EGYPT
SUDAN
ERITREA
YEMEN
DJIBOUTI
ETHIOPIA
DEM. REP. OF CONGO
UGANDA
KENYA
RWANDA
BURUNDI
TANZANIA
SEYCHELLES
COMOROS
ZAMBIA
MALAWI
ZIMBABWE
MADAGASCAR
MAURITIUS
MOZAMBIQUE
SWAZILAND
LESOTHO

KAZAKHSTAN
UZBEKISTAN
KYRGYZSTAN
TAJIKISTAN
MONGOLIA
CHINA
IRAN
PAKISTAN
NEPAL
BHUTAN
INDIA
BANGLADESH
BURMA
LAOS
THAILAND
VIETNAM
CAMBODIA
SRI LANKA
MALAYSIA
SINGAPORE
INDONESIA

JAPAN
SOUTH KOREA
Hong Kong SAR
PHILIPPINES

MICRONESIA, FED. STATES OF
KIRIBATI
SOLOMON ISLANDS
SAMOA
VANUATU
FIJI
TONGA

PAPUA NEW GUINEA
AUSTRALIA
NEW ZEALAND

**The annual income per capita of the richest country is**

# 80

**times that of the poorest**

**Inflation in Zimbabwe**
Rocketing inflation reached 100,000% by early 2008, with almost daily price rises, and shoppers exchanging piles of bank notes for a few groceries, if they could find any food at all.

| 20% | 19% | 18% | 17% | 15% | 15% | 13% | 11% |
| Haiti | Honduras | Armenia | Bosnia-Herz. | Nepal | Albania | Philippines | Gambia |

37

There is inequality everywhere. The income of the richest 1 percent of the world's population is equal to the income of the poorest 57 percent. Many people in rich countries live in great poverty, while some people in poor countries live in great wealth. Other kinds of inequality – in power, access to education, recognition of the rights of different groups – are often built on top of the basic income inequity. Measuring the latter thus offers an indication of some of the other potential divisions in a society.

**USA**
In 2008, there were 469 billionaires, and over 51 million people living in poverty.

**The richest 100 people own the equivalent of**

# 3%

**of the world annual GDP**

CANADA

USA

MEXICO

BAHAMAS

BELIZE

HAITI

DOMINICAN REP.

JAMAICA

GUATEMALA    HONDURAS

DOMINICA

EL SALVADOR

ST LUCIA

NICARAGUA

COSTA RICA

VENEZUELA

PANAMA

GUYANA

SURINAME

COLOMBIA

ECUADOR

PERU

BRAZIL

BOLIVIA

PARAGUAY

CHILE

ARGENTINA

URUGUAY

## In the hands of the few
Percentage of billionaires
by country of citizenship
*2008*

USA
41%

Russia
8%

China and
Hong Kong
6%

**There were
1,125 dollar
billionaires
in 2008.**

Germany 5%

India 5%

Turkey 3%

UK 3%

others
25%

Canada 2%

Japan 2%

## Poor people
## in rich countries
People whose income is less than half the median income as percentage of population
*2000–04*
selected countries

19%
Russia

17%
USA

16%
Ireland,
Israel

14%
Greece,
Spain

13%
Italy,
UK

12%
Australia,
Estonia,
Japan

11%
Canada

9%
Poland

8%
Austria,
Germany,
Romania,
Switzerland

7%
France, Hungary,
Netherlands
Sweden

## Map labels

NORWAY
SWEDEN
FINLAND
ESTONIA
RUSSIA
LATVIA
LITHUANIA
RUSSIA
UK
IRELAND
NETH.
GERMANY
BELGIUM
LUX.
POLAND
BELARUS
UKRAINE
AUSTRIA
HUNGARY
SWITZ.
SLOVENIA
MOLDOVA
ITALY
CROATIA
B-H
SERBIA
ROMANIA
MONT.
BULGARIA
SPAIN
ALBANIA
MACEDONIA
GREECE

RUSSIA
KAZAKHSTAN
MONGOLIA
UZBEKISTAN
KYRGYZSTAN
TURKMEN.
TAJIKISTAN
CHINA
SOUTH KOREA
GEORGIA
AZER.
TURKEY
ARMENIA
IRAN
ISRAEL
SYRIA
PALESTINE AUTHORITY
JORDAN
PAKISTAN
NEPAL
TUNISIA
MOROCCO
ALGERIA
EGYPT
INDIA
BANGLADESH
LAOS
THAILAND
VIETNAM
PHILIPPINES
CAMBODIA
YEMEN
SRI LANKA
SINGAPORE
MAURITANIA
MALI
SENEGAL
GAMBIA
BURKINA FASO
GUINEA
CÔTE D'IVOIRE
GHANA
BENIN
NIGERIA
CAMEROON
ETHIOPIA
UGANDA
RWANDA
BURUNDI
TANZANIA
INDONESIA
ZAMBIA
MALAWI
MADAGASCAR
NAMIBIA
BOTSWANA
MOZAMBIQUE
SWAZILAND
SOUTH AFRICA
LESOTHO

### Russia
In 2008, Russia had 87 dollar billionaires, and over 100,000 millionaires, while around 16% of the population lived below subsistence level.

## Distribution of wealth
*latest available 1998–2004*
Gini index

The Gini index measures the degree to which the distribution of wealth within a country is different from a perfectly equal distribution. The higher the index, the greater the inequality.

- 50 – 60    *most unequal*
- 40 – 49
- 30 – 39
- 20 – 29    *most equal*
- no data

● unemployment 10% or more
*latest available data 1996–2005*

### South Africa
There were 49,000 dollar millionaires in South Africa in 2007, a third of them women. The number of super-rich is increasing faster there than almost anywhere in the world.

6%
Demark, Norway

5%
Czech Republic, Finland

A good guide to the quality of life available in a country is to measure not just wealth but also health and education. The UN's Human Development Index (HDI) does this each year. It reveals the unsurprising insight that, to the extent that quality of life can be measured, richer countries offer more than poor ones. But among both rich and poor countries there are surprises. Some countries seem to be particularly effective at transforming their economic wealth into real benefit for their citizens. Many others are, however, much less effective – either because the political leadership lacks the will to do better, or because the country's history has not included proper investment in the foundations of education and good health care, so it lacks the capacity. Like all national-level statistics, a country's ranking on the HDI may obscure important internal differences. But when a country is ranked much lower on the HDI than its Gross National Income suggests it should be, this is a sign that there are severe social inequalities.

## Healthy water

Percentage of population with access to improved water source
*2004 or latest available data*

- fewer than 50%
- 50% – 69%
- 70% – 89%
- 90% or more
- no data

The proportion of people with access to a good source of water has increased in about half of all countries since 1990, but has declined in a few.

40

# Quality of Life

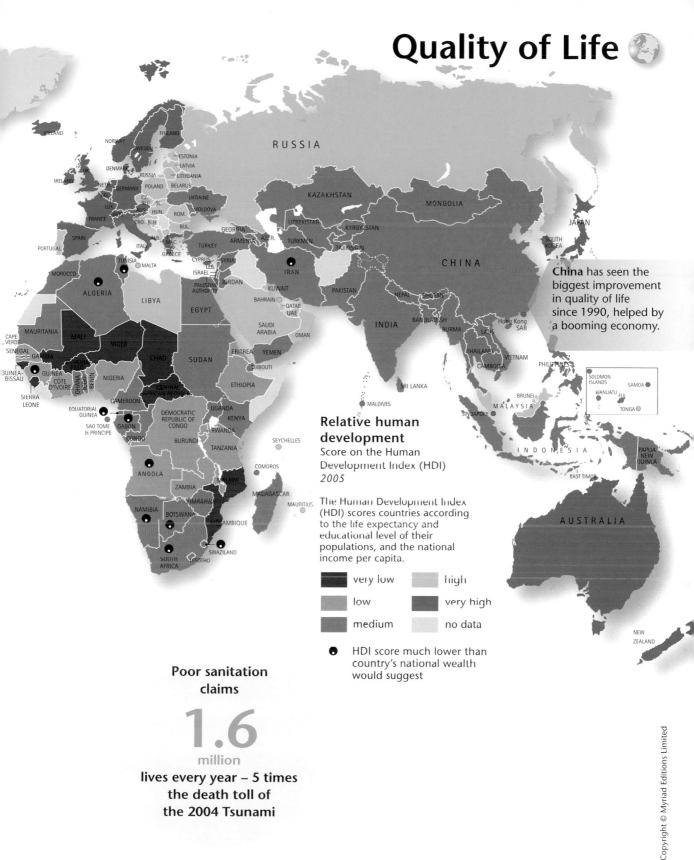

China has seen the biggest improvement in quality of life since 1990, helped by a booming economy.

## Relative human development

Score on the Human Development Index (HDI) *2005*

The Human Development Index (HDI) scores countries according to the life expectancy and educational level of their populations, and the national income per capita.

- very low
- low
- medium
- high
- very high
- no data

● HDI score much lower than country's national wealth would suggest

### Poor sanitation claims

## 1.6
million

lives every year – 5 times the death toll of the 2004 Tsunami

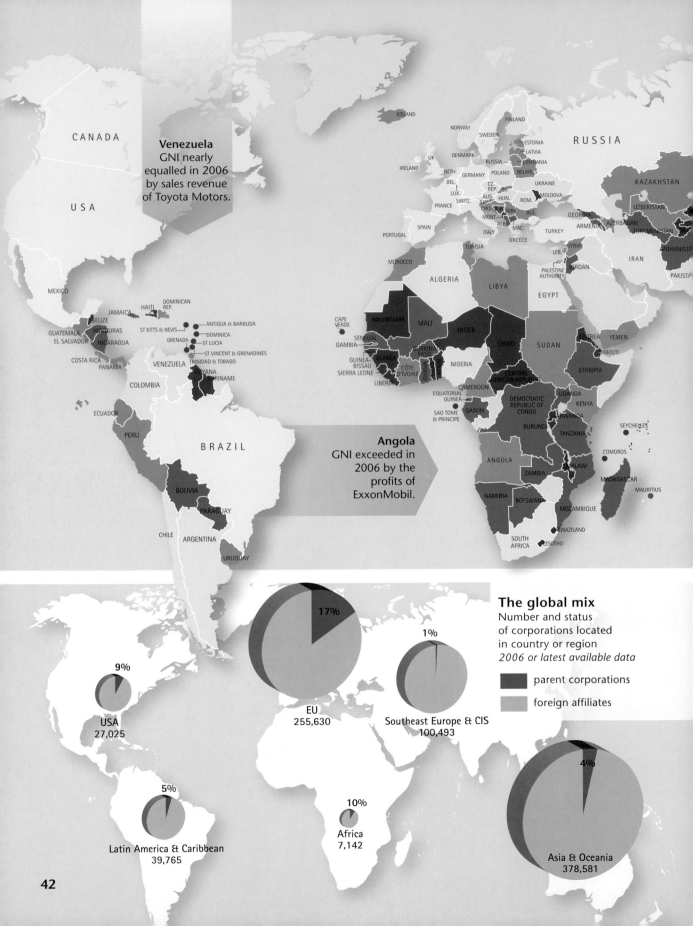

CANADA

USA

**Venezuela**
GNI nearly equalled in 2006 by sales revenue of Toyota Motors.

MEXICO

JAMAICA
HAITI
DOMINICAN REP.
BELIZE
GUATEMALA
EL SALVADOR
HONDURAS
NICARAGUA
ST KITTS & NEVIS
ANTIGUA & BARBUDA
DOMINICA
GRENADA
ST LUCIA
ST VINCENT & GRENADINES
COSTA RICA
PANAMA
VENEZUELA
TRINIDAD & TOBAGO
GUYANA
SURINAME

COLOMBIA

ECUADOR

PERU

BRAZIL

**Angola**
GNI exceeded in 2006 by the profits of ExxonMobil.

BOLIVIA

PARAGUAY

CHILE

ARGENTINA

URUGUAY

ICELAND
NORWAY
SWEDEN
FINLAND
RUSSIA
ESTONIA
LATVIA
DENMARK
LITHUANIA
UK
IRELAND
NETH.
GERMANY
RUSSIA
POLAND
BELARUS
BEL.
LUX.
CZ. REP.
UKRAINE
FRANCE
AUS.
SWITZ.
HUN.
SL.
MOLDOVA
CRO.
SERB.
ROM.
MONT.
BUL.
ALB.
MAC.
GEORGIA
SPAIN
ITALY
GREECE
TURKEY
ARMENIA
PORTUGAL

KAZAKHSTAN
UZBEKISTAN
AZERBAIJAN
TURKMENISTAN
AFGHANISTAN
IRAN
PAKISTAN

TUNISIA
SYRIA
LEB.
JORDAN
PALESTINE AUTHORITY
MOROCCO
ALGERIA
LIBYA
EGYPT

CAPE VERDE
MAURITANIA
MALI
NIGER
CHAD
SUDAN
ERITREA
YEMEN
SENEGAL
GAMBIA
BURKINA FASO
NIGERIA
DJIBOUTI
GUINEA-BISSAU
GUINEA
CÔTE D'IVOIRE
GHANA
SIERRA LEONE
LIBERIA
CENTRAL AFRICAN REPUBLIC
ETHIOPIA
EQUATORIAL GUINEA
CAMEROON
UGANDA
KENYA
SAO TOME & PRINCIPE
GABON
DEMOCRATIC REPUBLIC OF CONGO
RWANDA
SEYCHELLES
BURUNDI
TANZANIA
COMOROS
ANGOLA
MALAWI
MADAGASCAR
MAURITIUS
ZAMBIA
NAMIBIA
BOTSWANA
ZIMBABWE
MOZAMBIQUE
SWAZILAND
SOUTH AFRICA
LESOTHO

## The global mix
Number and status of corporations located in country or region
*2006 or latest available data*

■ parent corporations
■ foreign affiliates

9%
USA
27,025

17%
EU
255,630

1%
Southeast Europe & CIS
100,493

5%
Latin America & Caribbean
39,765

10%
Africa
7,142

4%
Asia & Oceania
378,581

# Transnationals

## Corporate wealth

Gross national income compared with sales revenue of selected transnationals
*2006*

GNI smaller than sales revenue of:

- Tata Motors ($5.2 billion)
- British Airways ($14.25 billion)
- Hewlett Packard ($94.08 billion)
- Wal-Mart ($348.6 billion)
- GNI larger than sales revenue of any transnational

Globalization of the world economy is not new, but it is continually advancing. Transnational corporations have bases in many countries. Their interests reach beyond national loyalties and their wealth far outreaches that of many countries. The sales revenue of Wal-Mart stores in 2006 was close to the GNI of Indonesia – the world's third most populous country – and exceeded the combined GNI of the poorest 49 states.

**Thailand**
GNI exceeded in 2006 by sales revenue of General Motors.

1.8 million people are employed by Wal-Mart. If each has two dependants, the company is responsible for the well-being of the equivalent of the population of Denmark.

## Global players

Corporations with presence in highest number of host countries and location of parent corporation
*2007*

|  |  |  |
|---|---|---|
| 103 | Deutsche Post | Germany |
| 96 | Royal Dutch/Shell Group | UK, Netherlands |
| 94 | Nestlé | Switzerland |
| 85 | Siemens | Germany |
| 84 | BASF | Germany |
| 76 | Bayer | Germany |
| 74 | Citigroup | USA |
| 72 | Procter & Gamble | USA |
| 66 | IBM | USA |
| 62 | Philips Electronics | Netherlands |
| 62 | Total | France |
| 62 | BP | UK |

# Foreign Investment

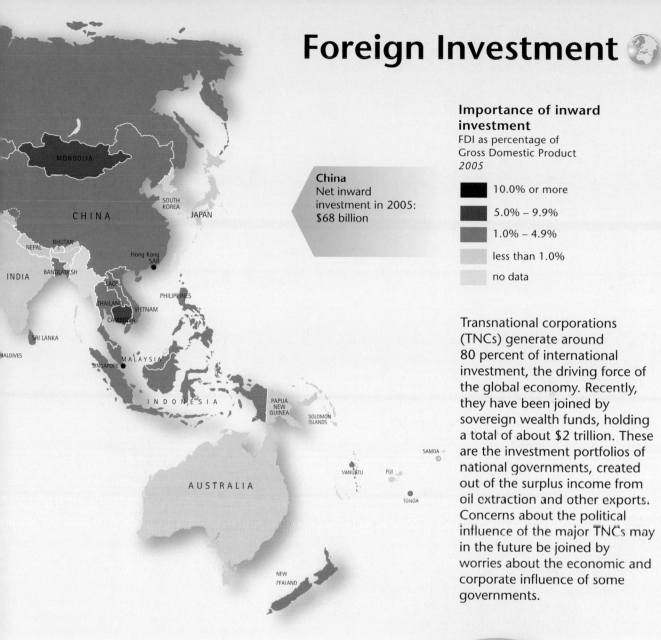

**China**
Net inward investment in 2005: $68 billion

## Importance of inward investment
FDI as percentage of Gross Domestic Product
*2005*

- 10.0% or more
- 5.0% – 9.9%
- 1.0% – 4.9%
- less than 1.0%
- no data

Transnational corporations (TNCs) generate around 80 percent of international investment, the driving force of the global economy. Recently, they have been joined by sovereign wealth funds, holding a total of about $2 trillion. These are the investment portfolios of national governments, created out of the surplus income from oil extraction and other exports. Concerns about the political influence of the major TNCs may in the future be joined by worries about the economic and corporate influence of some governments.

## Attractiveness to investors
UNCTAD assessment of performance and potential
*2005–07*

- **front-runners:** countries with high FDI potential and performance
- **above potential:** countries with low FDI potential but strong FDI performance
- **below potential:** countries with high FDI potential but low FDI performance
- **under-performers:** countries with both low FDI potential and performance
- no data

Multi-national companies from the larger developing nations are increasingly investing overseas. In 2008, the Indian company Tata bought Jaguar and Land Rover from Ford.

International trade continues to increase, and while comparisons over time are distorted by price inflation, the growth is nonetheless impressive. In recent years, services – actions carried out for money, rather than goods exchanged for money – have become an increasingly important part both of advanced national economies and of world trade. But for almost all countries, traded goods – merchandise – continues to be far more important. Some countries are so dependent on international trade that the combined value of imports and exports exceeds their national income. Yet the USA, which remains a key engine of the world economy, has a relatively low dependence on international trade. This gives it the capacity to recover quickly when the economic cycle turns down.

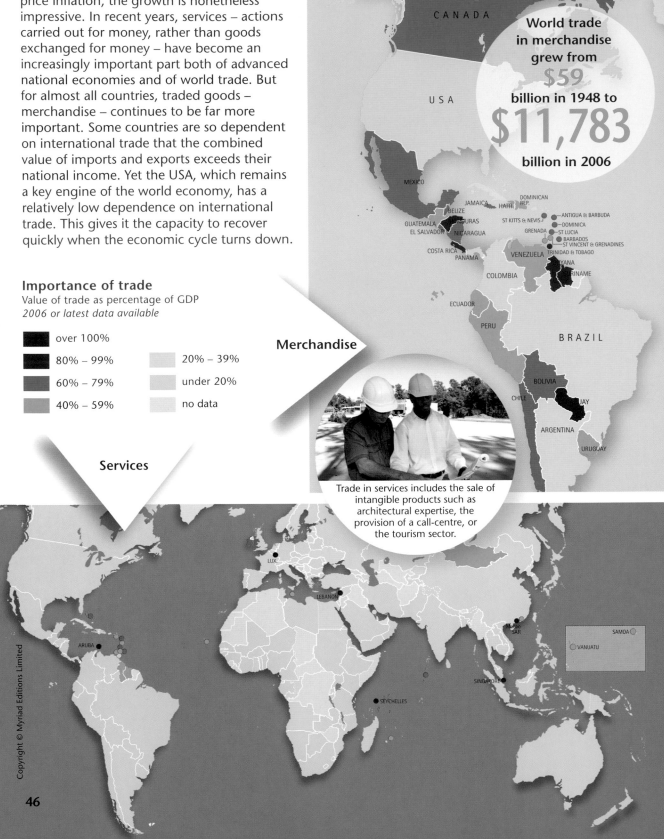

World trade in merchandise grew from $59 billion in 1948 to $11,783 billion in 2006

## Importance of trade
Value of trade as percentage of GDP
*2006 or latest data available*

- over 100%
- 80% – 99%
- 60% – 79%
- 40% – 59%
- 20% – 39%
- under 20%
- no data

**Merchandise**

**Services**

Trade in services includes the sale of intangible products such as architectural expertise, the provision of a call-centre, or the tourism sector.

# Trade

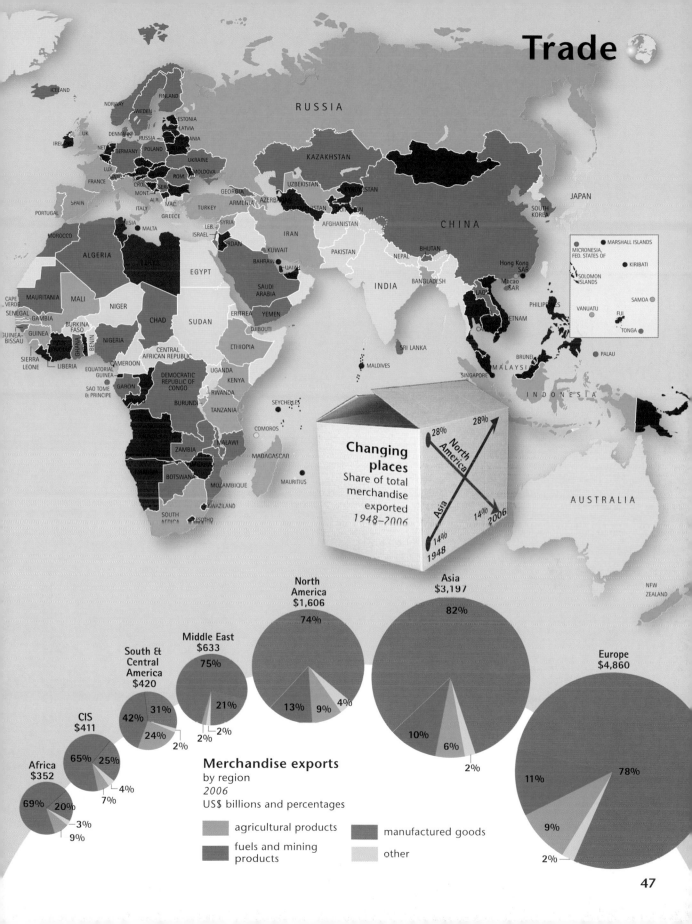

## Changing places
Share of total merchandise exported 1948–2006

North America
28% 28%

Asia
14% 14%

2006
1948

## Merchandise exports
by region
2006
US$ billions and percentages

- agricultural products
- fuels and mining products
- manufactured goods
- other

**Africa** $352
69% 20% 3% 9%

**CIS** $411
65% 25% 4% 7%

**South & Central America** $420
42% 31% 24% 2% 2%

**Middle East** $633
75% 21% 2% 2%

**North America** $1,606
74% 13% 9% 4%

**Asia** $3,197
82% 10% 6% 2%

**Europe** $4,860
78% 11% 9% 2%

Communications technology is essential for business, enabling those with access to tap into the global market. The communications sector itself represents a massive market, with cell-phone revenues in the USA and Japan each worth more than the GDP of around half the countries in the world. Internet-enabled cell phones are contributing substantially to this revenue.

Although internet access is still patchy in low-income countries, where there are few telephone landlines the cell phone is beginning to bridge the communications divide. In 2004, for the first time the number of cell-phone users in non-OECD countries equalled those in OECD countries.

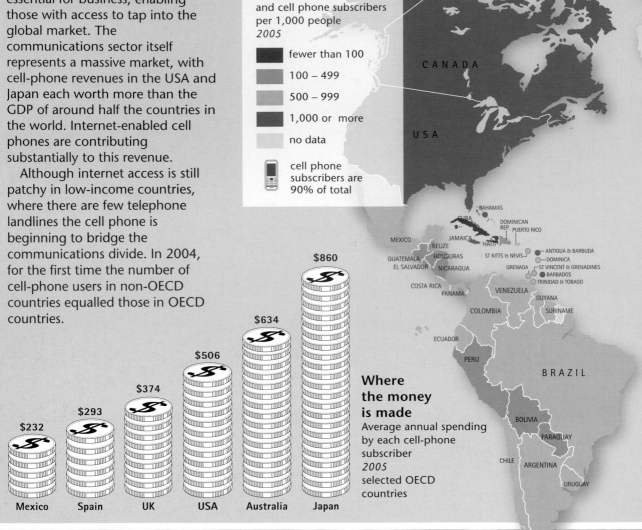

## Telephones
Number of fixed lines and cell phone subscribers per 1,000 people
*2005*

- fewer than 100
- 100 – 499
- 500 – 999
- 1,000 or more
- no data

cell phone subscribers are 90% of total

## Where the money is made
Average annual spending by each cell-phone subscriber
*2005*
selected OECD countries

- Mexico $232
- Spain $293
- UK $374
- USA $506
- Australia $634
- Japan $860

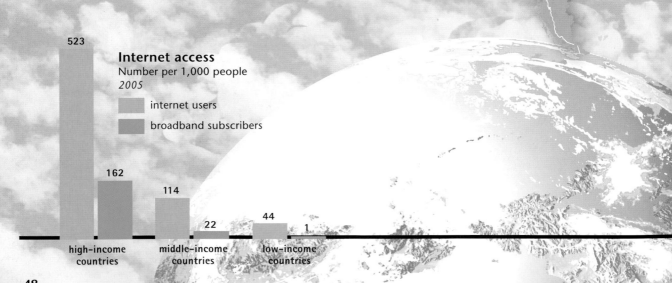

## Internet access
Number per 1,000 people
*2005*

- internet users
- broadband subscribers

| high-income countries | | middle-income countries | | low-income countries | |
|---|---|---|---|---|---|
| 523 | 162 | 114 | 22 | 44 | 1 |

# Communications

ICELAND
NORWAY
SWEDEN
FINLAND
UK
DENMARK
IRELAND
NETH.
GERMANY
POLAND
BELARUS
RUSSIA
ESTONIA
LATVIA
LITHUANIA
BEL.
LUX.
FRANCE
CZECH REP.
SLVK.
UKRAINE
SWITZ.
AUS.
HUN.
ROM.
MOLDOVA
ANDORRA
SPAIN
ITALY
CRO.
B-H
SERB.
MONT.
BUL.
GEORGIA
ARMENIA
AZERBAIJAN
PORTUGAL
ALB.
MAC.
GREECE
TURKEY
KAZAKHSTAN
MONGOLIA
RUSSIA

JAPAN
SOUTH KOREA

TUNISIA
MALTA
CYPRUS
LEB.
SYRIA
IRAQ
IRAN
KYRGYZSTAN
CHINA

MOROCCO
ISRAEL
JORDAN
PALESTINE AUTHORITY
KUWAIT
AFGHANISTAN
PAKISTAN

ALGERIA
EGYPT
SAUDI ARABIA
BAHRAIN
QATAR
UAE
OMAN
NEPAL
BHUTAN
Hong Kong SAR
Macao SAR
MICRONESIA, FED. STATES OF

CAPE VERDE
MAURITANIA
MALI
NIGER
CHAD
SUDAN
ERITREA
YEMEN
DJIBOUTI
INDIA
BANGLADESH
BURMA
LAOS
PHILIPPINES
SOLOMON ISLANDS

SENEGAL
GAMBIA
GUINEA
BURKINA FASO
GHANA
NIGERIA
CENTRAL AFRICAN REPUBLIC
ETHIOPIA
THAILAND
VIETNAM

CÔTE D'IVOIRE
CAMEROON
SOMALIA
SRI LANKA
BRUNEI
NEW CALEDONIA
FRENCH POLYNESIA

SAO TOME & PRINCIPE
GABON
CONGO
DEM. REP. OF CONGO
UGANDA
KENYA
RWANDA
BURUNDI
MALDIVES
MALAYSIA

EQUATORIAL GUINEA
TANZANIA
SEYCHELLES
SINGAPORE

ANGOLA
ZAMBIA
MALAWI
COMOROS
MADAGASCAR
MAURITIUS
INDONESIA

NAMIBIA
ZIMBABWE
BOTSWANA
MOZAMBIQUE
PAPUA NEW GUINEA

SOUTH AFRICA
SWAZILAND
LESOTHO

AUSTRALIA

NEW ZEALAND

In Africa, since 2000, the cell-phone network has expanded enormously, covering over a tenth of the population of many countries.

## Most popular internet search engines
Total number of searches made
*August 2007*

Total searches in August 2007:
61 billion

| | |
|---|---|
| 37 billion | Google |
| 8.5 billion | Yahoo |
| 3.2 billion | Baidu (China) |
| 2.1 billion | Microsoft |
| 2.0 billion | NHN (South Korea) |
| 1.3 billion | eBay |
| 1.2 billion | Time Warner |

## Searchers
Number of internet search engine users in each region
*August 2007*

258 million — Asia-Pacific
210 million — Europe
206 million — North America
30 million — MiddleEast & Africa

The **USA** is attempting to reduce its heavy reliance on imported fuels by investing in technology to convert plant and waste matter into biofuels.

**Germany**
Nearly a third of its gas comes from Russia, across Ukraine.

The International Energy Agency predicts an increase in global demand for energy of 50 percent by 2030, much of it from the booming economies of China and India.

The 1959 **Antarctic** Treaty has protected the continent from exploitation, but in the face of faltering oil supplies elsewhere, it may not survive untouched for ever.

CANADA

USA

MEXICO

CUBA

JAMAICA   HAITI   DOMINICAN REP.

GUATEMALA   HONDURAS
EL SALVADOR   NICARAGUA

COSTA RICA
PANAMA

TRINIDAD & TOBAGO

VENEZUELA

COLOMBIA

ECUADOR

PERU

BRAZIL

BOLIVIA

PARAGUAY

CHILE   ARGENTINA

URUGUAY

ICELAND

NORWAY   SWEDEN   FINLA

UK   DENMARK   ESTO
IRELAND   LITHUANIA
NETH.   RUSSIA
BEL.   GERMANY   POLAND
LUX.   CZ REP.   SLO
FRANCE   SWITZ   AUS.   HUN.
CRO   B-H
ALB.

PORTUGAL   SPAIN   ITALY   GREE

TUNISIA   MALTA
MOROCCO

ALGERIA   LIBYA

SENEGAL

CÔTE
D'IVOIRE   GHANA   TOGO   BENIN   NIGERIA

CAMEROON

GABON   DEM REP. CON

ANGOLA

NAMIBIA

BOTSWANA

SOU
AFRI

# Energy Trade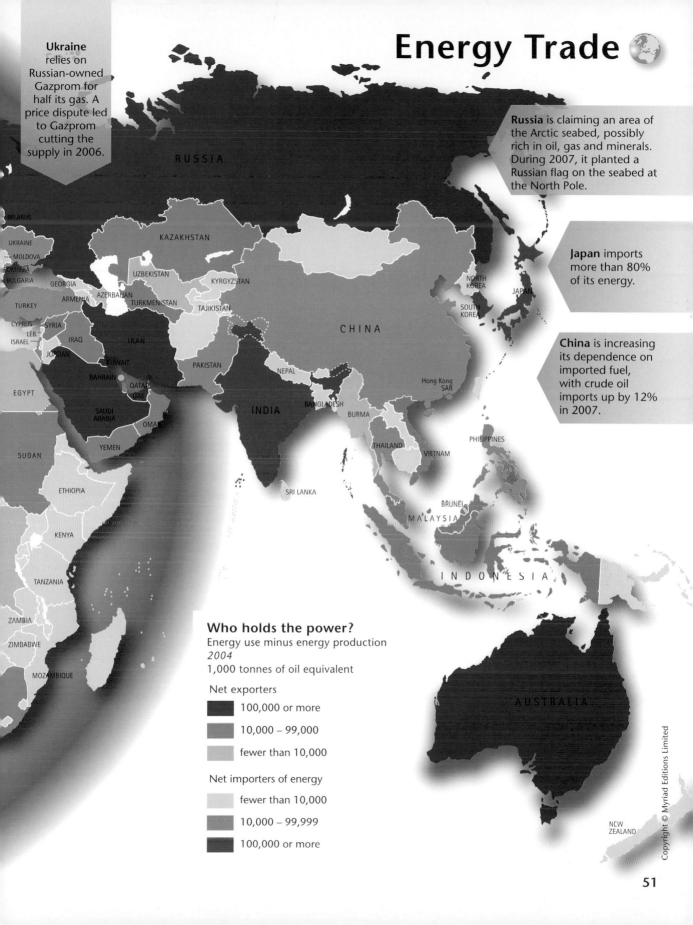

**Ukraine** relies on Russian-owned Gazprom for half its gas. A price dispute led to Gazprom cutting the supply in 2006.

**Russia** is claiming an area of the Arctic seabed, possibly rich in oil, gas and minerals. During 2007, it planted a Russian flag on the seabed at the North Pole.

**Japan** imports more than 80% of its energy.

**China** is increasing its dependence on imported fuel, with crude oil imports up by 12% in 2007.

RUSSIA

BELARUS
UKRAINE
MOLDOVA
ROMANIA
BULGARIA
GEORGIA
TURKEY
ARMENIA
CYPRUS
SYRIA
LEB.
ISRAEL
JORDAN
IRAQ
EGYPT
SUDAN
ETHIOPIA
KENYA
TANZANIA
ZAMBIA
ZIMBABWE
MOZAMBIQUE

KAZAKHSTAN
AZERBAIJAN
UZBEKISTAN
TURKMENISTAN
KYRGYZSTAN
TAJIKISTAN
IRAN
KUWAIT
BAHRAIN
QATAR
UAE
SAUDI ARABIA
OMAN
YEMEN
PAKISTAN

CHINA
NEPAL
INDIA
BANGLADESH
BURMA
SRI LANKA
THAILAND
VIETNAM

NORTH KOREA
SOUTH KOREA
JAPAN
Hong Kong SAR

PHILIPPINES
BRUNEI
MALAYSIA
INDONESIA

AUSTRALIA

NEW ZEALAND

## Who holds the power?

Energy use minus energy production
*2004*
1,000 tonnes of oil equivalent

**Net exporters**

- 100,000 or more
- 10,000 – 99,000
- fewer than 10,000

**Net importers of energy**

- fewer than 10,000
- 10,000 – 99,999
- 100,000 or more

51

## Importance of tourism
Receipts from overseas tourists as percentage of export earnings
*2005*

- 40% or more
- 20% – 39%
- 10% – 19%
- less than 10%
- no data

## Increasing popularity
More than 5 million additional overseas tourists a year
*2005, compared with 1995*

- 10 million or more *number given*
- 5 million – 9 million

The new-found wealth of many of China's citizens is enabling them to travel overseas. There were 31 million Chinese tourists abroad in 2005, seven times the number in 1995.

KAZAKHSTAN

KYRGYZSTAN

TAJIKISTAN

**27m**
CHINA

PAKISTAN

NEPAL

BANGLADESH

Macao SAR  Hong Kong SAR
**13m**

SOUTH KOREA  JAPAN

THAILAND  VIETNAM  PHILIPPINES
CAMBODIA

SRI LANKA
**9m** MALAYSIA

INDONESIA

## Country of origin
Countries generating highest number of overseas tourists
*2005*

The growing recognition of the damage tourism can do to the culture and environment of the places visited, has led to efforts at "responsible tourism."

VANUATU

AUSTRALIA

SAMOA

FRENCH POLYNESIA

France
22m

Malaysia
31m

Czech Republic
37m

Poland
41m

USA
64m

UK
66m

Germany
77m

Tourism is fundamental to the economy of many countries but is often a burden on local societies. The most beautiful location cannot sustain tourism without a well-developed transport, energy, water and sanitation infrastructure. As a result, most of the biggest tourist destinations are rich countries.

# Tourism

There were

## 40%

more international tourists in 2005, than in 1995

**Middle East & North Africa**
Over 20% of export earnings in the region arise from the tourist industry.

**Country of destination**
Countries attracting highest number of overseas tourists
*2005*

Map labels (cameras):

- UK **6m**
- RUSSIA **12m**
- **7m**
- UKRAINE **12m**
- FRANCE **16m**
- **13m**
- CROATIA **7m**
- ITALY **5m**
- SPAIN PORTUGAL **21m**
- EGYPT **5m**
- SAUDI ARABIA **6m**
- USA **6m**

Suitcases:

- Germany **22m**
- Mexico **22m**
- Russian Federation **22m**
- Hong Kong, China **23m**
- UK **30m**
- Italy **37m**
- China **47m**
- USA **49m**
- Spain **56m**
- France **76m**

Tourism often threatens the natural and architectural beauty that attracts the visitors. It is a potent form of cultural invasion, and in extreme circumstances armed groups have declared tourists to be legitimate targets for attack.

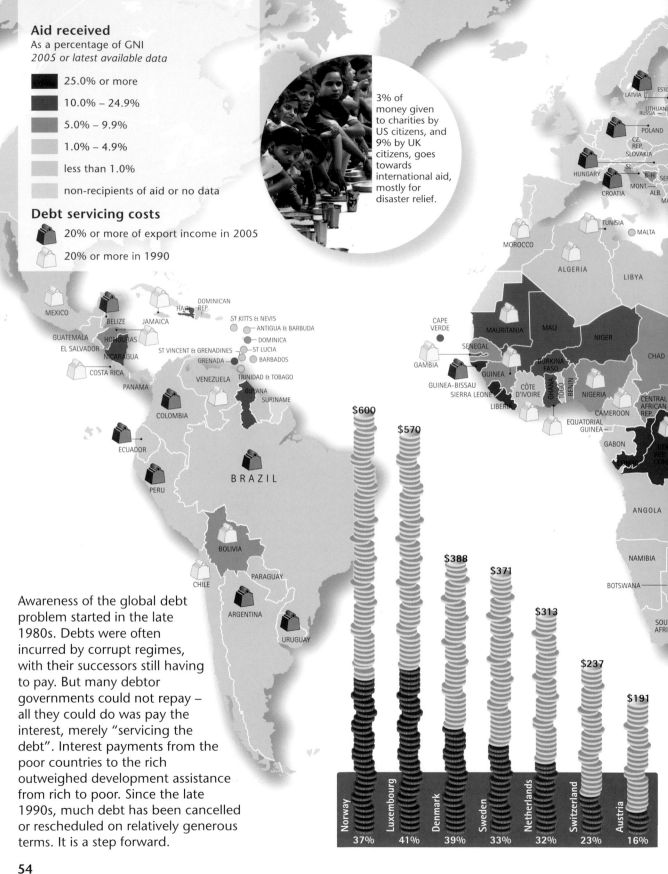

## Aid received
As a percentage of GNI
*2005 or latest available data*

- 25.0% or more
- 10.0% – 24.9%
- 5.0% – 9.9%
- 1.0% – 4.9%
- less than 1.0%
- non-recipients of aid or no data

## Debt servicing costs

- 20% or more of export income in 2005
- 20% or more in 1990

3% of money given to charities by US citizens, and 9% by UK citizens, goes towards international aid, mostly for disaster relief.

Awareness of the global debt problem started in the late 1980s. Debts were often incurred by corrupt regimes, with their successors still having to pay. But many debtor governments could not repay – all they could do was pay the interest, merely "servicing the debt". Interest payments from the poor countries to the rich outweighed development assistance from rich to poor. Since the late 1990s, much debt has been cancelled or rescheduled on relatively generous terms. It is a step forward.

| | | | | | | | |
|---|---|---|---|---|---|---|---|
| $600 | $570 | $388 | $371 | $313 | | $237 | $191 |
| Norway | Luxembourg | Denmark | Sweden | Netherlands | | Switzerland | Austria |
| 37% | 41% | 39% | 33% | 32% | | 23% | 16% |

# Debt and Aid

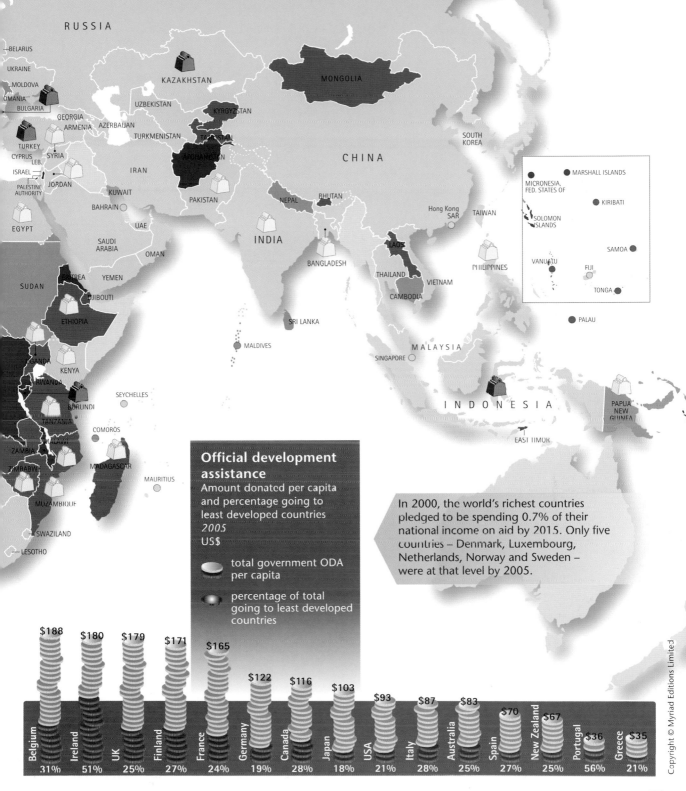

RUSSIA

- BELARUS
- UKRAINE
- MOLDOVA
- ROMANIA
- BULGARIA

GEORGIA
ARMENIA
AZERBAIJAN
TURKEY
CYPRUS
LEB.
SYRIA
ISRAEL
PALESTINE
AUTHORITY
JORDAN
EGYPT

KAZAKHSTAN
UZBEKISTAN
TURKMENISTAN
KYRGYZSTAN
TAJIKISTAN
AFGHANISTAN
IRAN
KUWAIT
BAHRAIN
UAE
SAUDI
ARABIA
OMAN
YEMEN

MONGOLIA

CHINA

SOUTH
KOREA

PAKISTAN
NEPAL
BHUTAN
INDIA
BANGLADESH
Hong Kong
SAR
TAIWAN

LAOS
THAILAND
VIETNAM
CAMBODIA

SUDAN
ERITREA
DJIBOUTI
ETHIOPIA
UGANDA
KENYA
RWANDA
BURUNDI
TANZANIA
SEYCHELLES
COMOROS
MALAWI
ZAMBIA
MADAGASCAR
MAURITIUS
ZIMBABWE
MOZAMBIQUE
SWAZILAND
LESOTHO

SRI LANKA
MALDIVES

SINGAPORE

MALAYSIA

MICRONESIA,
FED. STATES OF
MARSHALL ISLANDS
KIRIBATI
SOLOMON
ISLANDS
SAMOA
VANUATU
FIJI
TONGA
PALAU

INDONESIA

PHILIPPINES

PAPUA
NEW
GUINEA

EAST TIMOR

## Official development assistance
Amount donated per capita and percentage going to least developed countries
2005
US$

- total government ODA per capita
- percentage of total going to least developed countries

In 2000, the world's richest countries pledged to be spending 0.7% of their national income on aid by 2015. Only five countries – Denmark, Luxembourg, Netherlands, Norway and Sweden – were at that level by 2005.

| Country | Amount | Percentage |
|---|---|---|
| Belgium | $188 | 31% |
| Ireland | $180 | 51% |
| UK | $179 | 25% |
| Finland | $171 | 27% |
| France | $165 | 24% |
| Germany | $122 | 19% |
| Canada | $116 | 28% |
| Japan | $103 | 18% |
| USA | $93 | 21% |
| Italy | $87 | 28% |
| Australia | $83 | 25% |
| Spain | $70 | 27% |
| New Zealand | $67 | 25% |
| Portugal | $36 | 56% |
| Greece | $35 | 21% |

Graffiti on the wall of the Dheisheh Camp, Bethlehem, in the Occupied West Bank. Established by the UN in 1948, it is home to 11,000 Palestinians.

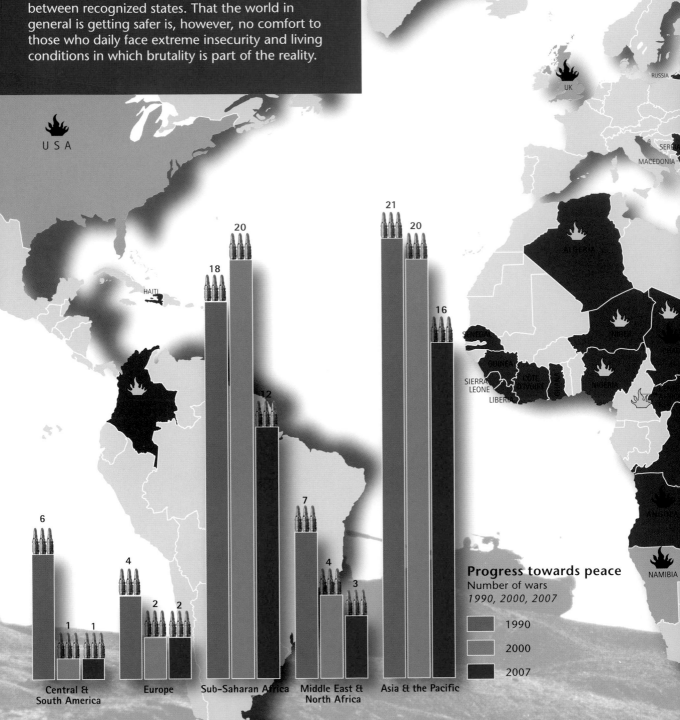

This is an era of growing peace, despite the war horrors that persist in Afghanistan, Darfur in Sudan, Iraq, and other regions. The frequency and lethality of wars has been declining since the end of the Cold War in 1989. Most wars since the end of World War II have been within states, or between states and their colonies, rather than between recognized states. That the world in general is getting safer is, however, no comfort to those who daily face extreme insecurity and living conditions in which brutality is part of the reality.

USA

RUSSIA

UK

SERBIA

MACEDONIA

HAITI

ALGERIA

SENEGAL

GUINEA

SIERRA LEONE

COTE D'IVOIRE

GHANA

NIGER

NIGERIA

LIBERIA

ANGOLA

NAMIBIA

**Progress towards peace**
Number of wars
*1990, 2000, 2007*

1990
2000
2007

6    1    1    Central & South America

4    2    2    Europe

18   20   12   Sub-Saharan Africa

7    4    3    Middle East & North Africa

21   20   16   Asia & the Pacific

58

# War in the 21st century

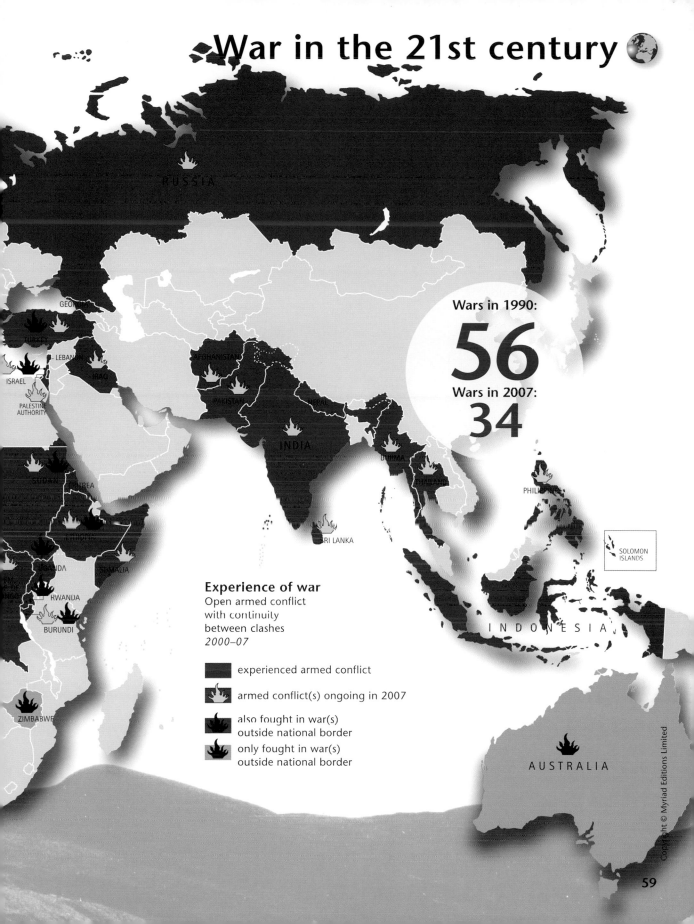

RUSSIA

GEORGIA

TURKEY

LEBANON

ISRAEL

IRAQ

PALESTINE
AUTHORITY

AFGHANISTAN

PAKISTAN

NEPAL

INDIA

SUDAN

ERITREA

ETHIOPIA

UGANDA

SOMALIA

RWANDA

BURUNDI

ZIMBABWE

BURMA

THAILAND

SRI LANKA

PHILIPPINES

SOLOMON
ISLANDS

INDONESIA

AUSTRALIA

**Wars in 1990:**

# 56

**Wars in 2007:**

# 34

## Experience of war
Open armed conflict
with continuity
between clashes
2000–07

- experienced armed conflict
- armed conflict(s) ongoing in 2007
- also fought in war(s)
  outside national border
- only fought in war(s)
  outside national border

## Child soldiers
2001–05

used in active combat by militias

RUSSIA
AFGHANISTAN
ISRAEL
IRAQ
PALESTINE AUTHORITY
BURMA
PHILIPPINES
CHAD   SUDAN
CENTRAL AFRICAN REP.
COLOMBIA
LIBERIA
CÔTE D'IVOIRE
UGANDA   SOMALIA
SRI LANKA
DEM. REP. OF CONGO — BURUNDI
INDONESIA
ANGOLA

Non-state wars occur where the state has a limited capacity to impose order – or has simply collapsed. This may happen alongside one or more internal wars. In some cases, the guerrillas and paramilitaries are supported by the government and used as deniable instruments of policy. In other cases, factions within the government support one side as part of their internal power struggle.

In all cases, the civilian population suffers. Although governments are capable of great brutality, most campaigns of violence against civilians are carried out by non-state forces. One form of abuse, in which militias lead the way though governments are also culpable, is forcing children to fight, often brutalizing them to reduce their resistance to committing violence. When peace returns, helping former child soldiers find a normal life is a delicate and challenging task.

## Non-state wars
2002–07

at least one armed conflict in which no state is involved

MEXICO
GUATEMALA
SENEGAL
COLOMBIA
ECUADOR
BRAZIL

**Colombia**
United Self-Defence Forces – broadly, pro-government, often organized by major landowners – against various leftwing groups, the largest being the Revolutionary Armed Forces of Colombia (FARC).

## Campaigns of violence against civilian populations
Number of campaigns by perpetrator
1989–2005

⎯⎯ non-state armed groups

⎯⎯ governments

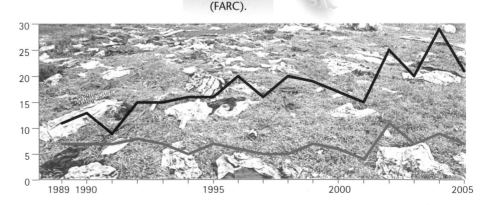

60

# Warlords and Militias

There are some wars – fought, as others are, for control of territory, resources or power – in which neither party is a state. Most of the fighting in Somalia since 1991 is a case in point. The parties to these wars are armed guerrilla groups and militias. These conflicts have only recently been recognized as a serious international problem, so information on them is patchy and does not go back very far.

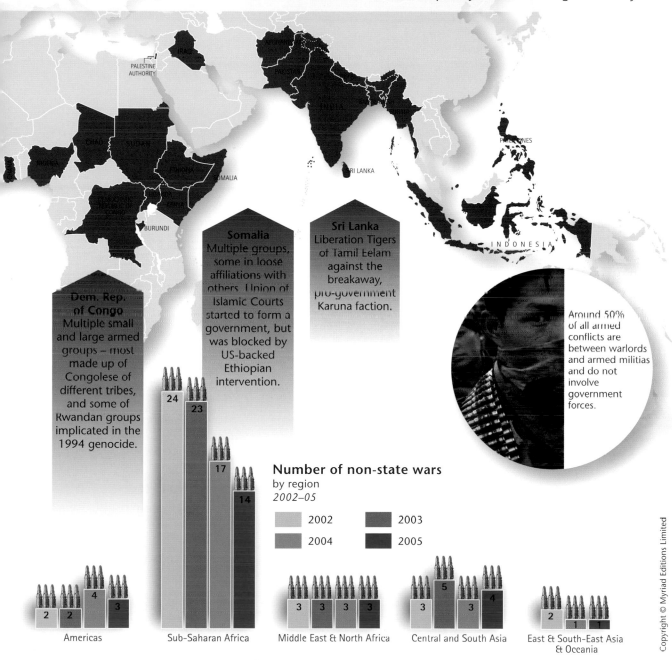

**Dem. Rep. of Congo**
Multiple small and large armed groups – most made up of Congolese of different tribes, and some of Rwandan groups implicated in the 1994 genocide.

**Somalia**
Multiple groups, some in loose affiliations with others. Union of Islamic Courts started to form a government, but was blocked by US-backed Ethiopian intervention.

**Sri Lanka**
Liberation Tigers of Tamil Eelam against the breakaway, pro-government Karuna faction.

Around 50% of all armed conflicts are between warlords and armed militias and do not involve government forces.

**Number of non-state wars**
by region
*2002–05*

- 2002
- 2003
- 2004
- 2005

**Americas**
2  2  4  3

**Sub-Saharan Africa**
24  23  17  14

**Middle East & North Africa**
3  3  3  3

**Central and South Asia**
3  5  3  4

**East & South-East Asia & Oceania**
2  1  1

**From 2002 to 2007, there was an increase in recorded terrorist incidents of**

# 750%

**New York and Washington DC, USA, September 2001**

Al Qaida terrorists crash three airliners into the World Trade Centre and the Pentagon, killing 2,973 people of more than 50 nationalities.

**London, UK, July 2005**

Four suicide bombers on public transport kill 52 people.

**Madrid, Spain, March 2004**

Bombs on four trains kill 191 people.

**Israel/Palestine**

Since 2000, Palestinian groups have used suicide bombings and rocket attacks against occupation by Israel, which responds with targeted killings, rocket strikes and army offensives. By 2007, 1,031 Israelis had been killed, 70% of them civilians. Of the 5,102 Palestinians killed, around half were not involved in the campaign.

**Algeria, 2007**

At least 150 people killed in campaign by al Qaida group.

Terrorism is a form of warfare – not an ideology but an instrument by which some groups try to advance their cause. The kind of attack usually described as terrorist is used predominantly by the weaker party, which may not have access to missiles, gunships and tanks. Governments, however, have also made covert use of terror tactics. Contemporary suicide bombing was pioneered by Tamil secessionists in Sri Lanka, but its most widespread use has been in the Middle East.

# Terrorism

### Moscow, Russia, October 2002
50 Chechen fighters hold 700 theatre-goers hostage. Rescue raid by Russian forces kills Chechens and over 100 hostages.

### Beslan, Russia, September 2004
Chechen fighters hold children and parents hostage in school. 336 hostages and 30 Chechens killed when Russian security forces storm school.

RUSSIA

### Baghdad, Iraq, August 2005
1,000 people die in human stampede when a rumoured sighting of a suicide bomber causes panic among Shi'a pilgrims.

### Ramadi & Fallujah, Iraq, March 2007
Insurgents detonate trucks filled with chlorine gas.

### Gujarat, India, 2002
29 Hindu worshippers shot dead by unknown gunmen.

LEBANON
ISRAEL
IRAQ
EGYPT
SAUDI ARABIA
PAKISTAN
INDIA

### Beirut, Lebanon, February 2005
Bomb kills former Prime Minister Rafiq Hariri and 20 others.

### Pakistan, 2007
**Karachi, October**
Bomb kills 140 supporters of ex-Prime Minister Benazir Bhutto on her return from exile.
**Rawalpindi, December**
Bhutto and 28 supporters killed in further attack.

### Riyadh, Saudi Arabia, May 2003
Suicide bomber kills 26 in attack on western housing complex.

SRI LANKA
KENYA

INDONESIA

### Bali, Indonesia, October 2002
200 holidaymakers killed in al Qaida bomb attack.

# 50%
of 14,500 recorded terrorist incidents in 2007 were in Iraq

### Sri Lanka, 1980s–2008
The Liberation Tigers of Tamil Eelam have killed, among others: a president of Sri Lanka; a former Prime Minister of India; 40 Sri Lankan politicians.

### Mombasa, Kenya, 2002
Al Qaida suicide bomb attack on hotel kills 3 Israelis and 10 Kenyans.

### Red Sea coast, Egypt
**Sharm el-Sheikh, 2005:** 88 dead
**Dahab, 2006:** 23 dead.

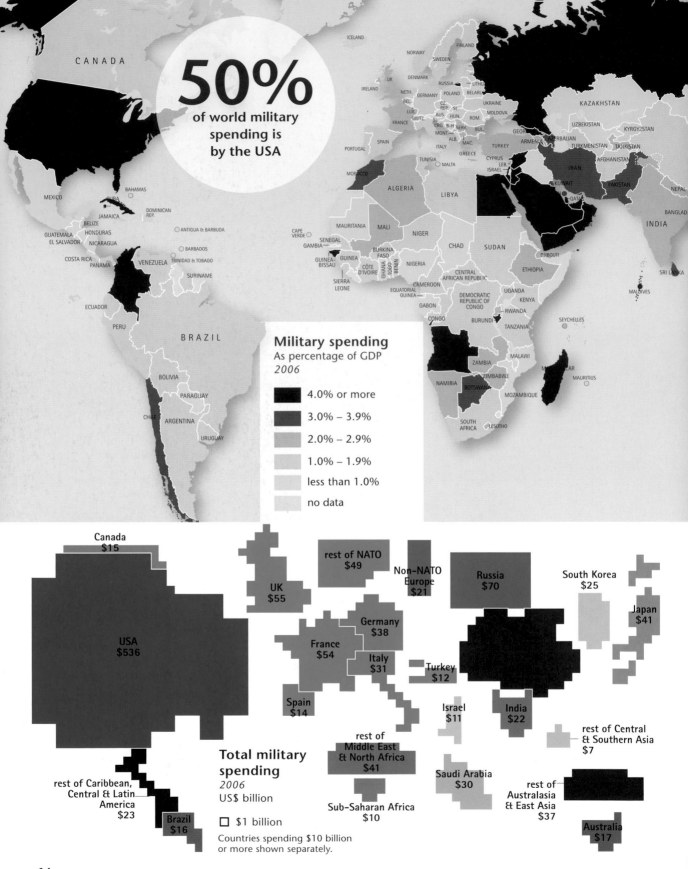

**50%**
of world military spending is by the USA

**Military spending**
As percentage of GDP
*2006*

- 4.0% or more
- 3.0% – 3.9%
- 2.0% – 2.9%
- 1.0% – 1.9%
- less than 1.0%
- no data

Canada $15
rest of NATO $49
UK $55
Non-NATO Europe $21
Russia $70
South Korea $25
Japan $41
USA $536
Germany $38
France $54
Italy $31
Turkey $12
Spain $14
Israel $11
India $22
rest of Caribbean, Central & Latin America $23
Brazil $16
rest of Middle East & North Africa $41
Sub-Saharan Africa $10
Saudi Arabia $30
rest of Central & Southern Asia $7
rest of Australasia & East Asia $37
Australia $17

**Total military spending**
*2006*
US$ billion

☐ $1 billion

Countries spending $10 billion or more shown separately.

# Military Spending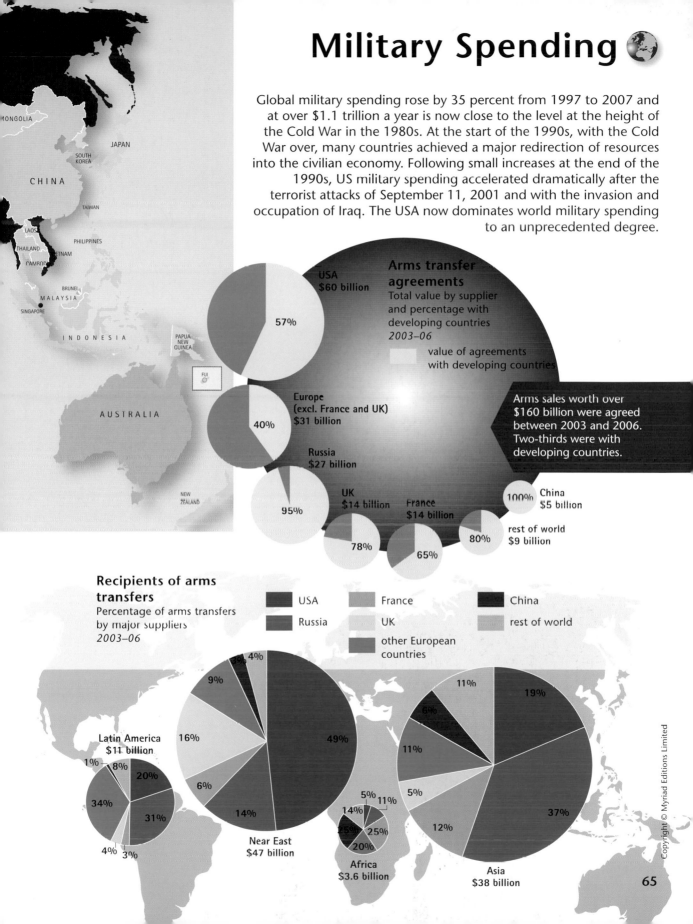

Global military spending rose by 35 percent from 1997 to 2007 and at over $1.1 trillion a year is now close to the level at the height of the Cold War in the 1980s. At the start of the 1990s, with the Cold War over, many countries achieved a major redirection of resources into the civilian economy. Following small increases at the end of the 1990s, US military spending accelerated dramatically after the terrorist attacks of September 11, 2001 and with the invasion and occupation of Iraq. The USA now dominates world military spending to an unprecedented degree.

## Arms transfer agreements
Total value by supplier and percentage with developing countries
2003–06

value of agreements with developing countries

Arms sales worth over $160 billion were agreed between 2003 and 2006. Two-thirds were with developing countries.

USA
$60 billion
57%

Europe (excl. France and UK)
$31 billion
40%

Russia
$27 billion
95%

UK
$14 billion
78%

France
$14 billion
65%

rest of world
$9 billion
80%

China
$5 billion
100%

## Recipients of arms transfers
Percentage of arms transfers by major suppliers
2003–06

USA
Russia
other European countries
France
UK
China
rest of world

Latin America
$11 billion
1%  8%
20%
34%
31%
4%  3%

Near East
$47 billion
4%
3%
9%
16%
6%
14%
49%

Africa
$3.6 billion
5%  11%
14%
25%
25%
20%

Asia
$38 billion
11%
6%
11%
5%
12%
19%
37%

65

**Warlords and militias**
Estimated number
in non-state groups
where known
*2008*

10,000 or more

fewer than 10,000

**USA**
1,498,000

CANADA

IRELAND

UK

NETH.

BELGIUM

DENMARK

SWEDEN

NORWAY

FINLAND

LATVIA

LITHUANIA

GERMANY

POLAND

BELARUS

**RUSSIA**
1,027,000

UKRAINE

CZ. REP.

SLO.

SWITZ.

AUSTRIA

HUN.

**FRANCE**
255,000

SL.

ITALY

CRO.

SERB.

ROMANIA

MOLDOVA

GEORGIA

AZERBAIJAN

ARMENIA

B-H

BULGARIA

**TURKEY**
510,000

MONT.

MAC.

ALB.

SPAIN

PORTUGAL

GREECE

CYPRUS

**SYRIA**
293,000

LEBANON

MEXICO

CUBA

DOMINICAN REP.

GUATEMALA

HONDURAS

NICARAGUA

EL SALVADOR

VENEZUELA

**COLOMBIA**
254,000

ECUADOR

PERU

**BRAZIL**
368,000

PARAGUAY

BOLIVIA

URUGUAY

CHILE

ARGENTINA

TUNISIA

MOROCCO

LIBYA

ALGERIA

NIGER

**EGYPT**
469,000

JORDAN

ISRAEL

SENEGAL

MAURITANIA

MALI

NIGERIA

SAUDI ARABIA

GUINEA-BISSAU

GUINEA

BURKINA FASO

SIERRA LEONE

CÔTE D'IVOIRE

GHANA

TOGO

BENIN

CHAD

SUDAN

CAMEROON

ERITREA

YEMEN

DJIBOUTI

GABON

ETHIOPIA

UGANDA

CONGO

KENYA

DEM. REP. OF CONGO

RWANDA

TANZANIA

BURUNDI

MALAWI

ZAMBIA

MOZAMBIQUE

ANGOLA

ZIMBABWE

MADAGASCAR

NAMIBIA

BOTSWANA

SOUTH AFRICA

66

# Armed Forces

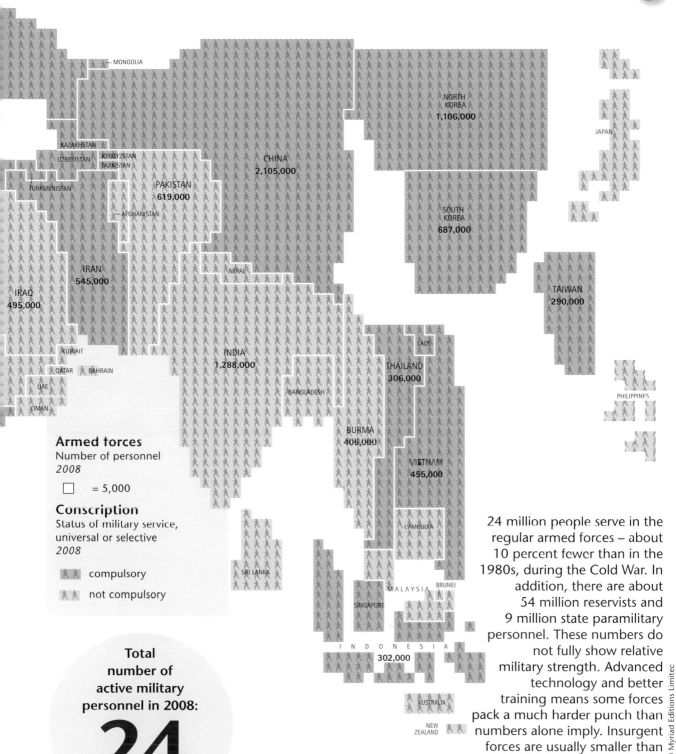

## Armed forces
Number of personnel
*2008*

□ = 5,000

## Conscription
Status of military service,
universal or selective
*2008*

🚶🚶 compulsory

🚶🚶 not compulsory

MONGOLIA

NORTH
KOREA
**1,106,000**

JAPAN

KAZAKHSTAN

UZBEKISTAN · KYRGYZSTAN
TAJIKISTAN

CHINA
**2,105,000**

TURKMENISTAN

PAKISTAN
**619,000**

AFGHANISTAN

SOUTH
KOREA
**687,000**

IRAN
**545,000**

NEPAL

TAIWAN
**290,000**

IRAQ
**495,000**

KUWAIT

LAOS

QATAR · BAHRAIN

INDIA
**1,288,000**

THAILAND
**306,000**

UAE

BANGLADESH

OMAN

PHILIPPINES

BURMA
**406,000**

VIETNAM
**455,000**

SRI LANKA

CAMBODIA

MALAYSIA · BRUNEI

SINGAPORE

I N D O N E S I A
**302,000**

AUSTRALIA

NEW
ZEALAND

## Total number of active military personnel in 2008:

# 24
million

24 million people serve in the regular armed forces – about 10 percent fewer than in the 1980s, during the Cold War. In addition, there are about 54 million reservists and 9 million state paramilitary personnel. These numbers do not fully show relative military strength. Advanced technology and better training means some forces pack a much harder punch than numbers alone imply. Insurgent forces are usually smaller than their opponents, but compensate through superior commitment and training.

Copyright © Myriad Editions Limited

67

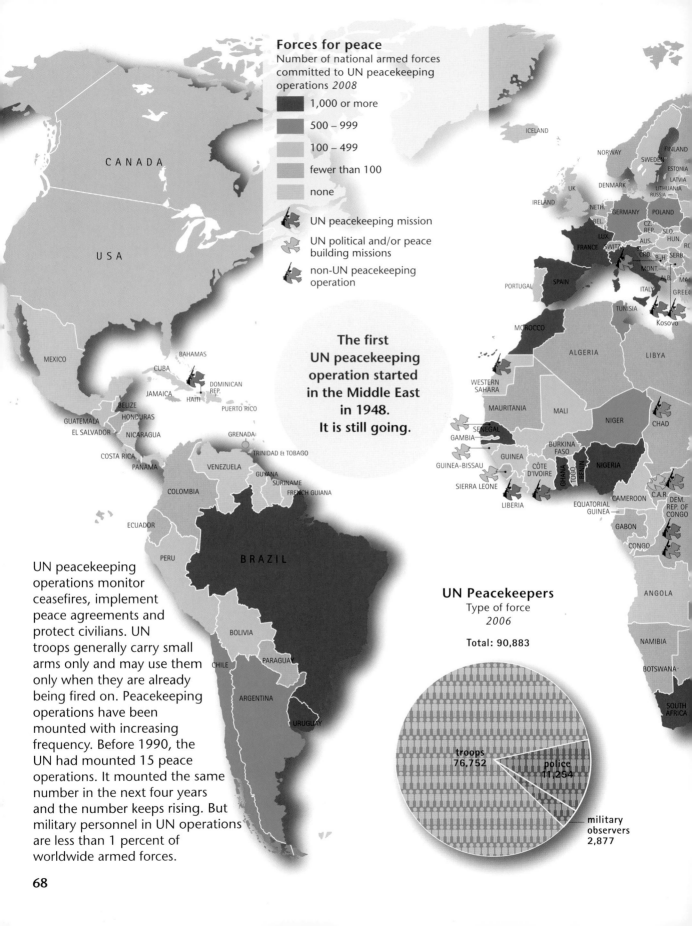

## Forces for peace

Number of national armed forces committed to UN peacekeeping operations *2008*

- 1,000 or more
- 500 – 999
- 100 – 499
- fewer than 100
- none

UN peacekeeping mission

UN political and/or peace building missions

non-UN peacekeeping operation

The first UN peacekeeping operation started in the Middle East in 1948. It is still going.

UN peacekeeping operations monitor ceasefires, implement peace agreements and protect civilians. UN troops generally carry small arms only and may use them only when they are already being fired on. Peacekeeping operations have been mounted with increasing frequency. Before 1990, the UN had mounted 15 peace operations. It mounted the same number in the next four years and the number keeps rising. But military personnel in UN operations are less than 1 percent of worldwide armed forces.

## UN Peacekeepers

Type of force *2006*

Total: 90,883

- troops 76,752
- police 11,254
- military observers 2,877

# Peacekeeping

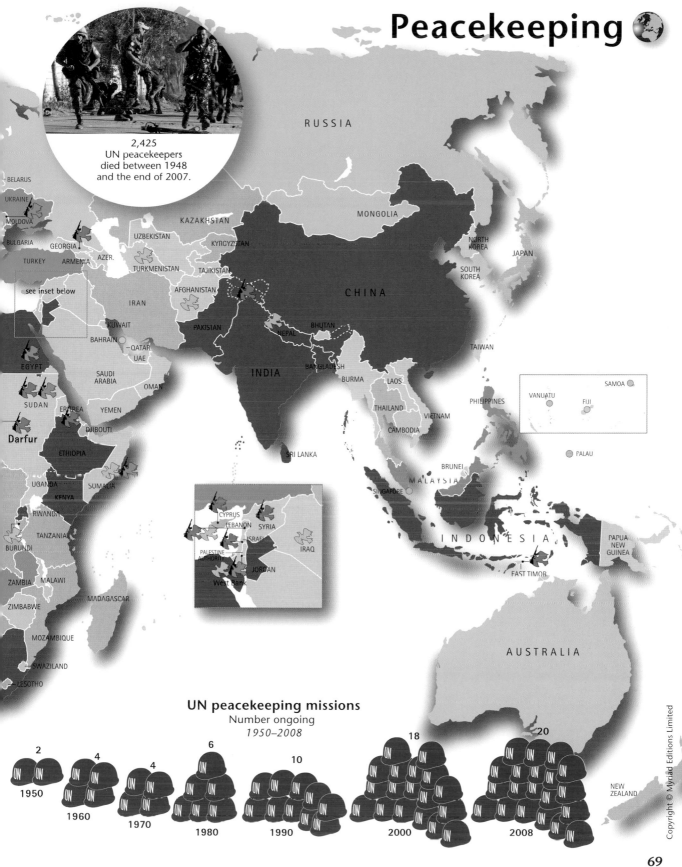

2,425
UN peacekeepers
died between 1948
and the end of 2007.

RUSSIA

BELARUS
UKRAINE
MOLDOVA
BULGARIA
GEORGIA
TURKEY
ARMENIA
AZER.

KAZAKHSTAN
UZBEKISTAN
KYRGYZSTAN
TURKMENISTAN
TAJIKISTAN
AFGHANISTAN

MONGOLIA

NORTH
KOREA
JAPAN
SOUTH
KOREA

see inset below

IRAN
KUWAIT
BAHRAIN
QATAR
UAE
SAUDI
ARABIA
OMAN
YEMEN

PAKISTAN

CHINA

BHUTAN
NEPAL

BANGLADESH
BURMA
INDIA

TAIWAN

EGYPT

SUDAN
ERITREA
Darfur
DJIBOUTI
ETHIOPIA

UGANDA
SUMALIA
KENYA
RWANDA
TANZANIA
BURUNDI

ZAMBIA
MALAWI
ZIMBABWE

MOZAMBIQUE
MADAGASCAR

SWAZILAND
LESOTHO

SRI LANKA

THAILAND

LAOS
VIETNAM
CAMBODIA

PHILIPPINES

VANUATU
FIJI
SAMOA

PALAU

BRUNEI
MALAYSIA
SINGAPORE

INDONESIA

EAST TIMOR

PAPUA
NEW
GUINEA

CYPRUS
LEBANON
SYRIA
ISRAEL
IRAQ
PALESTINE
AUTHORITY
JORDAN
West Bank

AUSTRALIA

NEW
ZEALAND

## UN peacekeeping missions
Number ongoing
*1950–2008*

2
1950

4
1960

4
1970

6
1980

10
1990

18
2000

20
2008

Far more information is available about wars today than only a few years ago. But one thing we do not know is how many people are killed. As researchers unearth more information, we discover how little we still know about human suffering in war.

The reasons for this uncertainty include the remote locations of much of the suffering, lack of interest by the international news media, deliberate deception and concealment by the parties to war.

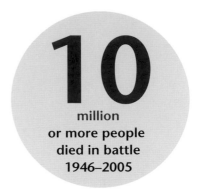

# 10
## million
## or more people died in battle 1946–2005

One measure of violence in war is "battle deaths" – people killed directly in combat. It does not include all people who die violently in war – such as in genocide – nor those who die because doctors have been killed, hospitals destroyed, medical supplies seized, crops devastated – all leading to rampant disease and starvation. Though incomplete, battle death numbers do reveal something important: the world has been getting less dangerous. There were 2.3 million battle deaths in the first five years after World War II, but in the five years between 2001 and 2005, battle deaths were 95 percent lower.

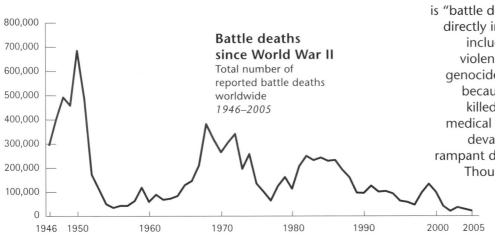

**Battle deaths since World War II**
Total number of reported battle deaths worldwide
*1946–2005*

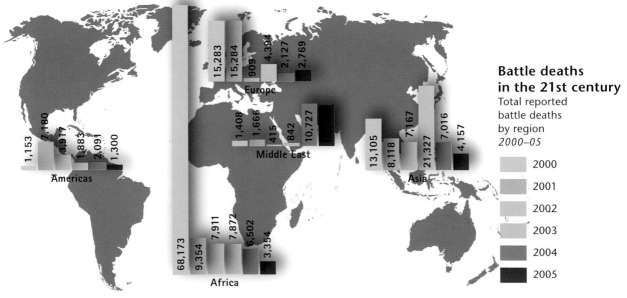

**Battle deaths in the 21st century**
Total reported battle deaths by region
*2000–05*

2000
2001
2002
2003
2004
2005

Americas
1,153
7,180
3,917
1,883
2,091
1,300

Europe
15,283
15,284
909
4,394
2,127
2,769

Middle East
1,408
1,666
415
842
10,727

Asia
13,105
8,118
7,167
21,327
7,016
4,157

Africa
68,173
9,354
7,911
7,872
6,502
3,354

# Casualties of War

The lack of war casualty figures that are both accurate and generally accepted is reflected in the discrepancies of 10:1 in estimates of the death toll in Iraq since March 2003. And views about the rights and wrongs of the US-led occupation of Iraq are inevitably coloured by estimates about the human costs. Such discrepancies in death tolls are not unusual, and are apparent in the range of figures given for many recent conflicts.

## Deaths in Iraq since March 2003
Estimates of number of deaths by different organizations

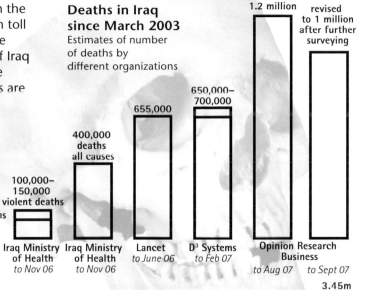

| 85,000 civilian deaths | 100,000–150,000 violent deaths | 400,000 deaths all causes | 655,000 | 650,000–700,000 | 1.2 million | revised to 1 million after further surveying |
|---|---|---|---|---|---|---|
| Iraq Body Count *to Dec 07* | Iraq Ministry of Health *to Nov 06* | Iraq Ministry of Health *to Nov 06* | Lancet *to June 06* | D³ Systems *to Feb 07* | Opinion Research Business *to Aug 07* | *to Sept 07* |

## The deadliest conflicts
Estimated war-related death tolls
11 major conflicts since 1945

— highest estimate
— common estimate
▓ median value
▒ lowest estimate

| 5.4m | 850,000 | 1.9m | 1.0m / 850,000 / 700,000 | 1.9m | 1.0m / 700,000 / 100,000 | 3.0m / 1.6m / 750,000 | 3.0m / 1.6m / 300,000 | 1.5m / 1.25m / 250,000 | 2.0m | 3.45m / 2.4m / 1.3m |
|---|---|---|---|---|---|---|---|---|---|---|
| Dem. Rep. Congo 1998– | Rwanda 1991–94 | Sudan excl. Darfur 1983– | Iran–Iraq 1980–88 | Afghanistan 1979–2001 | Mozambique 1975–92 | Cambodia 1975–78 | Bangladesh 1971 | Ethiopia 1962–92 | Vietnam 1960–75 | Korea 1950–53 |

# 1,367
people
**were reported killed by landmines in 2006**

## Persistent killers
Countries experiencing casualties from landmines and/or Explosive Remnants of War
*2006*

1,367 people were reported killed by landmines in 2006

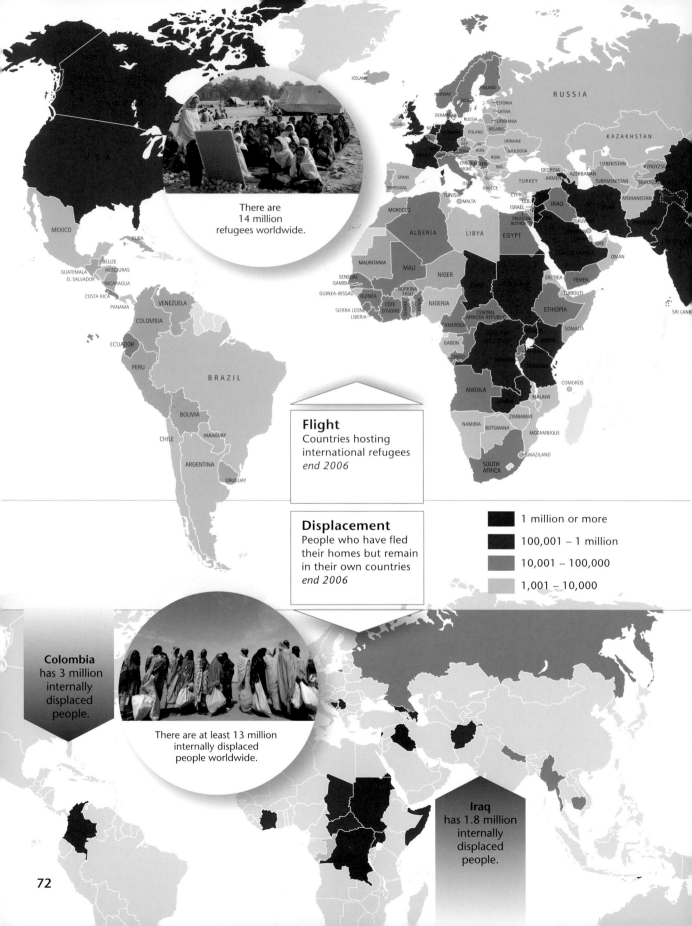

There are
14 million
refugees worldwide.

**Flight**
Countries hosting
international refugees
*end 2006*

**Displacement**
People who have fled
their homes but remain
in their own countries
*end 2006*

| | |
|---|---|
| ■ | 1 million or more |
| ■ | 100,001 – 1 million |
| ■ | 10,001 – 100,000 |
| ■ | 1,001 – 10,000 |

**Colombia**
has 3 million
internally
displaced
people.

There are at least 13 million
internally displaced
people worldwide.

**Iraq**
has 1.8 million
internally
displaced
people.

# Refugees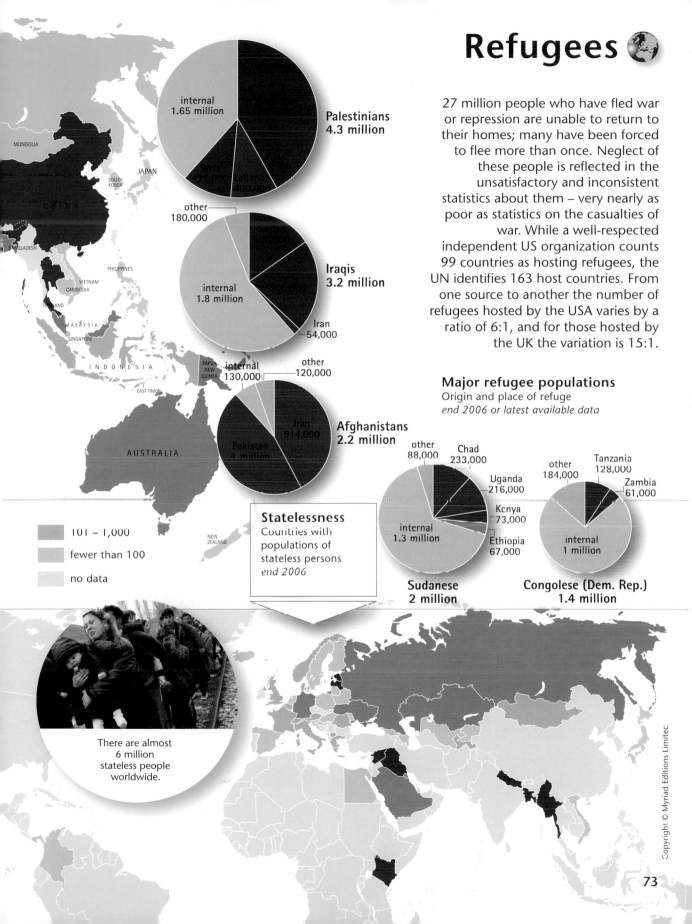

27 million people who have fled war or repression are unable to return to their homes; many have been forced to flee more than once. Neglect of these people is reflected in the unsatisfactory and inconsistent statistics about them – very nearly as poor as statistics on the casualties of war. While a well-respected independent US organization counts 99 countries as hosting refugees, the UN identifies 163 host countries. From one source to another the number of refugees hosted by the USA varies by a ratio of 6:1, and for those hosted by the UK the variation is 15:1.

## Palestinians
4.3 million

- internal 1.65 million
- Syria 425,000
- Lebanon 300,000

## Iraqis
3.2 million

- other 180,000
- Jordan 500,000
- Syria 700,000
- internal 1.8 million
- Iran 54,000

## Afghanistans
2.2 million

- internal 130,000
- other 120,000
- Iran 914,000
- Pakistan 1 million

## Major refugee populations
Origin and place of refuge
*end 2006 or latest available data*

## Sudanese
2 million

- other 88,000
- Chad 233,000
- Uganda 216,000
- Kenya 73,000
- Ethiopia 67,000
- internal 1.3 million

## Congolese (Dem. Rep.)
1.4 million

- other 184,000
- Tanzania 128,000
- Zambia 61,000
- internal 1 million

## Statelessness
Countries with populations of stateless persons
*end 2006*

Map legend:
- 101 – 1,000
- fewer than 100
- no data

There are almost 6 million stateless people worldwide.

**Nordic peace**
Denmark, Finland, Iceland, Norway, Sweden have low crime rates, good relations with each other, and small armed forces used abroad only for UN peacekeeping.

**North American contrast**
The USA scores poorly because of its engagement in wars, its high military spending, social violence and prison population. Canada is more peaceful at home; its forces are used only for UN peacekeeping.

**Change in Latin America**
Both Chile and Argentina are former dictatorships that went through years of violent political repression. The rise of peace in the past two decades is striking.

**Angolan rise**
Angola's GPI score improved substantially from 2007 to 2008, reflecting its continuing recovery from its struggle for independence, followed by 27 years of civil war that ended in 2002.

CANADA

USA

MEXICO

CUBA

JAMAICA    HAITI    DOMINICAN REP.

GUATEMALA    HONDURAS
EL SALVADOR    NICARAGUA

COSTA RICA
PANAMA

VENEZUELA

COLOMBIA

ECUADOR

PERU

BRAZIL

BOLIVIA

PARAGUAY

CHILE    ARGENTINA

URUGUAY

ICELAND

NORWAY    SWEDEN    FINLAND

ESTONIA

LATVIA

UK    DENMARK    LITHUANIA

IRELAND    RUSSIA

NETH.    POLAND

BEL    GERMANY

LUX.    CZ. REP.    SK

FRANCE    SWITZ.    AUS.    HUN.

CRO.    B-H    SERB.

PORTUGAL    SPAIN    ITALY    ALB.    MAC.

GREECE

TUNISIA

MOROCCO

ALGERIA    LIBYA

WESTERN SAHARA

MAURITANIA    MALI

SENEGAL

BURKINA FASO    CHAD

CÔTE
D'IVOIRE    GHANA    NIGERIA

CENTRAL
AFRICAN R

CAMEROON

EQUATORIAL
GUINEA

GABON    DEM.
REP. OF
CONGO

CONGO

ANGOLA

NAMIBIA

BOTSWANA

SOUTH
AFRICA

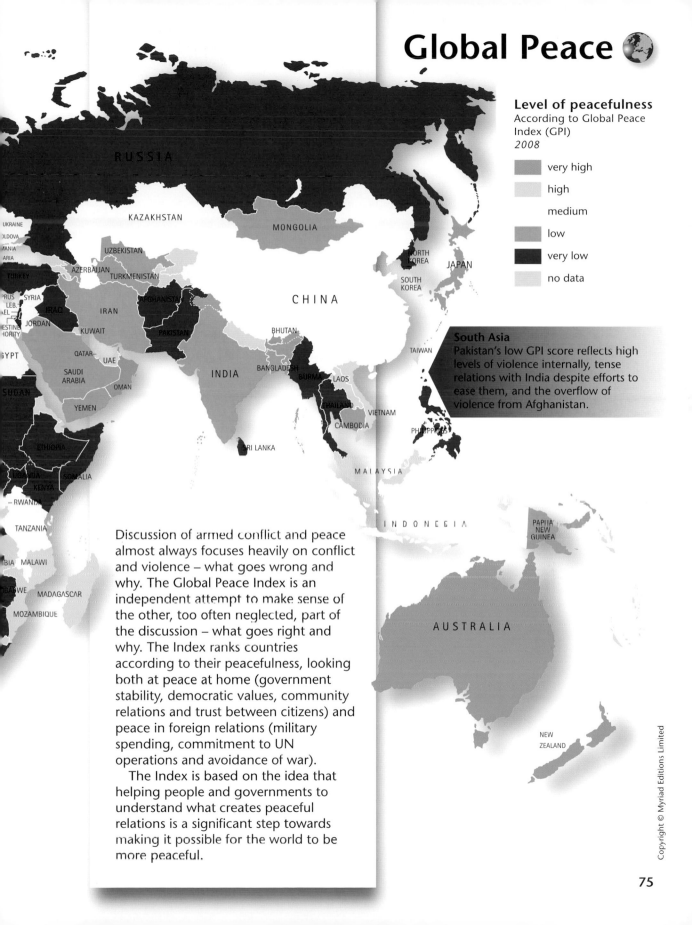

**Level of peacefulness**
According to Global Peace
Index (GPI)
*2008*

very high
high
medium
low
very low
no data

**South Asia**
Pakistan's low GPI score reflects high levels of violence internally, tense relations with India despite efforts to ease them, and the overflow of violence from Afghanistan.

Discussion of armed conflict and peace almost always focuses heavily on conflict and violence – what goes wrong and why. The Global Peace Index is an independent attempt to make sense of the other, too often neglected, part of the discussion – what goes right and why. The Index ranks countries according to their peacefulness, looking both at peace at home (government stability, democratic values, community relations and trust between citizens) and peace in foreign relations (military spending, commitment to UN operations and avoidance of war).

The Index is based on the idea that helping people and governments to understand what creates peaceful relations is a significant step towards making it possible for the world to be more peaceful.

On a wall in Senegal a message of hope – "Espoirs".

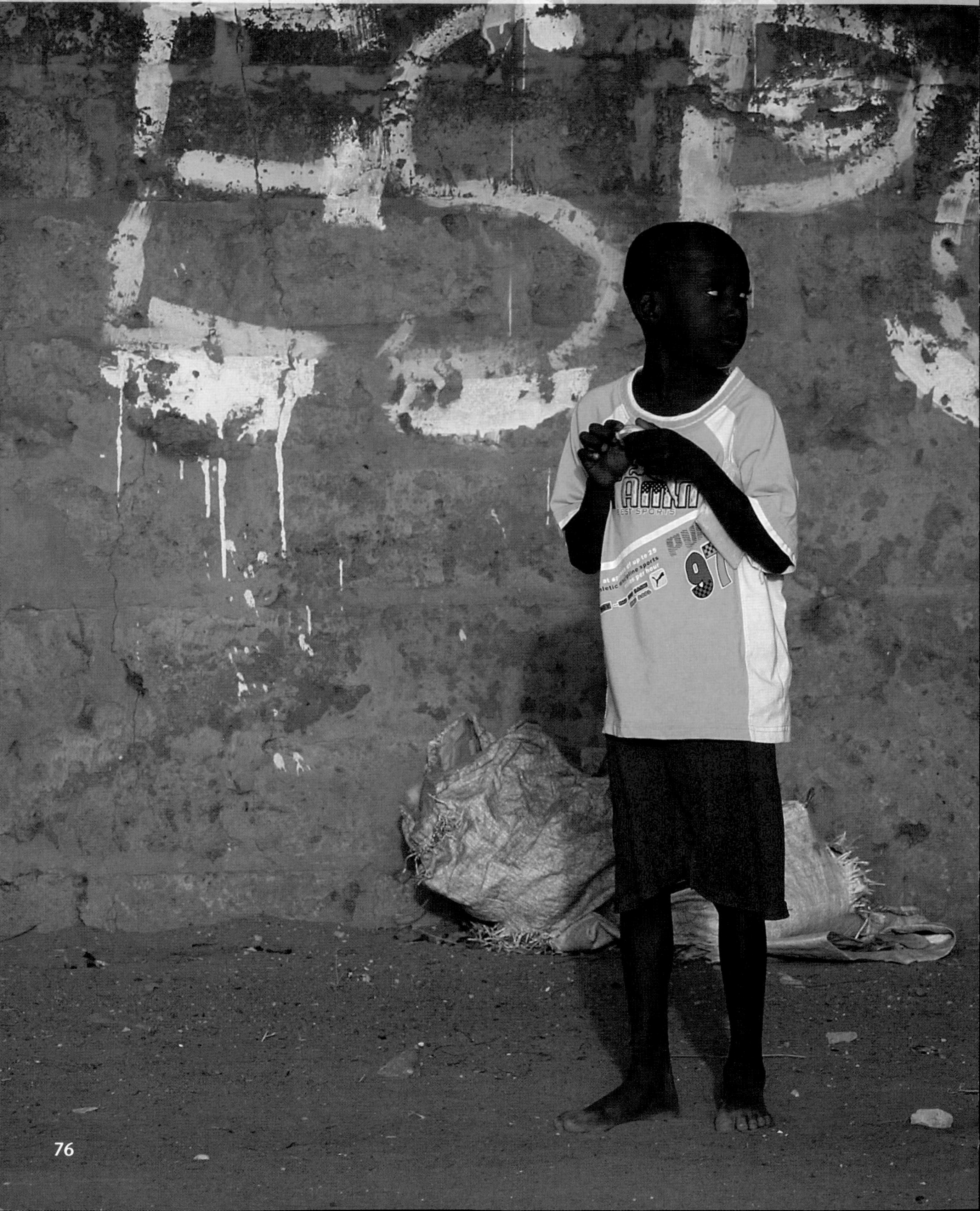

## Political systems
*2008*

**Legend:**
- established democracy
- weak, uncertain or transitional democracy
- effective or formal one-party rule
- military dictatorship
- monarchy or theocracy
- state of disorder
- dependent territory

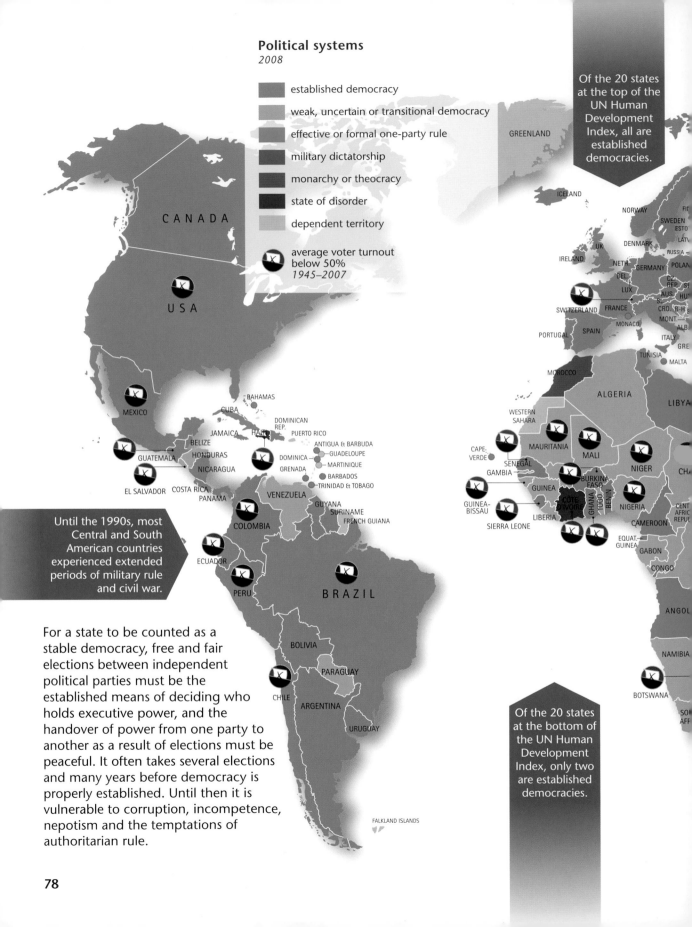 average voter turnout below 50% 1945–2007

GREENLAND

Of the 20 states at the top of the UN Human Development Index, all are established democracies.

ICELAND

NORWAY

FINLAND

SWEDEN

ESTONIA

IRELAND

UK

DENMARK

LATVIA

RUSSIA

NETH.

GERMANY

POLAND

BEL.

LUX.

CZ. REP.

SLOVAKIA

AUSTRIA

HUNGARY

SWITZERLAND

FRANCE

CRO.

B-H

SER.

MONT.

ALB.

PORTUGAL

SPAIN

MONACO

ITALY

GREECE

TUNISIA

MALTA

MOROCCO

ALGERIA

LIBYA

WESTERN SAHARA

MAURITANIA

MALI

NIGER

CHAD

CAPE VERDE

SENEGAL

GAMBIA

GUINEA

BURKINA FASO

NIGERIA

CENT. AFRIC. REPUB.

GUINEA-BISSAU

CÔTE D'IVOIRE

GHANA

TOGO

BENIN

CAMEROON

SIERRA LEONE

LIBERIA

EQUAT. GUINEA

GABON

CONGO

ANGOLA

NAMIBIA

BOTSWANA

SOUTH AFRICA

CANADA

USA

BAHAMAS

CUBA

MEXICO

JAMAICA

HAITI

BELIZE

GUATEMALA

HONDURAS

EL SALVADOR

NICARAGUA

COSTA RICA

PANAMA

DOMINICAN REP.

PUERTO RICO

ANTIGUA & BARBUDA

GUADELOUPE

DOMINICA

MARTINIQUE

GRENADA

BARBADOS

TRINIDAD & TOBAGO

VENEZUELA

GUYANA

SURINAME

FRENCH GUIANA

COLOMBIA

ECUADOR

PERU

BRAZIL

BOLIVIA

PARAGUAY

CHILE

ARGENTINA

URUGUAY

FALKLAND ISLANDS

Until the 1990s, most Central and South American countries experienced extended periods of military rule and civil war.

For a state to be counted as a stable democracy, free and fair elections between independent political parties must be the established means of deciding who holds executive power, and the handover of power from one party to another as a result of elections must be peaceful. It often takes several elections and many years before democracy is properly established. Until then it is vulnerable to corruption, incompetence, nepotism and the temptations of authoritarian rule.

Of the 20 states at the bottom of the UN Human Development Index, only two are established democracies.

# Political Systems

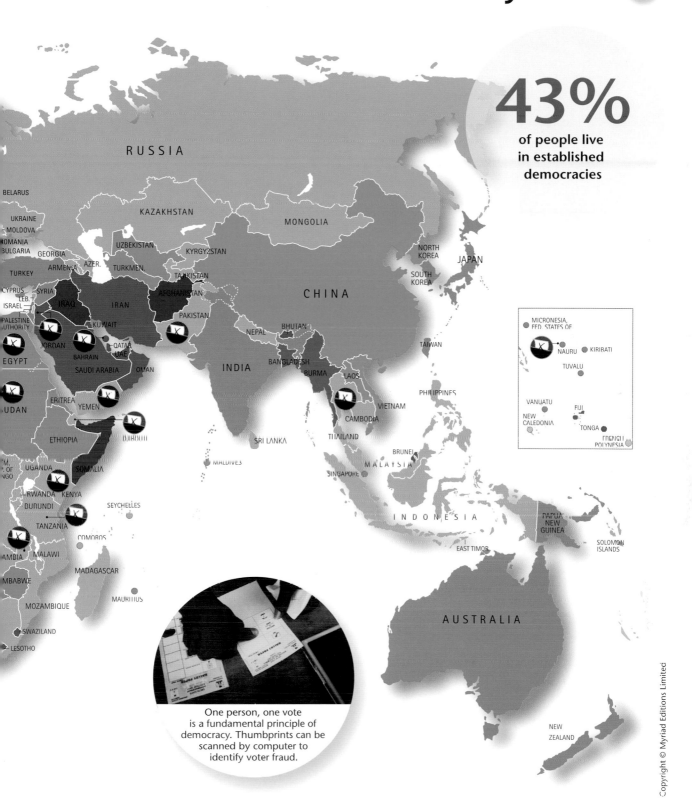

## 43%
of people live
in established
democracies

RUSSIA

BELARUS
UKRAINE
MOLDOVA
ROMANIA
BULGARIA
GEORGIA
TURKEY
ARMENIA
AZER.
CYPRUS
LEB.
SYRIA
ISRAEL
PALESTINE
AUTHORITY
IRAQ
EGYPT
JORDAN
KUWAIT
BAHRAIN
QATAR
UAE
SAUDI ARABIA
OMAN
SUDAN
ERITREA
YEMEN
ETHIOPIA
DJIBOUTI
DEM. OF
CONGO
UGANDA
SOMALIA
RWANDA
KENYA
BURUNDI
SEYCHELLES
TANZANIA
COMOROS
ZAMBIA
MALAWI
MADAGASCAR
MAURITIUS
ZIMBABWE
MOZAMBIQUE
SWAZILAND
LESOTHO

KAZAKHSTAN
UZBEKISTAN
TURKMEN.
TAJIKISTAN
AFGHANISTAN
IRAN
PAKISTAN
NEPAL
BHUTAN
INDIA
BANGLADESH
BURMA
SRI LANKA
MALDIVES

KYRGYZSTAN
MONGOLIA
CHINA
NORTH
KOREA
SOUTH
KOREA
JAPAN
TAIWAN
LAOS
VIETNAM
CAMBODIA
THAILAND
PHILIPPINES
BRUNEI
MALAYSIA
SINGAPORE
INDONESIA
EAST TIMOR
PAPUA
NEW
GUINEA
SOLOMON
ISLANDS

MICRONESIA,
FED. STATES OF
NAURU
KIRIBATI
TUVALU
VANUATU
FIJI
NEW
CALEDONIA
TONGA
FRENCH
POLYNESIA

AUSTRALIA

NEW
ZEALAND

One person, one vote
is a fundamental principle of
democracy. Thumbprints can be
scanned by computer to
identify voter fraud.

Copyright © Myriad Editions Limited

79

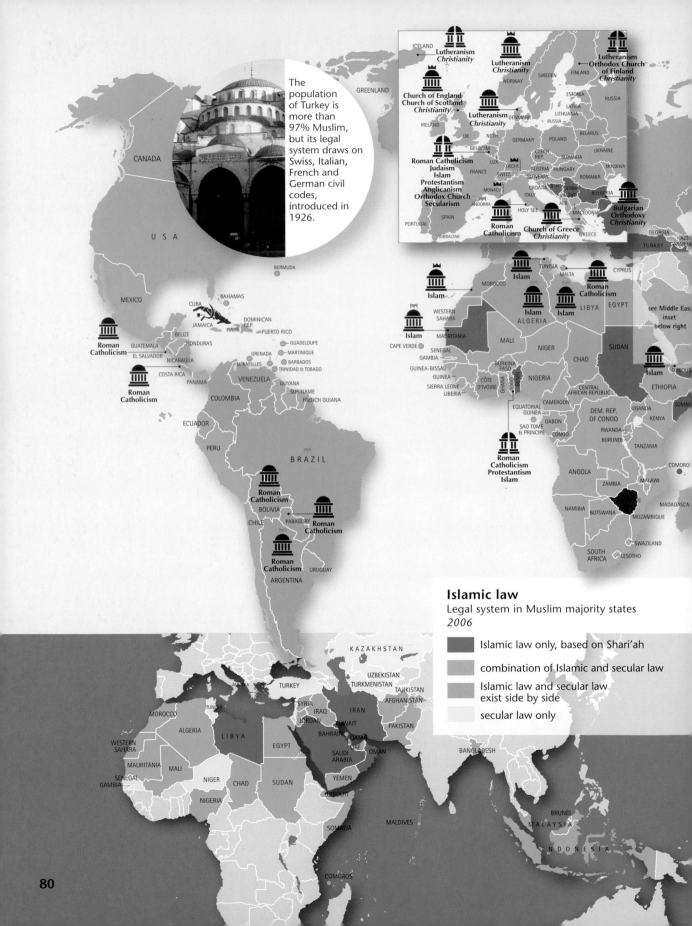

The population of Turkey is more than 97% Muslim, but its legal system draws on Swiss, Italian, French and German civil codes, introduced in 1926.

ICELAND

GREENLAND

CANADA

USA

Lutheranism
*Christianity*

Lutheranism
*Christianity*

NORWAY

SWEDEN

FINLAND

Lutheranism
Orthodox Church
of Finland
*Christianity*

RUSSIA

Church of England
Church of Scotland
*Christianity*

IRELAND

UK

DENMARK

ESTONIA
LATVIA
LITHUANIA
RUSSIA

Lutheranism
*Christianity*

NETH.
GERMANY

BELGIUM

BELARUS
POLAND

UKRAINE

Roman Catholicism
Judaism
Islam
Protestantism
Anglicanism
Orthodox Church
Secularism

FRANCE
LUX.
LIECHT.
SWITZ.
ANDORRA

CZECH
REP.
AUSTRIA
SLOVENIA
CROATIA
MONACO
ITALY

SLOVAKIA
HUNGARY

MOLDOVA
ROMANIA

BOS &
HERZ
SERBIA
MONT.
ALB.

BULGARIA
MACEDONIA

Bulgarian
Orthodoxy
*Christianity*

PORTUGAL
SPAIN

HOLY SEE

Roman
Catholicism

Church of Greece
*Christianity*

GREECE

GEORGIA
AZE.
ARMENIA
TURKEY

GIBRALTAR

MEXICO

BERMUDA

Roman
Catholicism

GUATEMALA
EL SALVADOR
HONDURAS
NICARAGUA
COSTA RICA
PANAMA

Roman
Catholicism

BAHAMAS
CUBA
JAMAICA
HAITI

DOMINICAN
REP.
PUERTO RICO

BELIZE

GRENADA
N. ANTILLES

GUADELOUPE
MARTINIQUE
BARBADOS
TRINIDAD & TOBAGO

VENEZUELA
COLOMBIA

GUYANA
SURINAME
FRENCH GUIANA

ECUADOR

PERU

BRAZIL

Roman
Catholicism

BOLIVIA

CHILE
PARAGUAY

Roman
Catholicism

Roman
Catholicism

URUGUAY

ARGENTINA

MOROCCO

Islam

Islam

WESTERN
SAHARA

Islam

TUNISIA

MALTA

Islam
ALGERIA

Islam
LIBYA

Roman
Catholicism

CYPRUS

LIBYA

EGYPT

see Middle East
inset
below right

MAURITANIA

CAPE VERDE

SENEGAL
GAMBIA
GUINEA-BISSAU
GUINEA
SIERRA LEONE
LIBERIA

Islam

MALI

BURKINA
FASO

CÔTE
D'IVOIRE
GHANA

NIGER

NIGERIA

CHAD

SUDAN

Islam

ETHIOPIA

DJIBOUTI

SOMALIA

CAMEROON

EQUATORIAL
GUINEA
SAO TOME
& PRINCIPE

GABON
CONGO

CENTRAL
AFRICAN REPUBLIC

DEM. REP.
OF CONGO

UGANDA

RWANDA
BURUNDI

KENYA

TANZANIA

Roman
Catholicism
Protestantism
Islam

ANGOLA

ZAMBIA

MALAWI

COMORO

MADAGASCAR

NAMIBIA
BOTSWANA

MOZAMBIQUE

SWAZILAND

SOUTH
AFRICA

LESOTHO

## Islamic law
Legal system in Muslim majority states
*2006*

Islamic law only, based on Shari'ah

combination of Islamic and secular law

Islamic law and secular law
exist side by side

secular law only

KAZAKHSTAN

UZBEKISTAN
TURKMENISTAN
TAJIKISTAN

TURKEY

ALGERIA
TUNISIA

SYRIA
IRAQ
JORDAN

IRAN
KUWAIT
BAHRAIN
QATAR
UAE
SAUDI
ARABIA
OMAN

AFGHANISTAN

PAKISTAN

BANGLADESH

MOROCCO

WESTERN
SAHARA

LIBYA

EGYPT

MAURITANIA
MALI
NIGER
CHAD
SUDAN

YEMEN

DJIBOUTI

SENEGAL
GAMBIA

NIGERIA

SOMALIA

MALDIVES

BRUNEI
MALAYSIA

INDONESIA

COMOROS

# Religious Freedom

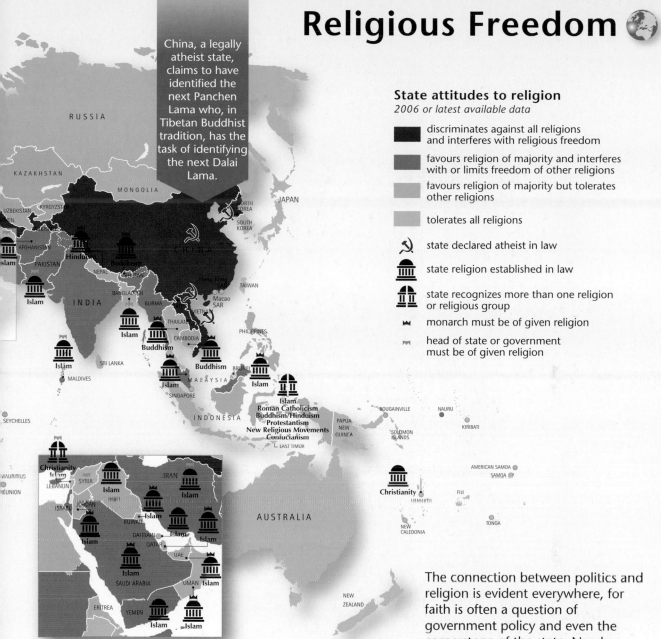

China, a legally atheist state, claims to have identified the next Panchen Lama who, in Tibetan Buddhist tradition, has the task of identifying the next Dalai Lama.

RUSSIA

KAZAKHSTAN

UZBEKISTAN
KYRGYZSTAN
AFGHANISTAN
Islam
PAKISTAN
Hinduism
Buddhism
MONGOLIA
CHINA
NORTH KOREA
SOUTH KOREA
JAPAN

NEPAL
BHUTAN
Hong Kong SAR
TAIWAN
INDIA
BANGLADESH
BURMA
Macao SAR
Islam
Buddhism
THAILAND
VIETNAM
CAMBODIA
Buddhism
PHILIPPINES
Islam
SRI LANKA
Buddhism
MALAYSIA
BRUNEI
Islam
MALDIVES
Islam
SINGAPORE

INDONESIA
Islam
Roman Catholicism
Buddhism/Hinduism
Protestantism
New Religious Movements
Confucianism
EAST TIMOR
PAPUA NEW GUINEA
BOUGAINVILLE
SOLOMON ISLANDS
NAURU
KIRIBATI

SEYCHELLES

Christianity
Islam
LEBANON
SYRIA
IRAN
Islam
Islam
MAURITIUS
RÉUNION
ISRAEL
JORDAN
KUWAIT
Islam
IRAQ
Islam
BAHRAIN
QATAR
Islam
UAE
SAUDI ARABIA
Islam
OMAN
Islam
ERITREA
YEMEN
Islam
Islam

AUSTRALIA

AMERICAN SAMOA
SAMOA
Christianity
VANUATU
FIJI
NEW CALEDONIA
TONGA

NEW ZEALAND

## State attitudes to religion
*2006 or latest available data*

- discriminates against all religions and interferes with religious freedom
- favours religion of majority and interferes with or limits freedom of other religions
- favours religion of majority but tolerates other religions
- tolerates all religions

- state declared atheist in law
- state religion established in law
- state recognizes more than one religion or religious group
- monarch must be of given religion
- head of state or government must be of given religion

The connection between politics and religion is evident everywhere, for faith is often a question of government policy and even the cornerstone of the state. Nearly a quarter of the world's states have formal links to a religion but what that means varies markedly. The establishment of an official religion can mean religious intolerance and persecution, but has also proven to be compatible with a secular state and religious tolerance. Religious freedom has increased since the end of the Cold War as the number of states intolerant of all religions has declined.

**1984**

**1994**

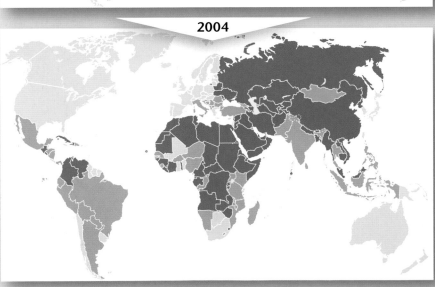

**2004**

## Freedom of the press
*2008*

- free press
- partly free
- not free
- no data
- ● journalists murdered in 2006

CANADA

USA

**10** MEXICO

BAHAMAS

CUBA

**3** DOMINICAN REP.

JAMAICA

HAITI

BELIZE

**2** GUATEMALA

HONDURAS

EL SALVADOR

NICARAGUA

ANTIGUA & BARBUDA

ST KITTS & NEVIS

DOMINICA

GRENADA

ST LUCIA

BARBADOS

ST VINCENT & GRENADIN

COSTA RICA

PANAMA

**5** VENEZUELA

TRINIDAD & TOBAGO

**5**

GUYANA

**6** SURINAME

**2** COLOMBIA

ECUADOR

PERU

**3** BRAZIL

BOLIVIA

PARAGUAY

**1** ARGENTINA

CHILE

URUGUAY

Only **18%** of the world's population have access to free press

82

# Press Freedom

ICELAND

NORWAY
SWEDEN
FINLAND

UK
IRELAND
DENMARK
NETH.
GERMANY
POLAND
BEL.
LUX.
LIECHT.
CZ.
REP.
SL.
AUS. HUN.
FRANCE
SWITZ.
SL.
CRO.
S.M.
ROM.
ANDORRA
MONACO
ITALY
MONT.
SERB.
BUL.

RUSSIA **4**

ESTONIA
LATVIA
LITHUANIA
RUSSIA
BELARUS
UKRAINE
MOLDOVA

KAZAKHSTAN

MONGOLIA

PORTUGAL
SPAIN
GEORGIA
ARMENIA
AZER.
**1**
UZBEKISTAN
**1**
KYRGYZSTAN
TURKMEN.
TAJIKISTAN

NORTH
KOREA
JAPAN
SOUTH
KOREA

TUNISIA
MALTA
GREECE
CYPRUS
TURKEY
**2**
SYRIA
LEBANON
ISRAEL
PALESTINE
AUTHORITY
JORDAN
IRAQ
**69**
AFGHANISTAN
**3**
PAKISTAN
**4**
CHINA **2**

MOROCCO
KUWAIT
BAHRAIN
IRAN
**1**
NEPAL
BHUTAN
Hong Kong
SAR
TAIWAN

ALGERIA
LIBYA
EGYPT
SAUDI
ARABIA
QATAR
UAE
OMAN
INDIA
**3**
BURMA
**1**
LAOS

MICRONESIA,
FED. STATES OF
MARSHALL ISLANDS
NAURU
KIRIBATI
SOLOMON
ISLANDS
TUVALU
VANUATU
FIJI
SAMOA
TONGA

CAPE
VERDE
MAURITANIA
MALI
NIGER
**1**
CHAD
SUDAN
ERITREA
YEMEN
**1**
BANGLADESH
THAILAND
VIETNAM
CAMBODIA

SENEGAL
GAMBIA
GUINEA-
BISSAU
GUINEA
BURKINA
FASO
BENIN
NIGERIA
**1**
DJIBOUTI
ETHIOPIA
PHILIPPINES
**13**

SIERRA LEONE
CÔTE
D'IVOIRE
GHANA
TOGO
CENTRAL
AFRICAN REPUBLIC
UGANDA
SOMALIA
**2**
SRI LANKA
**7**
MALDIVES
BRUNEI
MALAYSIA
PALAU

LIBERIA
CAMEROON
EQUATORIAL
GUINEA
GABON
CONGO
DEMOCRATIC
REPUBLIC OF
CONGO
**1**
RWANDA
BURUNDI
KENYA
SINGAPORE

SÃO TOMÉ
& PRINCIPE
TANZANIA
SEYCHELLES
INDONESIA
**1**

ANGOLA
ZAMBIA
MALAWI
COMOROS
MADAGASCAR
MAURITIUS
PAPUA
NEW
GUINEA

NAMIBIA
ZIMBABWE
BOTSWANA
MOZAMBIQUE
EAST TIMOR
AUSTRALIA

SOUTH
AFRICA
SWAZILAND
LESOTHO

NEW
ZEALAND

Freedom of the press and news media is an
essential element of a free society. Nowhere is
the press perfectly free, and arguably nor
should it be: most liberal societies agree that
hate speech should be restricted. But when
information and opinion critical of the state
cannot be published, citizens' freedom is at risk.

After a period of improvement in world press
freedom in the early 1990s, the next decade
saw a steady decline.

In many countries, measures to shackle the
press are backed by attacks on journalists.
Sometimes servants of the state carry out or
tacitly condone the attacks.

## Press freedom
Percentage of people
living under different
degrees of press freedom
*2006*

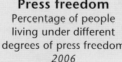

free press
18%

not free
42%

partly free
40%

Total population of
countries surveyed: 6.5 billion

The worse the human rights situation, the less possible it is to report all or even most abuses. Awareness of the issue is high, but extreme abuses of human rights continue. Although the International Criminal Court is now well established, many perpetrators of human rights abuses clearly count on impunity, and are only slowly being disabused of that notion. Extra-judicial execution is aimed against political opponents, prisoners of war and people regarded as socially undesirable.

**2001–08**
**Guantanamo**
The USA has detained 775 people without warrant. About 425 have been released without charge or transferred to native countries. About 270 remained in May 2008.

## Executions
Countries with highest number of reported executions
*2007*

**Total known executions: 1,252**

**Number of people known to be awaiting execution: 27,500**

|  | |
|---|---|
| USA | 42 |
| Pakistan | 135+ |
| Saudi Arabia | 143+ |
| Iran | 317+ |
| China | 470+ |

## Judicial killings
Status of death penalty
*2007*

- legal
- not legal

The number of countries where the death penalty is legal is gradually decreasing.

84

# Human Rights Abuses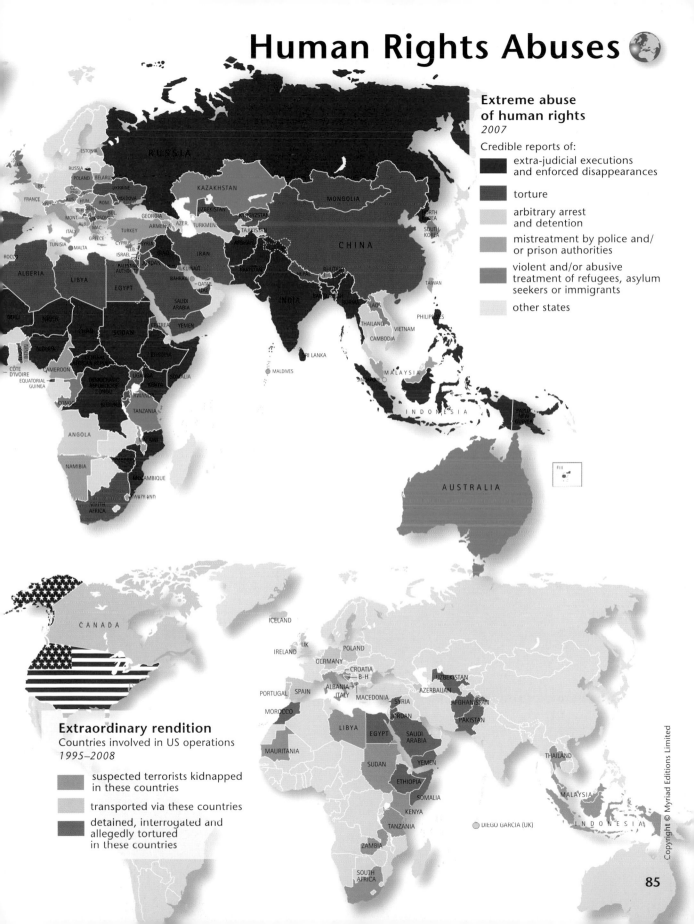

## Extreme abuse of human rights
*2007*

Credible reports of:

- extra-judicial executions and enforced disappearances
- torture
- arbitrary arrest and detention
- mistreatment by police and/or prison authorities
- violent and/or abusive treatment of refugees, asylum seekers or immigrants
- other states

## Extraordinary rendition
Countries involved in US operations
*1995–2008*

- suspected terrorists kidnapped in these countries
- transported via these countries
- detained, interrogated and allegedly tortured in these countries

Poverty, sexual and physical abuse, family breakdown, teenage pregnancy, homelessness, drug use and a lack of any alternatives, all put a child at risk of being trafficked. Traffickers promise employment in restaurants, hotels and homes but deliver children into all forms of exploitation. Victims often remain silent rather than risk deportation or institutionalization.

Trafficking can be linked to demand created by tourists and travellers. People who travel to sexually exploit children generally live in industrialized countries but exploit the underage poor in developing countries. However, this form of exploitation takes place within national borders all over the world.

**Mexico**
Over 16,000 children work as prostitutes, mostly in tourist destinations.

**Eastern Europe**
Girls as young as 13 are trafficked for sexual exploitation.

## Trafficking
Origins and destinations in Europe and Africa
*2008 or latest available data*

- country of origin
- country of destination
- country of origin and destination
- no data

Trafficking exists within many countries as well as across borders.

## Caribbean trafficking routes *2008*

**Guatemala** Between 1,000 and 1,500 babies and children are sold or trafficked each year for adoption in North America and Europe.

**Brazil**
Travel agencies or hotels facilitating child sex tourism risk being fined or losing their licence; perpetrators face 10 years imprisonment.

# Trafficking and Sex Tourism

**UK**
Paedophiles can be banned from destinations where they could be a risk to children.

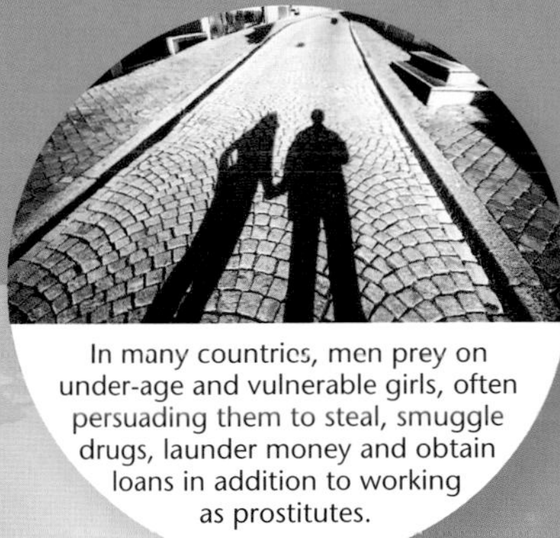


In many countries, men prey on under-age and vulnerable girls, often persuading them to steal, smuggle drugs, launder money and obtain loans in addition to working as prostitutes.


**Lithuania**
Maybe half of all prostitutes are minors. Ten-year-olds from children's homes have been used to make pornographic movies.

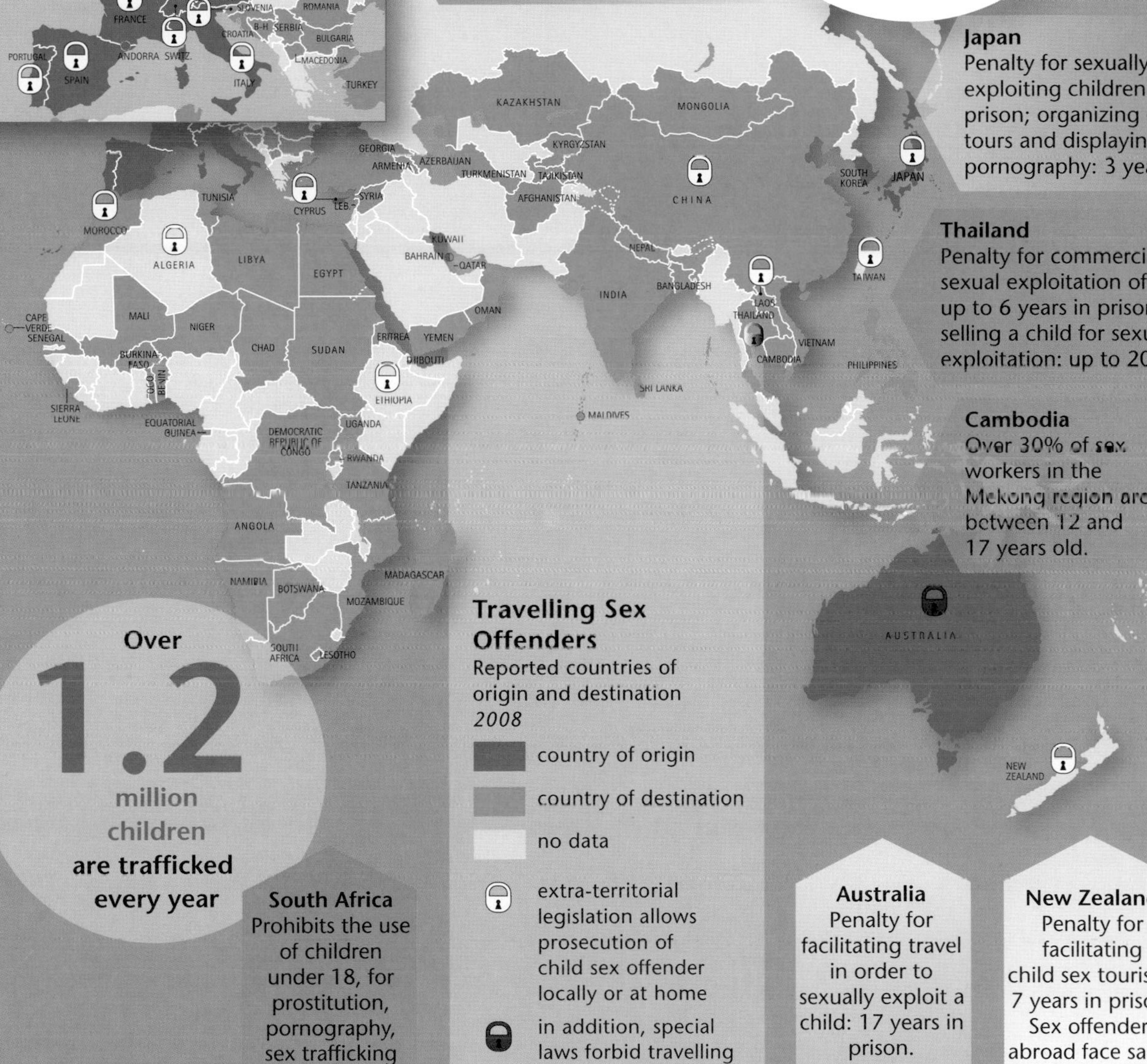


ICELAND
NORWAY
SWEDEN
FINLAND
ESTONIA
LATVIA
LITHUANIA
DENMARK
UK
IRELAND
NETH.
POLAND
BELGIUM
GERMANY
UKRAINE
LUXEMBOURG
SLOVAKIA
AUSTRIA
FRANCE
SLOVENIA
ROMANIA
CROATIA
B-H
SERBIA
BULGARIA
PORTUGAL
ANDORRA
SWITZ.
MACEDONIA
SPAIN
ITALY
TURKEY
KAZAKHSTAN
MONGOLIA
GEORGIA
KYRGYZSTAN
ARMENIA
AZERBAIJAN
TURKMENISTAN
TAJIKISTAN
SOUTH KOREA
JAPAN
TUNISIA
CYPRUS
LEB.
SYRIA
AFGHANISTAN
CHINA
MOROCCO
KUWAIT
BAHRAIN
QATAR
NEPAL
TAIWAN
ALGERIA
LIBYA
EGYPT
BANGLADESH
INDIA
LAOS
THAILAND
OMAN
CAPE VERDE
SENEGAL
MALI
NIGER
ERITREA
YEMEN
VIETNAM
CHAD
SUDAN
CAMBODIA
BURKINA FASO
TOGO
BENIN
DJIBOUTI
PHILIPPINES
ETHIOPIA
SRI LANKA
SIERRA LEONE
EQUATORIAL GUINEA
MALDIVES
UGANDA
DEMOCRATIC REPUBLIC OF CONGO
RWANDA
TANZANIA
ANGOLA
MADAGASCAR
NAMIBIA
BOTSWANA
MOZAMBIQUE
AUSTRALIA
SOUTH AFRICA
LESOTHO
NEW ZEALAND


**Japan**
Penalty for sexually exploiting children: 5 years in prison; organizing child sex tours and displaying child pornography: 3 years.

**Thailand**
Penalty for commercial sexual exploitation of a child: up to 6 years in prison; selling a child for sexual exploitation: up to 20 years.

**Cambodia**
Over 30% of sex workers in the Mekong region are between 12 and 17 years old.

**Over 1.2 million children are trafficked every year**

**Travelling Sex Offenders**
Reported countries of origin and destination
*2008*

- country of origin
- country of destination
- no data
- extra-territorial legislation allows prosecution of child sex offender locally or at home
- in addition, special laws forbid travelling with the intent of abusing children

**South Africa**
Prohibits the use of children under 18, for prostitution, pornography, sex trafficking or any other commercial exploitation.

**Australia**
Penalty for facilitating travel in order to sexually exploit a child: 17 years in prison.

**New Zealand**
Penalty for facilitating child sex tourism: 7 years in prison. Sex offenders abroad face same sentence as those at home.

## Children not in school

Percentage of school-age children
not attending school
by region and economic group
*2005*

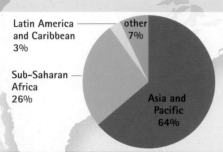

🧍 1 million children in school

🧍 1 million children not in school

World total **18%**

Latin America **6%**

Middle East and North Africa **19%**

West and Central Africa **45%**

Eastern and Southern Africa **39%**

Latin America and Caribbean **3%**

Sub-Saharan Africa **26%**

other **7%**

Asia and Pacific **64%**

## Where children are working

Regional distribution of economically active children aged 5 – 14 years
*2004*

The exclusion of the very poor from the benefits and rights that citizens should have according to international law begins in many countries with the non-registration of births. Left to one side by the state at the start of their lives, these children miss out on health care and education and head towards a life on the margins of society, often being exploited as child labourers.

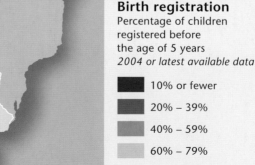

## Birth registration

Percentage of children registered before the age of 5 years
*2004 or latest available data*

- 10% or fewer
- 20% – 39%
- 40% – 59%
- 60% – 79%
- 80% or more
- no data

# Children's Rights

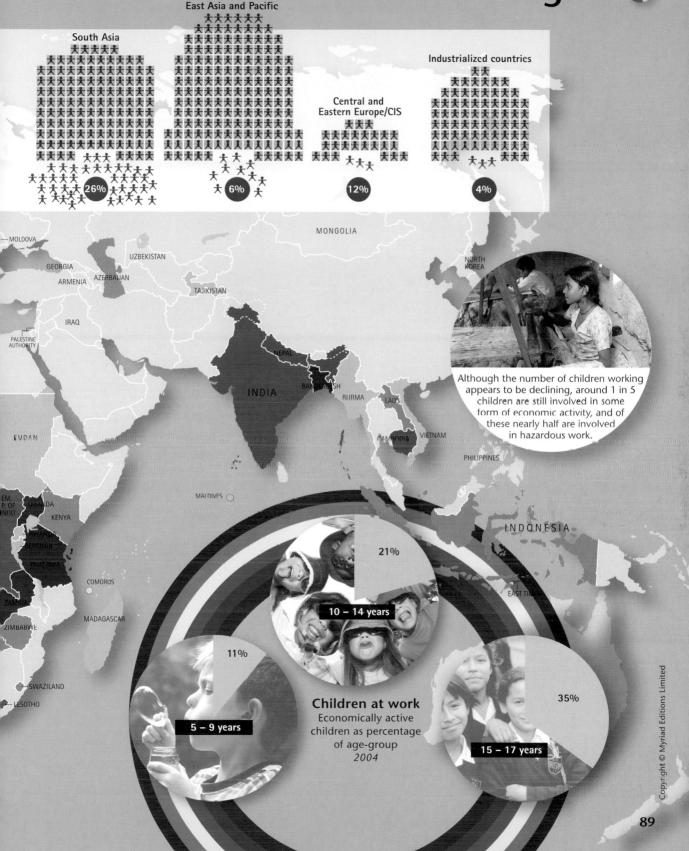

**South Asia**

**East Asia and Pacific**

**Industrialized countries**

**Central and Eastern Europe/CIS**

26%

6%

12%

4%

MOLDOVA
GEORGIA
ARMENIA
AZERBAIJAN
UZBEKISTAN
TAJIKISTAN
IRAQ
PALESTINE AUTHORITY
SUDAN
MONGOLIA
NORTH KOREA
NEPAL
INDIA
BANGLADESH
BURMA
LAOS
CAMBODIA
VIETNAM
PHILIPPINES
MALDIVES
DEM. REP. OF CONGO
UGANDA
KENYA
RWANDA
BURUNDI
TANZANIA
COMOROS
ZAMBIA
ZIMBABWE
MADAGASCAR
SWAZILAND
LESOTHO
INDONESIA
EAST TIMOR

Although the number of children working appears to be declining, around 1 in 5 children are still involved in some form of economic activity, and of these nearly half are involved in hazardous work.

21%

**10 – 14 years**

11%

**5 – 9 years**

35%

**15 – 17 years**

**Children at work**
Economically active children as percentage of age-group
*2004*

Recent economic improvements in many countries have still left women in a much worse position than men – and in some countries the position of women has declined since the early 1990s. Women are, in general, given less well-paid jobs than men, and get paid less than men even when doing the same job. Likewise, although women are participating more in politics than before, most political leaders are men.

## Equal rights

Score on the Gender-related Development Index (GDI) *2005*

- below 500 *least equal*
- 500 – 699
- 700 – 799
- 800 – 899
- 900 and above *most equal*
- no data

GDI rank compared with Human Development Index (HDI)

- ● GDI three or more places lower than HDI
- ○ GDI three or more places higher than HDI

The Gender Development Index (GDI) compares the life expectancy, literacy, school enrolment, and earned income of men and women within a country. The lower the GDI score, the worse the gender equality.

## National parliament

Proportion of seats held by women *2006*

- none
- 1% – 10%
- 11% – 20%
- 21% – 30%
- more than 30%
- no data

CANADA

● U S A

MEXICO

BAHAMAS

CUBA

JAMAICA

DOMINICAN REP.

CAPE VERDE

GUATEMALA
EL SALVADOR
HONDURAS
NICARAGUA

COSTA RICA
PANAMA

BARBADOS
TRINIDAD & TOBAGO

VENEZUELA

GUYANA
SURINAME

COLOMBIA

PERU

○ B R A Z I L

BOLIVIA

PARAGUAY

CHILE
ARGENTINA

URUGUAY

In Norway it is a legal requirement that
**40%**
of company board members are women

Only
**35**
countries have ever had a woman head of government

**Spain**
In April 2008, 50% of the cabinet were women.

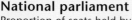

# Women's Rights

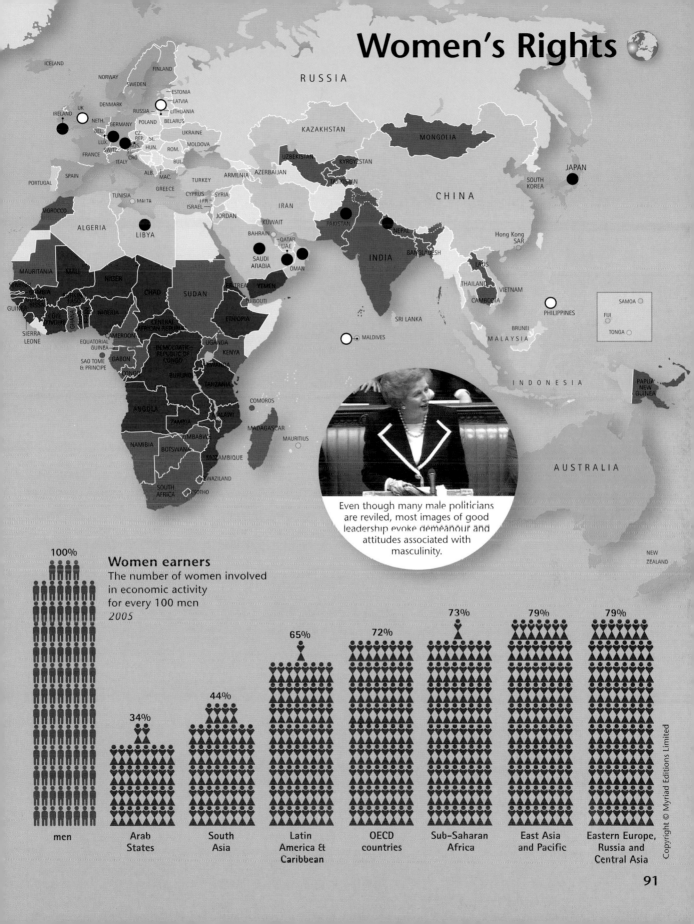

ICELAND · NORWAY · FINLAND · SWEDEN · ESTONIA · LATVIA · LITHUANIA · RUSSIA · DENMARK · IRELAND · UK · NETH. · GERMANY · POLAND · BELARUS · CZ. REP. · SL · BEL. · LUX. · SWITZ. · AUS. · HUN. · ROM. · MOLDOVA · UKRAINE · FRANCE · ITALY · CRO. · BUL. · ALB. · MAC. · PORTUGAL · SPAIN · GREECE · CYPRUS · TURKEY · ARMENIA · AZERBAIJAN · TUNISIA · MALTA · ISRAEL · I.FR · SYRIA · JORDAN · IRAN · MOROCCO · ALGERIA · LIBYA · KUWAIT · BAHRAIN · QATAR · UAE · SAUDI ARABIA · OMAN · MAURITANIA · MALI · NIGER · CHAD · SUDAN · ERITREA · YEMEN · DJIBOUTI · ETHIOPIA · SENEGAL · GAMBIA · GUINEA-BISSAU · GUINEA · SIERRA LEONE · CÔTE D'IVOIRE · GHANA · NIGERIA · CAMEROON · CENTRAL AFRICAN REPUBLIC · EQUATORIAL GUINEA · SAO TOME & PRINCIPE · GABON · CONGO · DEMOCRATIC REPUBLIC OF CONGO · UGANDA · KENYA · RWANDA · BURUNDI · TANZANIA · ANGOLA · ZAMBIA · MALAWI · ZIMBABWE · NAMIBIA · BOTSWANA · MOZAMBIQUE · SOUTH AFRICA · SWAZILAND · LESOTHO · COMOROS · MADAGASCAR · MAURITIUS · RUSSIA · KAZAKHSTAN · UZBEKISTAN · KYRGYZSTAN · TAJIKISTAN · MONGOLIA · CHINA · PAKISTAN · NEPAL · INDIA · BANGLADESH · SRI LANKA · MALDIVES · JAPAN · SOUTH KOREA · Hong Kong SAR · LAOS · THAILAND · VIETNAM · CAMBODIA · PHILIPPINES · BRUNEI · MALAYSIA · INDONESIA · SAMOA · FIJI · TONGA · PAPUA NEW GUINEA · AUSTRALIA · NEW ZEALAND

Even though many male politicians are reviled, most images of good leadership evoke demeanour and attitudes associated with masculinity.

## Women earners
The number of women involved in economic activity for every 100 men
*2005*

| men | Arab States | South Asia | Latin America & Caribbean | OECD countries | Sub-Saharan Africa | East Asia and Pacific | Eastern Europe, Russia and Central Asia |
|-----|------------|-----------|---------------------------|----------------|--------------------|-----------------------|----------------------------------------|
| 100% | 34% | 44% | 65% | 72% | 73% | 79% | 79% |

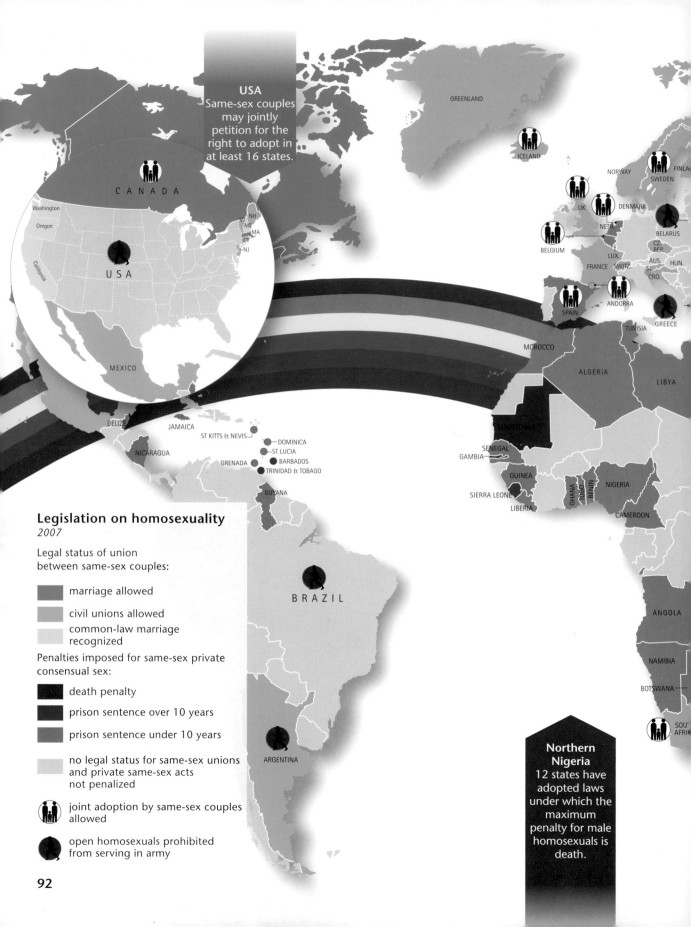

**USA**
Same-sex couples may jointly petition for the right to adopt in at least 16 states.

GREENLAND

ICELAND

NORWAY

SWEDEN

FINLA

UK

DENMARK

BELGIUM

NETH.

BELARUS

CZ. REP.

LUX.

FRANCE    SWITZ.

AUS.    HUN.

SI.

CRO.

SPAIN

ANDORRA

GREECE

CANADA

Washington

Oregon

California

USA

NH

ME

MA

CT

NJ

MEXICO

TUNISIA

MOROCCO

ALGERIA

LIBYA

BELIZE

JAMAICA

ST KITTS & NEVIS

DOMINICA

ST LUCIA

BARBADOS

TRINIDAD & TOBAGO

GRENADA

NICARAGUA

GUYANA

MAURITANIA

SENEGAL

GAMBIA

GUINEA

SIERRA LEONE

LIBERIA

GHANA

TOGO

BENIN

NIGERIA

CAMEROON

BRAZIL

ANGOLA

NAMIBIA

BOTSWANA

SOU

AFRI

ARGENTINA

# Legislation on homosexuality
*2007*

Legal status of union between same-sex couples:

- marriage allowed
- civil unions allowed
- common-law marriage recognized

Penalties imposed for same-sex private consensual sex:

- death penalty
- prison sentence over 10 years
- prison sentence under 10 years
- no legal status for same-sex unions and private same-sex acts not penalized
- joint adoption by same-sex couples allowed
- open homosexuals prohibited from serving in army

**Northern Nigeria**
12 states have adopted laws under which the maximum penalty for male homosexuals is death.

# Gay Rights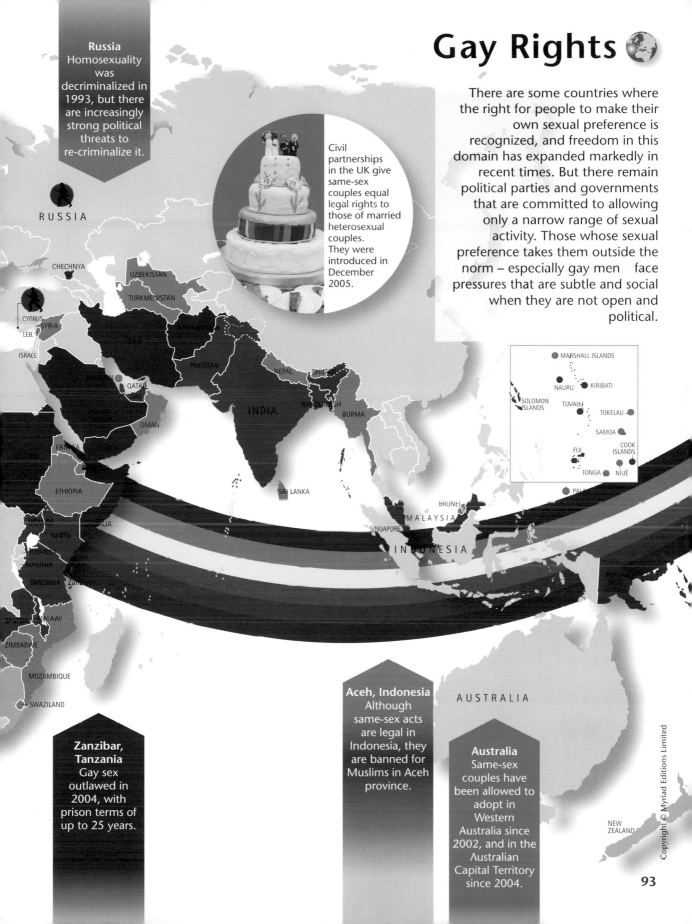

There are some countries where the right for people to make their own sexual preference is recognized, and freedom in this domain has expanded markedly in recent times. But there remain political parties and governments that are committed to allowing only a narrow range of sexual activity. Those whose sexual preference takes them outside the norm – especially gay men   face pressures that are subtle and social when they are not open and political.

**Russia**
Homosexuality was decriminalized in 1993, but there are increasingly strong political threats to re-criminalize it.

RUSSIA

CHECHNYA

UZBEKISTAN

TURKMENISTAN

CYPRUS
SYRIA
LEB.
ISRAEL

IRAN

AFGHANISTAN

PAKISTAN

NEPAL

BHUTAN

BAHRAIN
QATAR
UAE
SAUDI
ARABIA
OMAN

YEMEN

INDIA

BANGLADESH

BURMA

ERITREA

ETHIOPIA

SRI LANKA

KENYA

RWANDA
BURUNDI

TANZANIA  Zanzibar

ZAMBIA  MALAWI

ZIMBABWE

MOZAMBIQUE

SWAZILAND

Civil partnerships in the UK give same-sex couples equal legal rights to those of married heterosexual couples. They were introduced in December 2005.

MARSHALL ISLANDS

NAURU  KIRIBATI

SOLOMON
ISLANDS  TUVALU

TOKELAU

SAMOA

FIJI  COOK
ISLANDS

TONGA  NIUE

PALAU

BRUNEI

MALAYSIA

SINGAPORE

INDONESIA

PAPUA
NEW
GUINEA

AUSTRALIA

NEW ZEALAND

**Zanzibar, Tanzania**
Gay sex outlawed in 2004, with prison terms of up to 25 years.

**Aceh, Indonesia**
Although same-sex acts are legal in Indonesia, they are banned for Muslims in Aceh province.

**Australia**
Same-sex couples have been allowed to adopt in Western Australia since 2002, and in the Australian Capital Territory since 2004.

93

Fighter graffiti on a hospital wall in eastern Chad. The area is destabilized by refugees and militia from the crisis in neighbouring Darfur, Sudan.

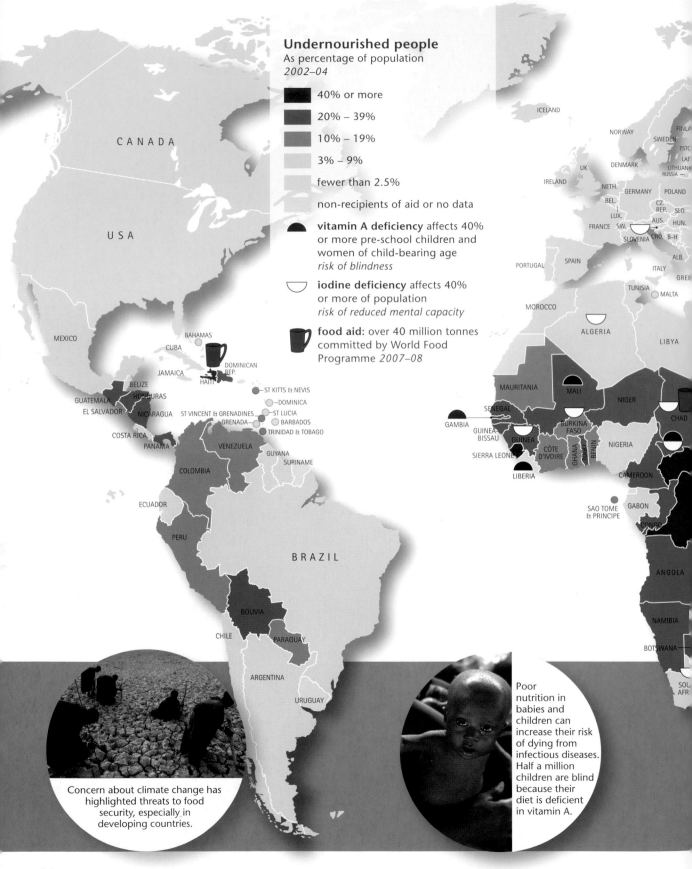

## Undernourished people
As percentage of population
*2002–04*

- 40% or more
- 20% – 39%
- 10% – 19%
- 3% – 9%
- fewer than 2.5%
- non-recipients of aid or no data

**vitamin A deficiency** affects 40% or more pre-school children and women of child-bearing age *risk of blindness*

**iodine deficiency** affects 40% or more of population *risk of reduced mental capacity*

**food aid:** over 40 million tonnes committed by World Food Programme *2007–08*

CANADA

USA

MEXICO

BAHAMAS
CUBA
JAMAICA
HAITI
DOMINICAN REP.
BELIZE
GUATEMALA
HONDURAS
EL SALVADOR
NICARAGUA
COSTA RICA
PANAMA
ST KITTS & NEVIS
DOMINICA
ST VINCENT & GRENADINES
ST LUCIA
GRENADA
BARBADOS
TRINIDAD & TOBAGO

VENEZUELA
COLOMBIA
GUYANA
SURINAME
ECUADOR
PERU
BRAZIL
BOLIVIA
PARAGUAY
CHILE
ARGENTINA
URUGUAY

ICELAND
NORWAY
SWEDEN
FINL
ESTO
LAT
LITHUAN
RUSSIA
UK
DENMARK
IRELAND
NETH.
GERMANY
POLAND
BEL.
CZ. REP.
SLO.
LUX.
AUS.
HUN.
FRANCE
SW.
SLOVENIA
CRO.
B-H
ALB.
PORTUGAL
SPAIN
ITALY
GREI
TUNISIA
MALTA
MOROCCO
ALGERIA
LIBYA

MAURITANIA
MALI
NIGER
CHAD
SENEGAL
GAMBIA
BURKINA FASO
GUINEA-BISSAU
GUINEA
CÔTE D'IVOIRE
GHANA
TOGO
BENIN
NIGERIA
SIERRA LEONE
LIBERIA
CAMEROON
SAO TOME & PRINCIPE
GABON
CONGO
ANGOLA
NAMIBIA
BOTSWANA
SOL
AFR

Concern about climate change has highlighted threats to food security, especially in developing countries.

Poor nutrition in babies and children can increase their risk of dying from infectious diseases. Half a million children are blind because their diet is deficient in vitamin A.

96

# Malnutrition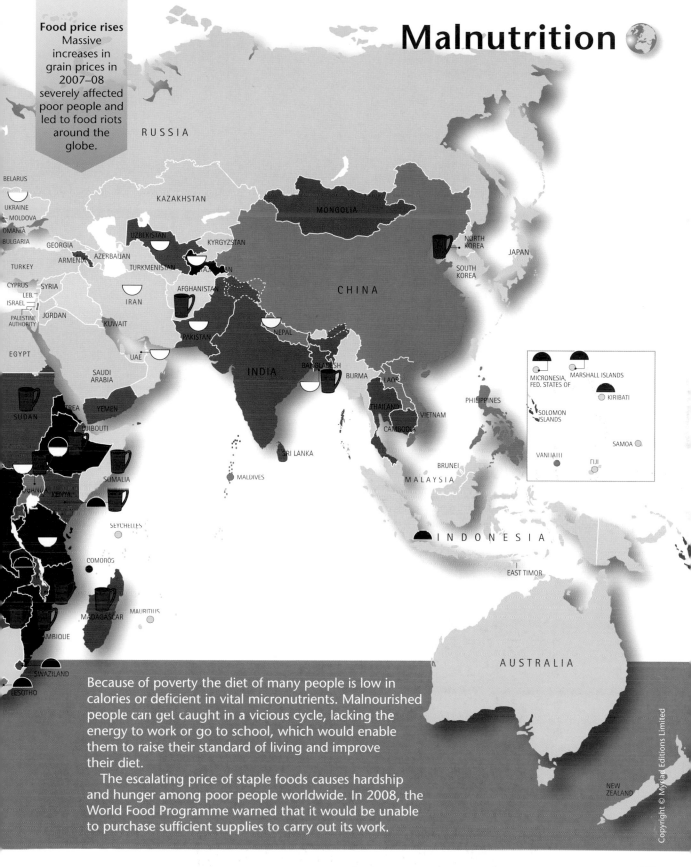

**Food price rises**
Massive increases in grain prices in 2007–08 severely affected poor people and led to food riots around the globe.

Because of poverty the diet of many people is low in calories or deficient in vital micronutrients. Malnourished people can get caught in a vicious cycle, lacking the energy to work or go to school, which would enable them to raise their standard of living and improve their diet.

The escalating price of staple foods causes hardship and hunger among poor people worldwide. In 2008, the World Food Programme warned that it would be unable to purchase sufficient supplies to carry out its work.

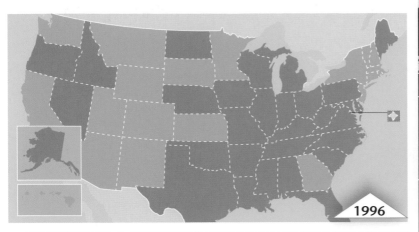

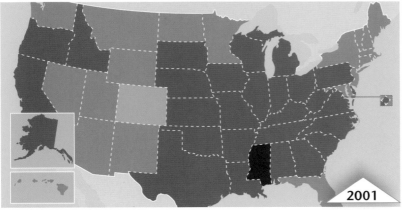

## America's spreading obesity
Percentage of adults who are obese *1996, 2001, 2006*

- ■ 25% or more
- ■ 20% – 24%
- ■ 15% – 19%
- ■ 10% – 14%
- □ no data

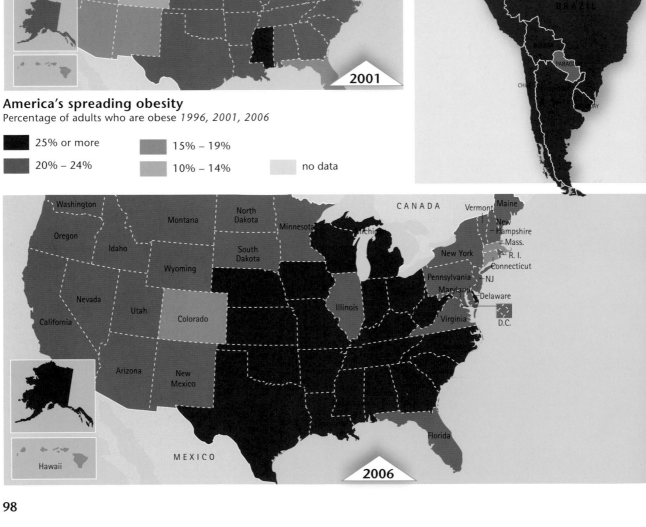

USA
19% of children aged 6–11 were obese in 2004.

# Obesity

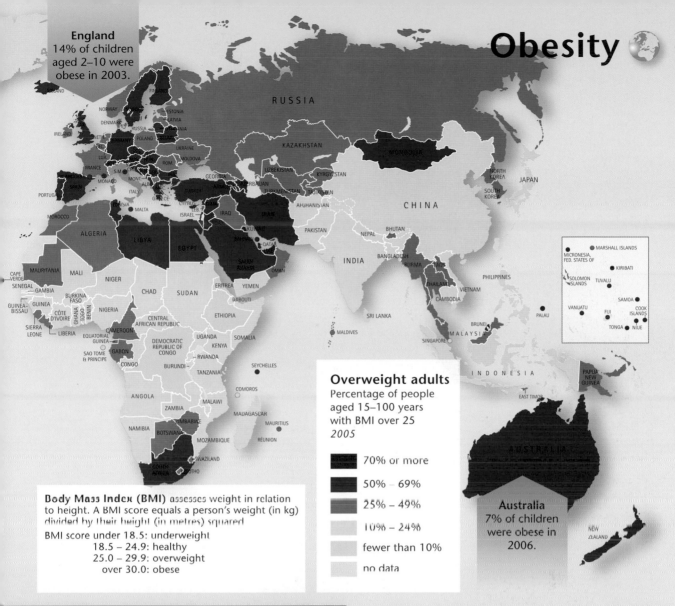

**England**
14% of children aged 2–10 were obese in 2003.

RUSSIA

KAZAKHSTAN

MONGOLIA

NORTH KOREA

JAPAN

SOUTH KOREA

CHINA

UZBEKISTAN

KYRGYZSTAN

TURKMENISTAN

TAJIKISTAN

AFGHANISTAN

PAKISTAN

NEPAL

BHUTAN

INDIA

BANGLADESH

BURMA

LAOS

THAILAND

VIETNAM

CAMBODIA

PHILIPPINES

SRI LANKA

MALDIVES

BRUNEI

MALAYSIA

SINGAPORE

INDONESIA

EAST TIMOR

PAPUA NEW GUINEA

MICRONESIA, FED. STATES OF

MARSHALL ISLANDS

KIRIBATI

SOLOMON ISLANDS

TUVALU

SAMOA

VANUATU

PALAU

FIJI

COOK ISLANDS

TONGA

NIUE

AUSTRALIA

NEW ZEALAND

**Australia**
7% of children were obese in 2006.

ICELAND

NORWAY

DENMARK

RUSSIA

IRELAND

NETH.

GERMANY

POLAND

FINLAND

ESTONIA

LATVIA

LITHUANIA

UKRAINE

LUX.

FRANCE

BELARUS

MOLDOVA

GEORGIA

AZERBAIJAN

ROM.

MONACO

S.M.

SWITZ.

MONT.

ALB.

GREECE

ITALY

TURKEY

ARMENIA

CYPRUS

LEB.

SYRIA

IRAQ

IRAN

ISRAEL

JORDAN

KUWAIT

QATAR

U.A.E.

OMAN

SAUDI ARABIA

YEMEN

PORTUGAL

SPAIN

TUNISIA

MALTA

MOROCCO

ALGERIA

LIBYA

EGYPT

CAPE VERDE

MAURITANIA

MALI

NIGER

CHAD

SUDAN

ERITREA

DJIBOUTI

SENEGAL

GAMBIA

GUINEA-BISSAU

GUINEA

BURKINA FASO

CÔTE D'IVOIRE

GHANA

TOGO

BENIN

NIGERIA

SIERRA LEONE

LIBERIA

CAMEROON

CENTRAL AFRICAN REPUBLIC

ETHIOPIA

SOMALIA

EQUATORIAL GUINEA

SAO TOME & PRINCIPE

GABON

CONGO

DEMOCRATIC REPUBLIC OF CONGO

UGANDA

KENYA

RWANDA

BURUNDI

TANZANIA

SEYCHELLES

ANGOLA

ZAMBIA

MALAWI

COMOROS

MADAGASCAR

MAURITIUS

RÉUNION

NAMIBIA

ZIMBABWE

BOTSWANA

MOZAMBIQUE

SWAZILAND

SOUTH AFRICA

LESOTHO

## Overweight adults

Percentage of people aged 15–100 years with BMI over 25
*2005*

- 70% or more
- 50% – 69%
- 25% – 49%
- 10% – 24%
- fewer than 10%
- no data

**Body Mass Index (BMI)** assesses weight in relation to height. A BMI score equals a person's weight (in kg) divided by their height (in metres) squared

BMI score under 18.5: underweight
18.5 – 24.9: healthy
25.0 – 29.9: overweight
over 30.0: obese

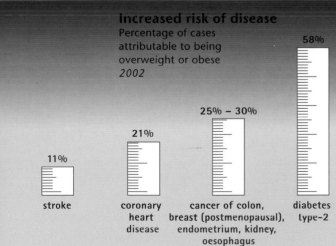

## Increased risk of disease

Percentage of cases attributable to being overweight or obese
*2002*

- 11% — stroke
- 21% — coronary heart disease
- 25% – 30% — cancer of colon, breast (postmenopausal), endometrium, kidney, oesophagus
- 58% — diabetes type-2

Worldwide, people are eating more meat, dairy products and sugary foods, and their weight is increasing as a consequence. Even in countries where the majority of people are undernourished, those who can afford it are over-eating, their extra flesh often seen as a prestigious indication of their wealth. In rich countries, cheap processed foods are high in animal fats and sugars, so a poor diet is more likely to lead to weight gain. Obesity leads to an increased risk of several serious diseases. The likely consequences are serious, not only for the individuals concerned but for society as a whole as health services struggle to cope with the increased strain.

A cigarette is the only legal consumer product that kills through normal use. And the full health and economic impacts of the increasing popularity of cigarettes over the last 50 years are yet to be felt. Half of the 650 million people who currently smoke will eventually be killed by the habit.

With advertising controls being tightened in industrialized countries, tobacco companies are increasingly seeking to expand into developing countries in an effort to maintain sales.

The number of young smokers around the world is increasing, with 25% of them trying their first cigarette before the age of ten.

## Deaths
Increasing deaths due to tobacco
*1950–2030 projected*

— industrialized countries
— developing countries

7 million
*projected*

3 million
*projected*

2.1 million

2.1 million

1.3 million

0.3 million

0.2 million

| 1950 | 1975 | 2000 | 2025–30 |

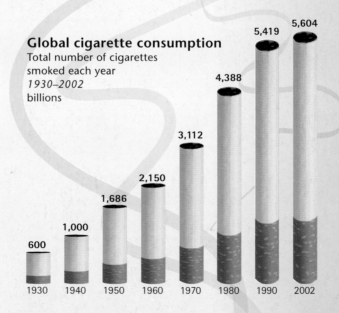

## Global cigarette consumption
Total number of cigarettes smoked each year
*1930–2002*
billions

5,604

5,419

4,388

3,112

2,150

1,686

1,000

600

| 1930 | 1940 | 1950 | 1960 | 1970 | 1980 | 1990 | 2002 |

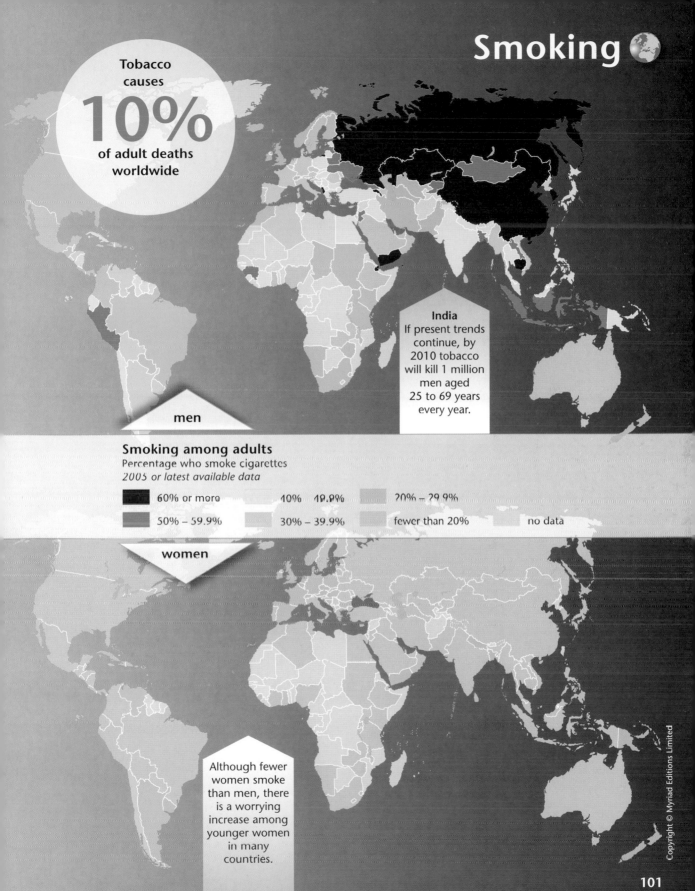

# Smoking

**Tobacco causes**

# 10%

**of adult deaths worldwide**

**India**
If present trends continue, by 2010 tobacco will kill 1 million men aged 25 to 69 years every year.

men

### Smoking among adults
Percentage who smoke cigarettes
*2005 or latest available data*

- 60% or more
- 50% – 59.9%
- 40% – 49.9%
- 30% – 39.9%
- 20% – 29.9%
- fewer than 20%
- no data

women

Although fewer women smoke than men, there is a worrying increase among younger women in many countries.

In 2002, there were 10.9 million new cancer cases in the world, and 6.7 million deaths. The most common cancers worldwide are lung, breast, large intestine (colon and rectum), stomach and prostate. Liver cancer is the most common cancer for men in several African countries, although Kaposi sarcoma has become the most common in those countries severely affected by the AIDS epidemic.

The risk of getting cancer is higher in the industrialized world, but in the developing world lack of treatment means that it is more likely to be fatal.

## Sex differences
New cancer cases by sex 2002 thousands

♂ male — female ♀

| male | | female |
|---|---|---|
| 965 | lung | 387 |
| | breast (female) | 1,151 |
| 550 | colon and rectum | 473 |
| 603 | stomach | 331 |
| 679 | prostate | |
| 442 | liver | 184 |
| | cervix and uterus | 493 |
| 315 | oesophagus | 147 |
| 274 | bladder | 83 |
| | ovary | 204 |
| 171 | leukaemia | 129 |
| 175 | non-Hodgkin lymphoma | 125 |
| 176 | oral cavity | 98 |
| 125 | pancreas | 107 |
| 129 | kidney | 79 |

## Differences around the world
New cancer cases in industrialized and developing countries 2002 thousands

- industrialized countries
- developing countries

**46%** of new cancer cases occur in industrialized countries, home to **19%** of the world's population

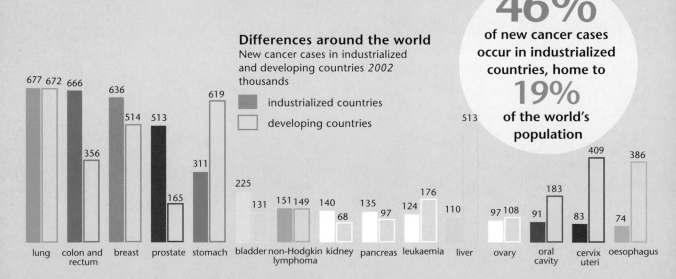

| | industrialized | developing |
|---|---|---|
| lung | 677 | 672 |
| colon and rectum | 666 | 356 |
| breast | 636 | 514 |
| prostate | 513 | 165 |
| stomach | 311 | 619 |
| bladder | 225 | 131 |
| non-Hodgkin lymphoma | 151 | 149 |
| kidney | 140 | 68 |
| pancreas | 135 | 97 |
| leukaemia | 124 | 176 |
| liver | 513 | 110 |
| ovary | 97 | 108 |
| oral cavity | 91 | 183 |
| cervix uteri | 83 | 409 |
| oesophagus | 74 | 386 |

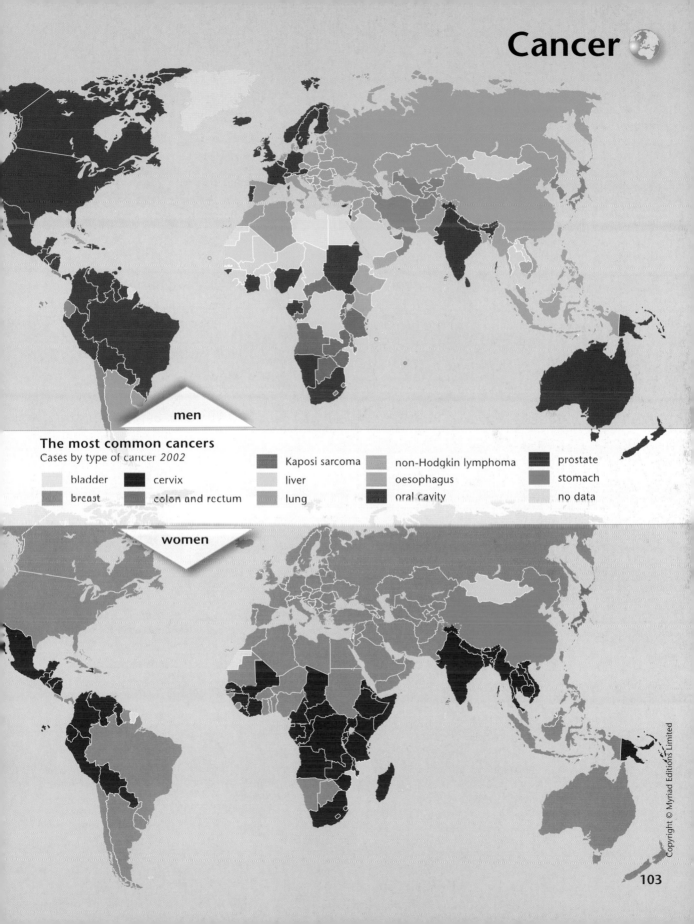

**men**

## The most common cancers
Cases by type of cancer *2002*

| | | | |
|---|---|---|---|
| bladder | Kaposi sarcoma | non-Hodgkin lymphoma | prostate |
| breast | liver | oesophagus | stomach |
| cervix | lung | oral cavity | no data |
| colon and rectum | | | |

**women**

Every day during 2007 over 6,800 people became infected with HIV, and over 5,700 people died from AIDS, mostly because of inadequate access to HIV prevention and treatment services. Sub-Saharan Africa is the worst-affected region, with widespread infection having a devastating social and economic impact.

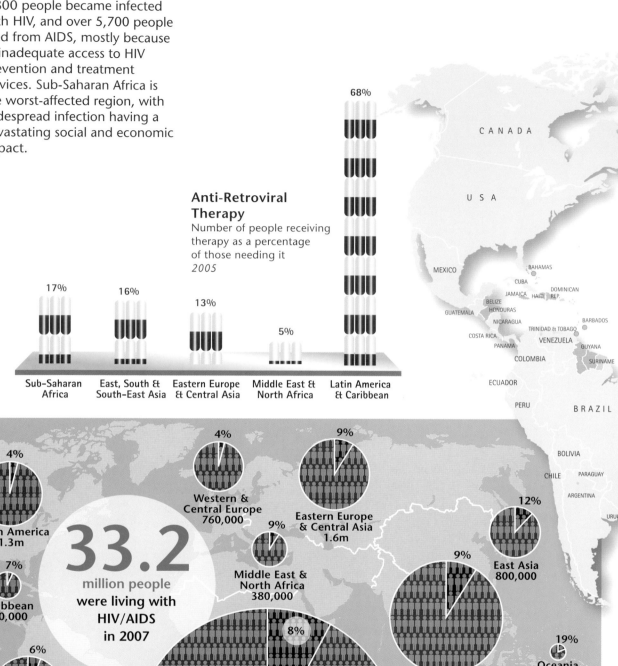

### Anti-Retroviral Therapy

Number of people receiving therapy as a percentage of those needing it
*2005*

68%

17% — Sub-Saharan Africa

16% — East, South & South-East Asia

13% — Eastern Europe & Central Asia

5% — Middle East & North Africa

68% — Latin America & Caribbean

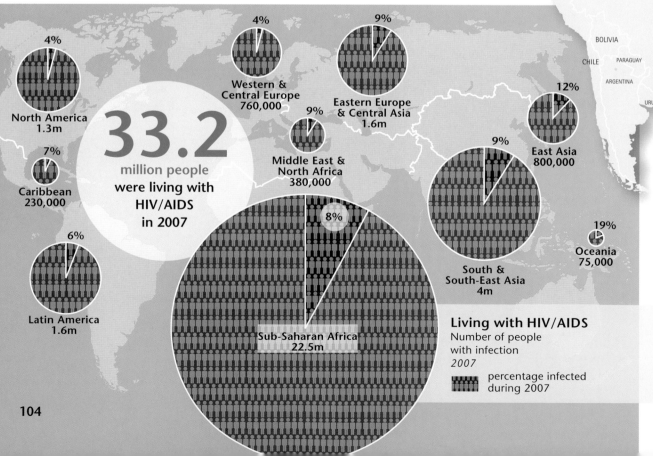

4%
North America
1.3m

7%
Caribbean
230,000

6%
Latin America
1.6m

4%
Western & Central Europe
760,000

9%
Middle East & North Africa
380,000

9%
Eastern Europe & Central Asia
1.6m

12%
East Asia
800,000

9%
South & South-East Asia
4m

19%
Oceania
75,000

**33.2**
million people
**were living with HIV/AIDS in 2007**

8%
Sub-Saharan Africa
22.5m

### Living with HIV/AIDS

Number of people with infection
*2007*

percentage infected during 2007

104

# HIV/AIDS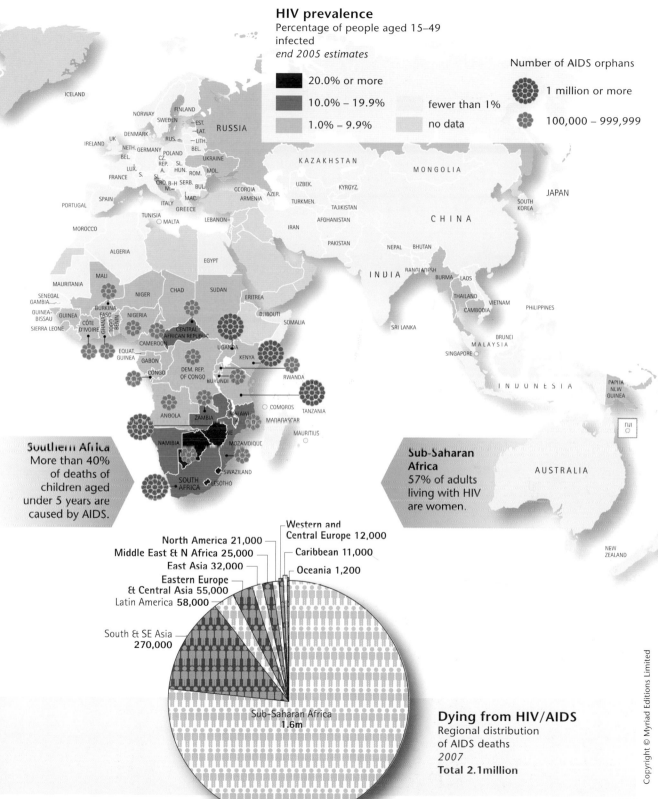

## HIV prevalence
Percentage of people aged 15–49 infected
*end 2005 estimates*

| | |
|---|---|
| ⬛ | 20.0% or more |
| ⬛ | 10.0% – 19.9% |
| ⬛ | 1.0% – 9.9% |

fewer than 1%

no data

**Number of AIDS orphans**

1 million or more

100,000 – 999,999

### Southern Africa
More than 40% of deaths of children aged under 5 years are caused by AIDS.

### Sub-Saharan Africa
57% of adults living with HIV are women.

## Dying from HIV/AIDS
Regional distribution of AIDS deaths
*2007*
**Total 2.1million**

North America 21,000
Middle East & N Africa 25,000
East Asia 32,000
Eastern Europe & Central Asia 55,000
Latin America 58,000
South & SE Asia 270,000
Western and Central Europe 12,000
Caribbean 11,000
Oceania 1,200
Sub-Saharan Africa 1.6m

Copyright © Myriad Editions Limited

105

Women and children search for edible roots in a river bed during the dry season in Burkina Faso. Conditions are made worse by over-grazing, infestations, and changes in weather due to climate change.

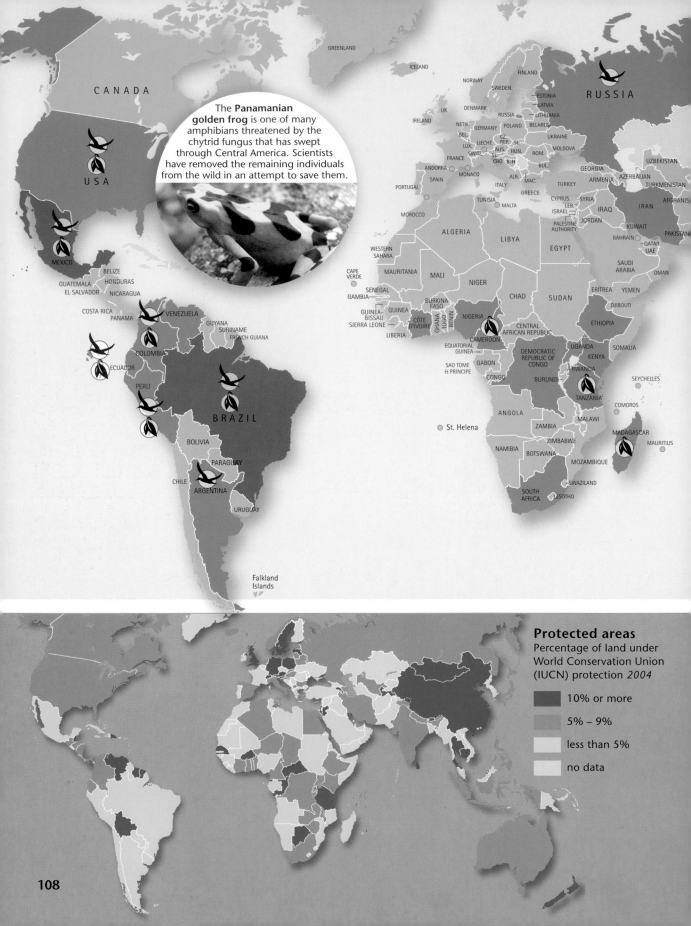

The **Panamanian golden frog** is one of many amphibians threatened by the chytrid fungus that has swept through Central America. Scientists have removed the remaining individuals from the wild in an attempt to save them.

CANADA

USA

MEXICO
BELIZE
GUATEMALA
EL SALVADOR
HONDURAS
NICARAGUA
COSTA RICA
PANAMA
VENEZUELA
GUYANA
SURINAME
FRENCH GUIANA
COLOMBIA
ECUADOR
PERU
BRAZIL
BOLIVIA
PARAGUAY
CHILE
ARGENTINA
URUGUAY
Falkland
Islands

GREENLAND

ICELAND
NORWAY
SWEDEN
FINLAND
DENMARK
UK
IRELAND
NETH.
GERMANY
POLAND
BELARUS
BEL.
LIECHT.
CZ. REP.
UKRAINE
LUX.
SL.
AUS.
HUN.
MOLDOVA
ANDORRA
FRANCE
SWITZ.
CRO.
B-H
ROM.
SPAIN
MONACO
ITALY
BUL.
PORTUGAL
SAN MARINO
ALB.
MAC.
GREECE
TURKEY
GEORGIA
ARMENIA
AZERBAIJAN
MOROCCO
TUNISIA
MALTA
CYPRUS
SYRIA
LEB.
ISRAEL
IRAQ
IRAN
PALESTINE AUTHORITY
JORDAN
KUWAIT
ESTONIA
LATVIA
LITHUANIA
RUSSIA
UZBEKISTAN
TURKMENISTAN
AFGHANIS
PAKISTAN
BAHRAIN
QATAR
UAE
SAUDI ARABIA
OMAN
RUSSIA

WESTERN SAHARA
ALGERIA
LIBYA
EGYPT
CAPE VERDE
MAURITANIA
MALI
NIGER
CHAD
SUDAN
ERITREA
YEMEN
DJIBOUTI
SENEGAL
GAMBIA
GUINEA-BISSAU
GUINEA
BURKINA FASO
BENIN
NIGERIA
CENTRAL AFRICAN REPUBLIC
ETHIOPIA
SIERRA LEONE
CÔTE D'IVOIRE
GHANA
TOGO
LIBERIA
EQUATORIAL GUINEA
SAO TOME & PRINCIPE
GABON
CONGO
CAMEROON
DEMOCRATIC REPUBLIC OF CONGO
UGANDA
RWANDA
BURUNDI
KENYA
SOMALIA
TANZANIA
SEYCHELLES
COMOROS
ANGOLA
ZAMBIA
MALAWI
MADAGASCAR
MAURITIUS
NAMIBIA
ZIMBABWE
BOTSWANA
MOZAMBIQUE
SWAZILAND
SOUTH AFRICA
LESOTHO
St. Helena

## Protected areas

Percentage of land under World Conservation Union (IUCN) protection *2004*

- 10% or more
- 5% – 9%
- less than 5%
- no data

# Biodiversity

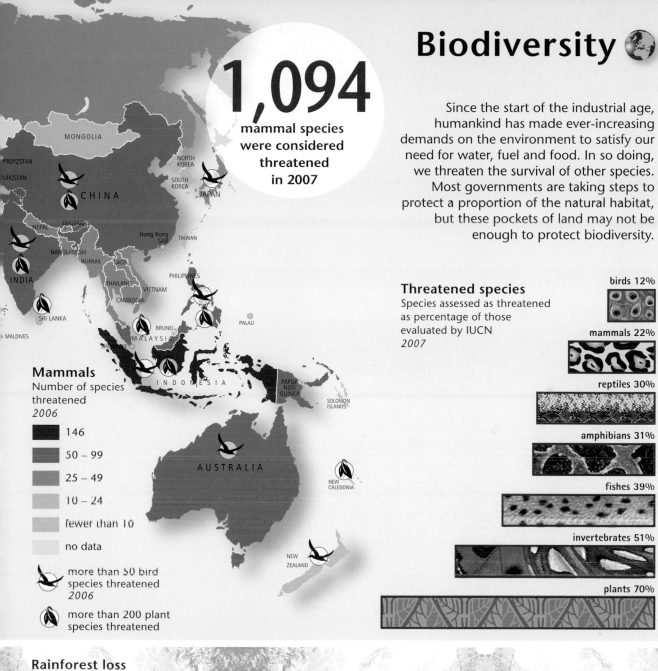

## 1,094
mammal species were considered threatened in 2007

Since the start of the industrial age, humankind has made ever-increasing demands on the environment to satisfy our need for water, fuel and food. In so doing, we threaten the survival of other species. Most governments are taking steps to protect a proportion of the natural habitat, but these pockets of land may not be enough to protect biodiversity.

### Mammals
Number of species threatened
*2006*

- 146
- 50 – 99
- 25 – 49
- 10 – 24
- fewer than 10
- no data

more than 50 bird species threatened 2006

more than 200 plant species threatened

### Threatened species
Species assessed as threatened as percentage of those evaluated by IUCN
*2007*

birds 12%

mammals 22%

reptiles 30%

amphibians 31%

fishes 39%

invertebrates 51%

plants 70%

### Rainforest loss
*1990–2005*

square kilometres lost

area lost as percentage of total rainforest in region

| Region | Square kilometres lost | Percentage lost |
| --- | --- | --- |
| Thailand | 14,450 | 9% |
| Malaysia | 14,860 | 7% |
| Cameroon | 33,000 | 13% |
| Philippines | 34,120 | 32% |
| Congo, D.R. | 69,210 | 5% |
| Burma | 69,970 | 18% |
| Indonesia | 280,720 | 24% |
| Brazil | 423,290 | 8% |

One in four people live in areas with insufficient water to support them. This means that water is being used at an unsustainable level, with rivers running dry, underground aquifers being drained to make up the shortfall, and energy being used to desalinate water. Throughout much of Sub-Saharan Africa, even where water is available, the infrastructure needed to get it to people is absent or poorly maintained. As a result, countries that are comparatively well off in water actually use relatively little. The problem is not the availability of the resource, but a shortfall in the ability to govern its use so as to benefit the majority of people.

## Water available
Annual renewable water resources *2007*
cubic meters per capita

- fewer than 1,000
- 1,000 – 1,999
- 2,000 – 2,999
- more than 3,000
- no data
- **!** dependent on upstream neighbours for 75% or more of water supply

# 70%
**of food emergencies in developing countries are caused by drought**

## Water used
Amount used each year for industries, agricultural and domestic purposes
*2007 or latest available data*
cubic meters per capita

- fewer than 250
- 250 – 499
- 500 – 1,000
- 1,000 – 1,999
- more than 2,000
- no data

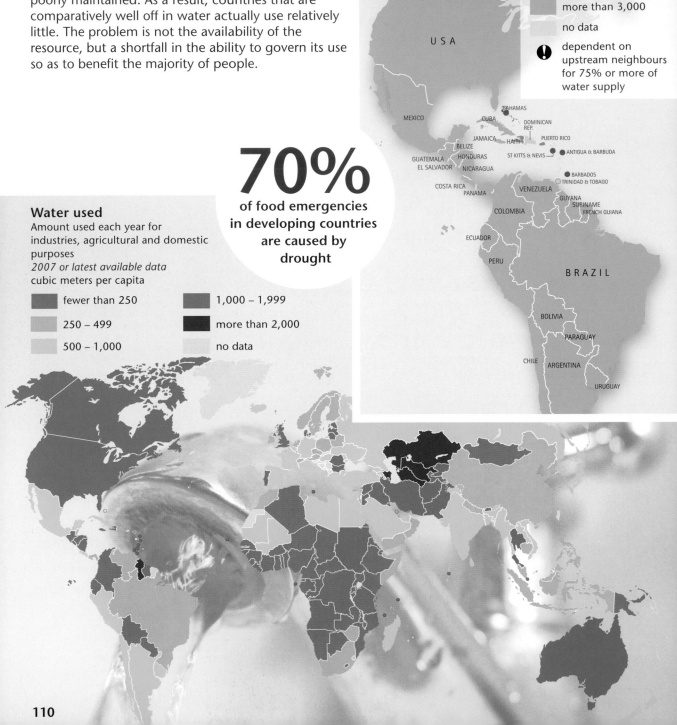

# Water Resources

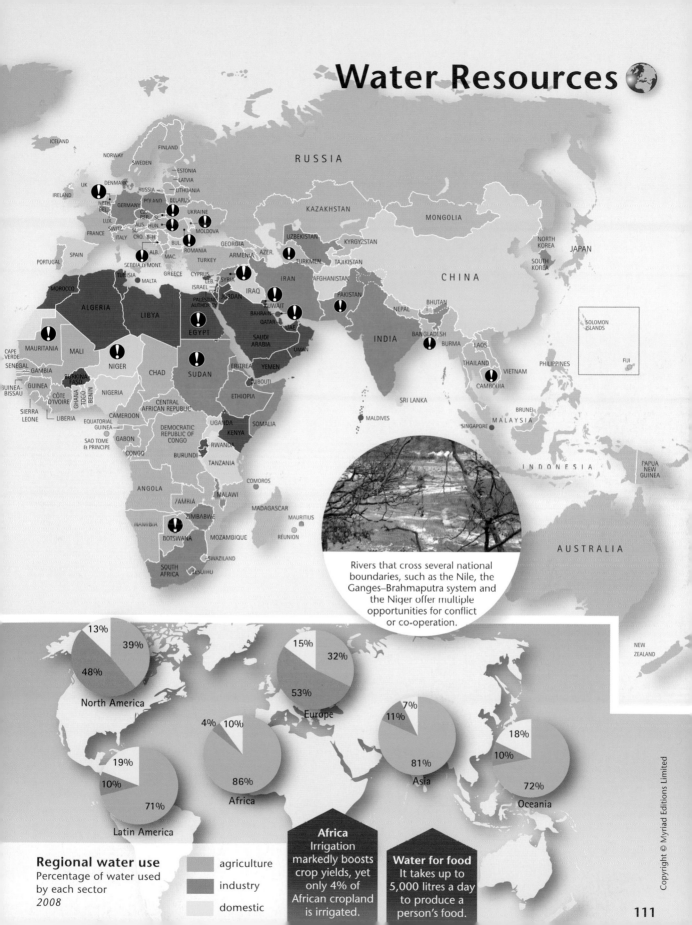

RUSSIA

ICELAND
NORWAY
FINLAND
SWEDEN
ESTONIA
LATVIA
UK DENMARK
IRELAND
RUSSIA
LITHUANIA
BELARUS
NETH. GERMANY POLAND UKRAINE
BEL.
LUX. CZ. SL.
FRANCE SWITZ. AUS. HUN. MOLDOVA
ITALY CRO. B-H.
SERBIA & MONT. BUL. ROMANIA
ALB. MAC.
PORTUGAL SPAIN GREECE
MALTA CYPRUS GEORGIA
TUNISIA LEB. SYRIA ARMENIA AZER.
MOROCCO ISRAEL JORDAN IRAQ IRAN
PALESTINE
AUTHORITY
ALGERIA LIBYA EGYPT KUWAIT
BAHRAIN
QATAR UAE
SAUDI
ARABIA OMAN

KAZAKHSTAN
MONGOLIA
UZBEKISTAN
KYRGYZSTAN
TURKMEN. TAJIKISTAN
AFGHANISTAN CHINA
TURKEY
PAKISTAN
NEPAL BHUTAN
NORTH
KOREA JAPAN
SOUTH
KOREA

CAPE
VERDE
MAURITANIA MALI NIGER CHAD SUDAN
SENEGAL
GAMBIA
GUINEA- GUINEA BURKINA ERITREA YEMEN
BISSAU FASO BENIN NIGERIA
SIERRA CÔTE TOGO CENTRAL DJIBOUTI
LEONE D'IVOIRE GHANA AFRICAN REPUBLIC ETHIOPIA
LIBERIA
EQUATORIAL CAMEROON
GUINEA UGANDA SOMALIA
SAO TOME GABON KENYA
& PRINCIPE CONGO DEMOCRATIC RWANDA
REPUBLIC OF BURUNDI
CONGO TANZANIA

INDIA
BURMA
LAOS
THAILAND VIETNAM
CAMBODIA
SRI LANKA
MALDIVES

SOLOMON
ISLANDS

PHILIPPINES
FIJI
BRUNEI
MALAYSIA
SINGAPORE

INDONESIA PAPUA
NEW
GUINEA

ANGOLA ZAMBIA MALAWI
COMOROS
MADAGASCAR
NAMIBIA ZIMBABWE MAURITIUS
BOTSWANA MOZAMBIQUE RÉUNION
SWAZILAND
SOUTH LESOTHO
AFRICA

AUSTRALIA

NEW
ZEALAND

Rivers that cross several national
boundaries, such as the Nile, the
Ganges–Brahmaputra system and
the Niger offer multiple
opportunities for conflict
or co-operation.

## Regional water use
Percentage of water used
by each sector
*2008*

- agriculture
- industry
- domestic

### North America
13%
39%
48%

### Europe
15%
32%
53%

### Latin America
19%
10%
71%

### Africa
4%
10%
86%

### Asia
7%
11%
81%

### Oceania
18%
10%
72%

**Africa**
Irrigation
markedly boosts
crop yields, yet
only 4% of
African cropland
is irrigated.

**Water for food**
It takes up to
5,000 litres a day
to produce a
person's food.

Waste is one of the great unspoken problems of our time. It is an issue that reaches from the actions of individuals to the operation of large-scale industry. Non-stop growth in garbage is consuming landfill sites faster than they can be created. Commercial enterprises have stepped in, and recycling rubbish has become a global business worth billions of dollars, yet still the problem mounts. At one end of the scale lie the plastic bags that supermarkets give away for free and that end up in the sea, killing dolphins. At the other end lies industrial pollution and the unresolved problem of disposing of the radioactive waste products of nuclear power.

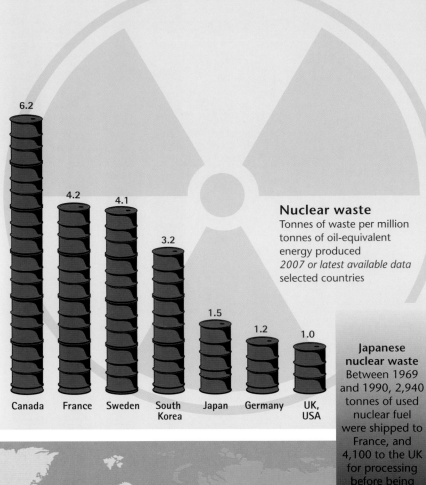

## Nuclear waste

Tonnes of waste per million tonnes of oil-equivalent energy produced
*2007 or latest available data* selected countries

| Canada | France | Sweden | South Korea | Japan | Germany | UK, USA |
|--------|--------|--------|-------------|-------|---------|---------|
| 6.2 | 4.2 | 4.1 | 3.2 | 1.5 | 1.2 | 1.0 |

**Japanese nuclear waste** Between 1969 and 1990, 2,940 tonnes of used nuclear fuel were shipped to France, and 4,100 to the UK for processing before being returned to Japan for storage.

**US nuclear waste** Between 1968 and 2002, over 47,000 tonnes of uranium was processed.

## Nuclear power
*Jan 2008*

- operates 50 or more commercial nuclear power stations
- operates fewer than 50 commercial nuclear power stations
- plans or proposes to operate commercial nuclear power station

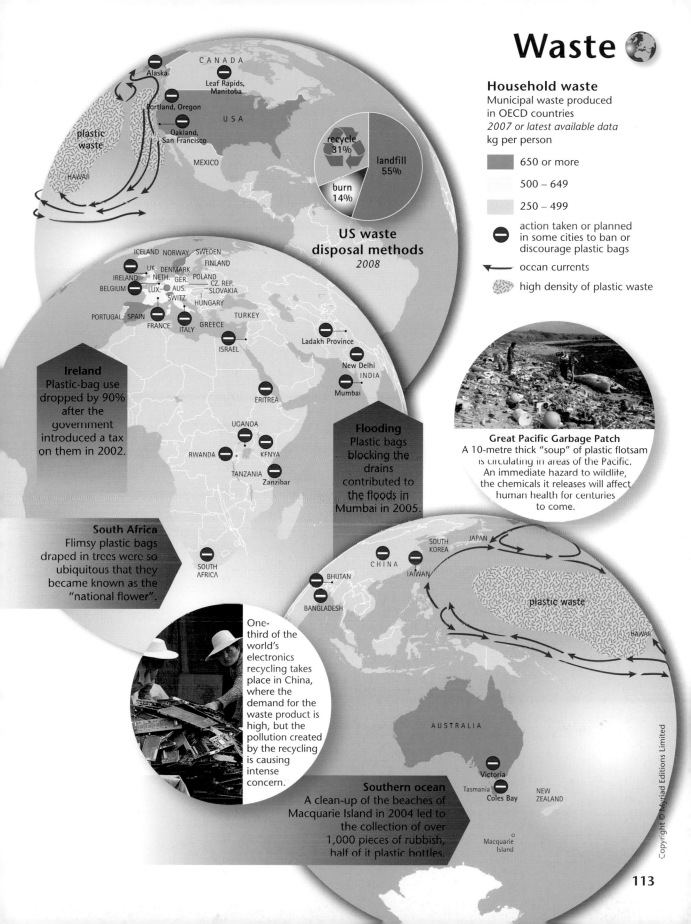

# Waste

## Household waste
Municipal waste produced in OECD countries
*2007 or latest available data*
kg per person

- 650 or more
- 500 – 649
- 250 – 499
- ⊖ action taken or planned in some cities to ban or discourage plastic bags
- ← ocean currents
- high density of plastic waste

### US waste disposal methods
*2008*

- recycle 31%
- landfill 55%
- burn 14%

CANADA

Alaska

Leaf Rapids, Manitoba

Portland, Oregon

USA

Oakland, San Francisco

plastic waste

HAWAII

MEXICO

ICELAND  NORWAY  SWEDEN

FINLAND

UK  DENMARK

IRELAND  NETH.  GER.  POLAND

BELGIUM  LUX.  AUS.  CZ. REP.

SWITZ.  I  SLOVAKIA

HUNGARY

PORTUGAL  SPAIN

FRANCE  ITALY  GREECE

TURKEY

ISRAEL

Ladakh Province

New Delhi

INDIA

ERITREA

Mumbai

UGANDA

RWANDA  KENYA

TANZANIA  Zanzibar

SOUTH AFRICA

### Ireland
Plastic-bag use dropped by 90% after the government introduced a tax on them in 2002.

### South Africa
Flimsy plastic bags draped in trees were so ubiquitous that they became known as the "national flower".

### Flooding
Plastic bags blocking the drains contributed to the floods in Mumbai in 2005.

### Great Pacific Garbage Patch
A 10-metre thick "soup" of plastic flotsam is circulating in areas of the Pacific. An immediate hazard to wildlife, the chemicals it releases will affect human health for centuries to come.

One-third of the world's electronics recycling takes place in China, where the demand for the waste product is high, but the pollution created by the recycling is causing intense concern.

SOUTH KOREA  JAPAN

CHINA  TAIWAN

BHUTAN

BANGLADESH

plastic waste

HAWAII

AUSTRALIA

Victoria

Tasmania  Coles Bay

NEW ZEALAND

Macquarie Island

### Southern ocean
A clean-up of the beaches of Macquarie Island in 2004 led to the collection of over 1,000 pieces of rubbish, half of it plastic bottles.

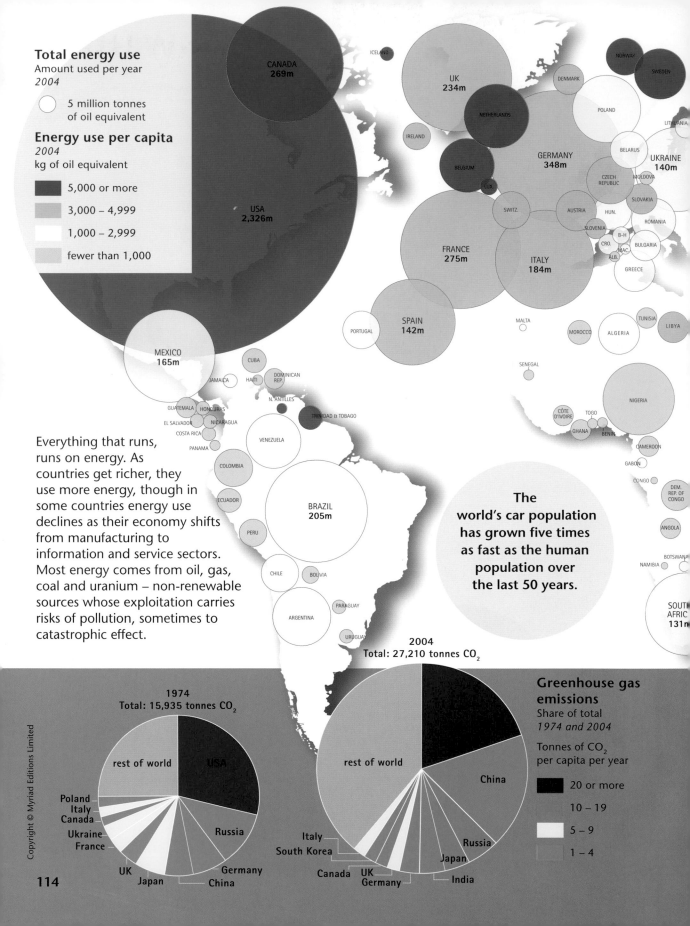

## Total energy use
Amount used per year
*2004*

◯ 5 million tonnes
of oil equivalent

## Energy use per capita
*2004*
kg of oil equivalent

- 5,000 or more
- 3,000 – 4,999
- 1,000 – 2,999
- fewer than 1,000

CANADA
269m

ICELAND

UK
234m

DENMARK

NORWAY

SWEDEN

NETHERLANDS

IRELAND

POLAND

LITHUANIA

BELARUS

UKRAINE
140m

BELGIUM

GERMANY
348m

CZECH
REPUBLIC

MOLDOVA

USA
2,326m

LUX.

SWITZ.

AUSTRIA

HUN.

SLOVAKIA

ROMANIA

SLOVENIA

B-H

CRO.

MAC.

BULGARIA

FRANCE
275m

ITALY
184m

ALB.

GREECE

MEXICO
165m

SPAIN
142m

MALTA

PORTUGAL

TUNISIA

LIBYA

MOROCCO

ALGERIA

CUBA

DOMINICAN
REP.

SENEGAL

JAMAICA

HAITI

N. ANTILLES

NIGERIA

GUATEMALA

HONDURAS

TRINIDAD & TOBAGO

CÔTE
D'IVOIRE

TOGO

EL SALVADOR

NICARAGUA

COSTA RICA

VENEZUELA

GHANA

BENIN

PANAMA

CAMEROON

COLOMBIA

GABON

Everything that runs,
runs on energy. As
countries get richer, they
use more energy, though in
some countries energy use
declines as their economy shifts
from manufacturing to
information and service sectors.
Most energy comes from oil, gas,
coal and uranium – non-renewable
sources whose exploitation carries
risks of pollution, sometimes to
catastrophic effect.

ECUADOR

BRAZIL
205m

CONGO

DEM.
REP. OF
CONGO

PERU

ANGOLA

CHILE

BOLIVIA

The
world's car population
has grown five times
as fast as the human
population over
the last 50 years.

BOTSWANA

NAMIBIA

PARAGUAY

SOUTH
AFRICA
131m

ARGENTINA

URUGUAY

2004
Total: 27,210 tonnes $CO_2$

---

1974
Total: 15,935 tonnes $CO_2$

rest of world

USA

Poland
Italy
Canada

Ukraine
France

Russia

UK

Japan

China

Germany

rest of world

China

Italy
South Korea

Russia

Canada

Japan

UK
Germany

India

## Greenhouse gas emissions
Share of total
*1974 and 2004*

Tonnes of $CO_2$
per capita per year

- 20 or more
- 10 – 19
- 5 – 9
- 1 – 4

# Energy Use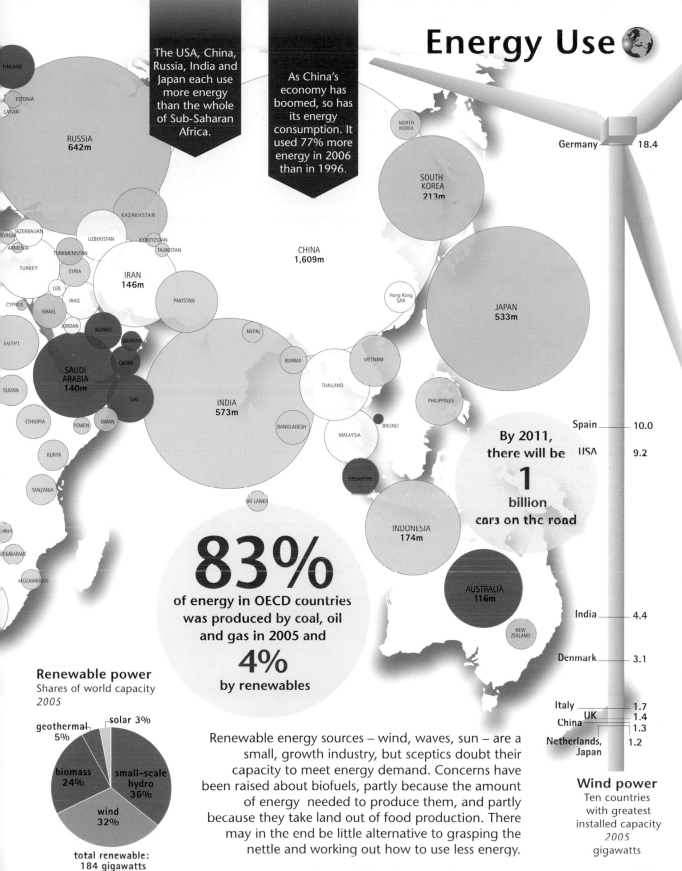

The USA, China, Russia, India and Japan each use more energy than the whole of Sub-Saharan Africa.

As China's economy has boomed, so has its energy consumption. It used 77% more energy in 2006 than in 1996.

FINLAND

ESTONIA

LATVIA

RUSSIA 642m

KAZAKHSTAN

ORGIA

AZERBAIJAN

ARMENIA

TURKMENISTAN

UZBEKISTAN

KYRGYZSTAN

TAJIKISTAN

TURKEY

SYRIA

IRAN 146m

CYPRUS

LEB.

IRAQ

PAKISTAN

ISRAEL

JORDAN

KUWAIT

BAHRAIN

NEPAL

EGYPT

QATAR

SAUDI ARABIA 140m

UAE

SUDAN

OMAN

INDIA 573m

ETHIOPIA

YEMEN

BANGLADESH

KENYA

TANZANIA

SRI LANKA

...RIA

ZIMBABWE

MOZAMBIQUE

NORTH KOREA

SOUTH KOREA 213m

CHINA 1,609m

Hong Kong SAR

JAPAN 533m

BURMA

VIETNAM

THAILAND

PHILIPPINES

MALAYSIA

BRUNEI

SINGAPORE

INDONESIA 174m

AUSTRALIA 116m

NEW ZEALAND

By 2011, there will be

# 1 billion cars on the road

# 83%
of energy in OECD countries was produced by coal, oil and gas in 2005 and
# 4%
by renewables

## Renewable power
Shares of world capacity
*2005*

- geothermal 5%
- solar 3%
- biomass 24%
- small-scale hydro 36%
- wind 32%

total renewable:
184 gigawatts

Renewable energy sources – wind, waves, sun – are a small, growth industry, but sceptics doubt their capacity to meet energy demand. Concerns have been raised about biofuels, partly because the amount of energy needed to produce them, and partly because they take land out of food production. There may in the end be little alternative to grasping the nettle and working out how to use less energy.

| | |
|---|---|
| Germany | 18.4 |
| Spain | 10.0 |
| USA | 9.2 |
| India | 4.4 |
| Denmark | 3.1 |
| Italy | 1.7 |
| UK | 1.4 |
| China | 1.3 |
| Netherlands, Japan | 1.2 |

## Wind power
Ten countries with greatest installed capacity
*2005*
gigawatts

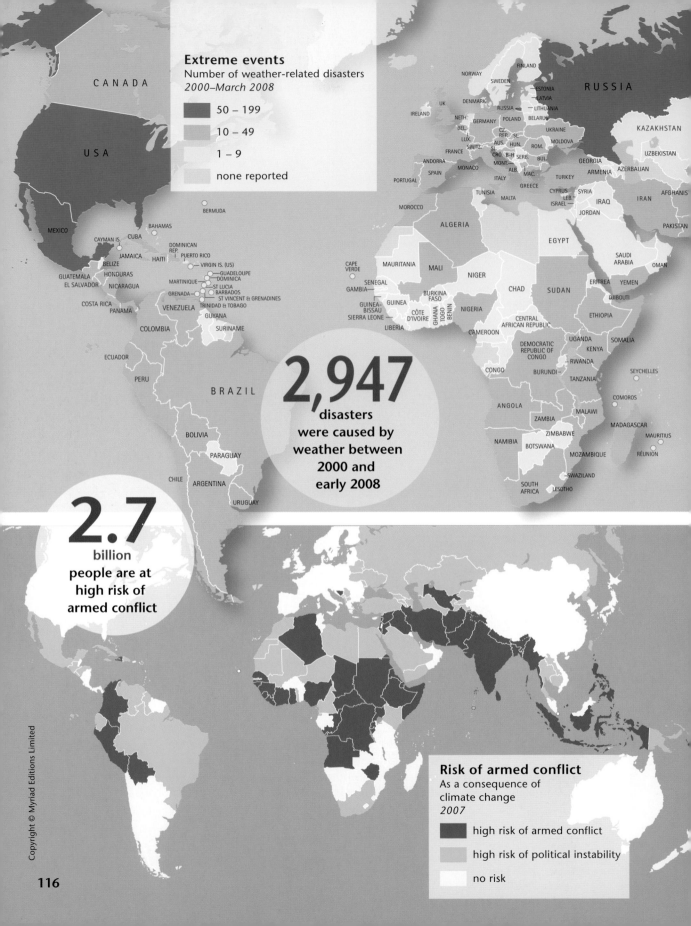

**Extreme events**
Number of weather-related disasters
*2000–March 2008*

- 50 – 199
- 10 – 49
- 1 – 9
- none reported

**2,947**
disasters
were caused by
weather between
2000 and
early 2008

**2.7**
billion
people are at
high risk of
armed conflict

**Risk of armed conflict**
As a consequence of
climate change
*2007*

- high risk of armed conflict
- high risk of political instability
- no risk

# Climate Change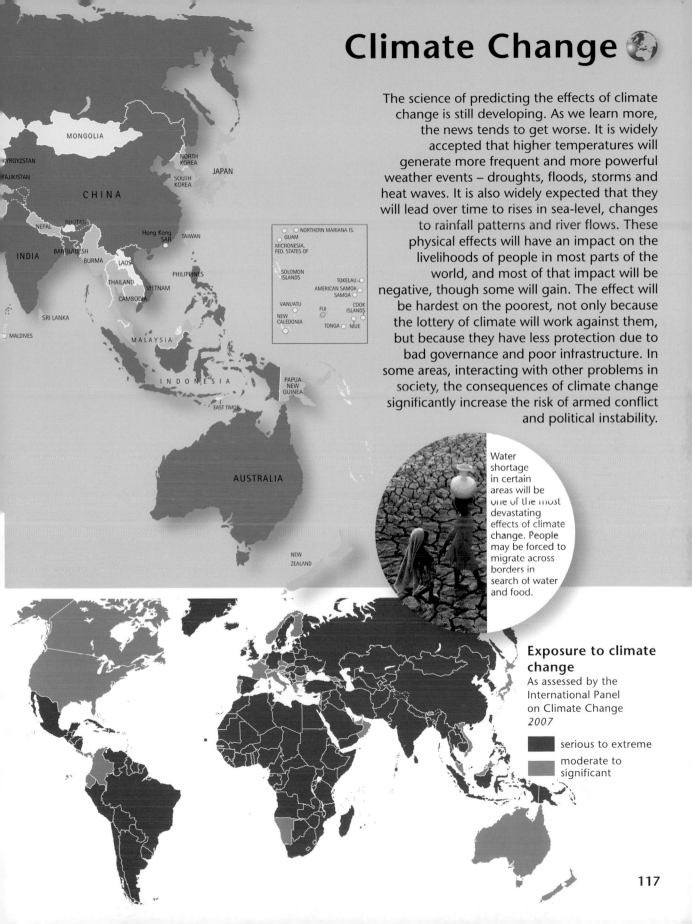

The science of predicting the effects of climate change is still developing. As we learn more, the news tends to get worse. It is widely accepted that higher temperatures will generate more frequent and more powerful weather events – droughts, floods, storms and heat waves. It is also widely expected that they will lead over time to rises in sea-level, changes to rainfall patterns and river flows. These physical effects will have an impact on the livelihoods of people in most parts of the world, and most of that impact will be negative, though some will gain. The effect will be hardest on the poorest, not only because the lottery of climate will work against them, but because they have less protection due to bad governance and poor infrastructure. In some areas, interacting with other problems in society, the consequences of climate change significantly increase the risk of armed conflict and political instability.

Water shortage in certain areas will be one of the most devastating effects of climate change. People may be forced to migrate across borders in search of water and food.

## Exposure to climate change

As assessed by the International Panel on Climate Change *2007*

- serious to extreme
- moderate to significant

117

## Extinction

Current trends suggest that between 20% and 33% of all species are at risk of extinction by 2100. Some research suggests 50% are at risk. That would be a mass extinction on the scale of the end of the age of the dinosaurs.

## Canadian polar bears

Arctic sea ice is shrinking by about 8% each decade. This affects seals, who breed on ice, and polar bears, who hunt seals. Polar bear populations are starting to show a marked decline.

## European heatwave

In the European heatwave of 2003, 35,000–52,000 people died from heat-related causes. By the 2040s, half of Europe's summers will be that hot.

## Alaskan permafrost

A temperature increase of 3°–4°C since 1950 is having a visible effect in Alaska. Roads and buildings in some areas are subsiding as the permafrost melts.

## North American Mosquito

Mosquitoes are entering their winter dormancy 9 days later than in the 1970s, prolonging the period during which they can spread disease.

## Atlantic hurricanes

Since the late 1970s, hurricanes have become 70% more energetic. Since the mid-1990s both hurricanes and major storms have become more frequent.

## Tropical Andes

On current trends, all Peru's glaciers below 5,500 metres altitude (most of them) will melt by 2015. Two-thirds of Peru's population depends on glacial melt for water. There will be a surfeit of water followed by severe continuing shortage.

## Floods in Bolivia

Heavy rain and flooding early in 2006 affected around 17,500 people.

## Drought in southern Brazil

Drought conditions in 2006 led to a 10% decrease in soybean yield.

Scientific consensus has been growing that climate change is happening, that it is caused by the global warming created by greenhouse gases – primarily carbon dioxide – produced by human activity, that its effects are being felt already, and that most of its consequences are negative for today's societies. There are some scientists who question each of these conclusions, but observed changes in the climate in different parts of the world are consistent with the theories, models and projections of global warming, and are not adequately explained by any alternative theories and models.

For non-scientists, the safe bet is that climate change is real and reflected in items that make the news headlines – natural disasters, food crises, record summers and more. The question – and the challenge before us – is whether political leaders will deploy the formidable store of human knowledge to mitigate and adapt to climate change, enabling us slowly to work our way towards a global environment we can confidently say is sustainable.

## South Atlantic hurricane

The first hurricane ever observed in the South Atlantic hit Brazil in 2004.

## Larsen B ice shelf

In 2002, 1,250 square miles (3,250 sq km) of ice shelf broke away from the Antarctic Peninsula. This was followed by an unexpectedly rapid increase in the rate of glacial flow and ice sheet retreat.

# Warning Signs

### Siberian melt

Average temperatures in the west have risen by 3°C since the 1960s, leading to melting of the permafrost.

### Drought in China

In 2006, severe drought in the north led to 12% of the nation's agriculture being affected. Severe drought in the south affected 18 million people.

### Time-lag

Carbon dioxide and the other greenhouse gases stay in the atmosphere for a long time. We are living with the consequences of emissions since the industrial revolution in the early 19th century. In 100 years' time, the world will be living with the consequences of ours.

### European butterfly ranges

Of 35 European non-migratory butterfly species studied, 22 shifted their ranges north by 20–150 miles (35–240 km) during the 20th century, and only one shifted south.

### Floods in China

Heavy rain led to severe flooding and landslides in June 2006, affecting 17 million people in southern China.

### Changing patterns of disease

Flooding in eastern Africa in 2007 created new breeding sites for mosquitoes, causing Rift Valley Fever epidemics and increased malaria.

### Asian summer monsoon

Heavy rain and flooding in parts of northern India, Nepal and Bangladesh in 2004 left 1,800 dead and millions stranded. Floods hit again in 2007, leaving over 4,000 dead and 6 million homeless.

### South Asian cyclone

In 2008, cyclone Nargis struck the Irrawaddy delta region of Burma, killing at least 100,000 people, and having a devastating effect on the homes and livelihoods of 1.4 million more.

### Drought in Africa

In 2006 at least 11 million people were affected by food shortages caused by drought in Burundi, Djibouti, Eritrea, Ethiopia, Kenya, Somalia and Tanzania.

### Coral bleaching

Warm seas in 1998 bleached coral in the Australian Great Barrier Reef, destroyed 90% of the coral in the Maldives in the Indian Ocean, and caused scarring visible from space. The scale of the damage was unprecedented. Further and worse damage occurred in 2000 (Fiji), 2002 (Great Barrier Reef) and 2005 (Caribbean).

### South Asian heatwave

More than 1,500 fatalities in India and Pakistan in 2003 were caused by temperatures over 50°C.

### Madagascan lemurs

Lemurs are among animals producing their young at what is now the "wrong" time. Their breeding season is no longer synchronized with the growing season and the availability of food, putting their survival at risk.

### Drought in Australia

A decade of drought has severely affected cattle farmers and reduced rice production by 98%, contributing to international rice shortages, price increases and the gathering food crisis of 2008.

Children in a public primary school in Rwanda where the average class size is 60.

| Countries | Official capital | Land area 1,000 hectares 2008 | Population 1,000s 2005 | Population Urban as % of total 2006 | Migrants People born outside country (excl. refugees) as % of population 2005 | Life expectancy at birth 2005 |
|---|---|---|---|---|---|---|
| Afghanistan | Kabul | 65,209 | 29,929 | 23% | 0.1% | 47.0 |
| Albania | Tirane | 2,740 | 3,563 | 46% | 2.6% | 75.5 |
| Algeria | Algiers | 238,174 | 32,532 | 64% | 0.7% | 71.7 |
| Angola | Luanda | 124,670 | 11,191 | 54% | 0.4% | 41.4 |
| Antigua and Barbuda | Saint John's | 44 | 69 | 40% | 22.4% | 75.3 |
| Argentina | Buenos Aires | 273,669 | 39,538 | 90% | 3.9% | 74.8 |
| Armenia | Yerevan | 2,820 | 2,983 | 64% | 7.8% | 73.3 |
| Australia | Canberra | 768,230 | 20,090 | 88% | 20.3% | 80.6 |
| Austria | Vienna | 8,245 | 8,185 | 66% | 15.1% | 79.4 |
| Azerbaijan | Baku | 8,266 | 7,912 | 52% | 2.2% | 72.3 |
| Bahamas | Nassau | 1,001 | 302 | 91% | 9.8% | 71.0 |
| Bahrain | Al-Manámah | 71 | 688 | 97% | 40.7% | 74.9 |
| Bangladesh | Dhaka | 13,017 | 144,320 | 26% | 0.7% | 63.9 |
| Barbados | Bridgetown | 43 | 279 | 53% | 9.7% | 74.9 |
| Belarus | Mensk | 20,748 | 10,300 | 73% | 12.2% | 68.5 |
| Belgium | Brussels | 3,023 | 10,364 | 97% | 6.9% | 79.5 |
| Belize | Belmopan | 2,281 | 279 | 49% | 15.0% | 71.8 |
| Benin | Porto-Novo | 11,062 | 7,460 | 41% | 2.1% | 55.0 |
| Bhutan | Thimphu | 4,700 | 2,232 | 11% | 0.5% | 63.5 |
| Bolivia | La Paz | 108,438 | 8,858 | 65% | 1.3% | 64.8 |
| Bosnia and Herzegovina | Sarajevo | 5,120 | 4,025 | 46% | 1.0% | 74.4 |
| Botswana | Gaborone | 56,673 | 1,545 | 58% | 4.5% | 35.0 |
| Brazil | Brasilia | 845,942 | 186,113 | 85% | 0.3% | 71.2 |
| Brunei | Bandar Seri Begawan | 527 | 372 | 74% | 33.2% | 77.0 |
| Bulgaria | Sofia | 10,864 | 7,450 | 70% | 1.3% | 72.6 |
| Burkina Faso | Ouagadougou | 27,360 | 13,925 | 19% | 5.8% | 48.5 |
| Burma | Nay Pyi Taw | 65,755 | 42,909 | 31% | 0.2% | 61.1 |
| Burundi | Bujumbura | 2,568 | 6,371 | 10% | 1.3% | 44.6 |
| Cambodia | Phnom Penh | 17,652 | 13,607 | 20% | 2.2% | 57.0 |
| Cameroon | Yaoundé | 46,540 | 16,380 | 55% | 0.8% | 46.1 |
| Canada | Ottawa | 909,351 | 32,805 | 80% | 18.9% | 80.2 |
| Cape Verde | Praia | 403 | 418 | 58% | 2.2% | 70.7 |
| Central African Republic | Bangui | 62,300 | 3,800 | 38% | 1.9% | 39.4 |
| Chad | N'Djamena | 125,920 | 9,826 | 26% | 4.5% | 44.0 |
| Chile | Santiago | 74,880 | 15,981 | 88% | 1.4% | 78.2 |
| China | Beijing | 932,749 | 1,306,314 | 41% | 0.0% | 71.8 |
| Colombia | Santafé de Bogotá | 110,950 | 42,954 | 73% | 0.3% | 72.8 |
| Comoros | Moroni | 186 | 671 | 38% | 8.4% | 62.6 |
| Congo | Brazzaville | 34,150 | 3,039 | 61% | 7.2% | 52.8 |
| Congo, Dem. Rep. | Kinshasa | 226,705 | 60,085 | 33% | 0.9% | 44.0 |
| Cook Islands | Avarua | 24 | 21 | – | 17.0% | – |
| Costa Rica | San José | 5,106 | 4,016 | 62% | 10.2% | 78.9 |
| Côte d'Ivoire | Yamoussoukro | 31,800 | 17,693 | 45% | 13.1% | 46.2 |
| Croatia | Zagreb | 5,592 | 4,496 | 57% | 14.5% | 75.7 |
| Cuba | Havana | 10,982 | 11,347 | 75% | 0.7% | 77.3 |
| Cyprus | Lefkosia (Nicosia) | 924 | 780 | 70% | 13.9% | 79.3 |
| Czech Republic | Prague | 7,726 | 10,241 | 74% | 4.4% | 75.9 |

# Indicators of Wellbeing

| Gross National Income GNI per capita 2005–06 current international $ | Water % with access to improved source 2004 | Literacy % of adult population who are literate 2005 | Education Net enrolment in primary school 2005 or latest available | Maternal mortality Deaths in childbirth per 100,000 live births 2006 | Undernourished people As % of population 2002–04 | Countries |
|---|---|---|---|---|---|---|
| – | – | – | – | – | – | Afghanistan |
| 5,840 | 96% | 99% | – | 17 | 6% | Albania |
| 6,900 | 85% | 70% | 97% | 38 | 4% | Algeria |
| 2,360 | 53% | 67% | – | 260 | 35% | Angola |
| 13,500 | 91% | 86% | – | 11 | – | Antigua and Barbuda |
| 15,390 | 96% | 97% | 99% | 16 | 3% | Argentina |
| 5,890 | 92% | 99% | 79% | 24 | 24% | Armenia |
| 34,060 | 100% | – | 97% | 6 | <2.5% | Australia |
| 35,130 | 100% | – | 97% | 5 | <2.5% | Austria |
| 5,960 | 77% | 99% | 85% | 88 | 7% | Azerbaijan |
| – | 97% | – | 91% | 14 | 8% | Bahamas |
| 18,770 | – | 87% | 97% | 10 | – | Bahrain |
| 2,340 | 74% | 48% | 94% | 69 | 30% | Bangladesh |
| – | 100% | – | 98% | 12 | <2.5% | Barbados |
| 8,810 | 100% | 100% | 89% | 13 | 4% | Belarus |
| 35,090 | – | – | 99% | 4 | <2.5% | Belgium |
| 6,650 | 91% | 75% | 94% | 16 | 4% | Belize |
| 1,160 | 67% | 35% | 78% | 148 | 12% | Benin |
| 5,690 | 62% | 47% | – | 70 | – | Bhutan |
| 2,890 | 85% | 87% | 94% | 61 | 23% | Bolivia |
| – | 97% | 97% | – | 15 | 9% | Bosnia and Herzegovina |
| 12,250 | 95% | 81% | 85% | 124 | 32% | Botswana |
| 8,800 | 90% | 89% | 95% | 20 | 7% | Brazil |
| – | – | 93% | 93% | 9 | 4% | Brunei |
| 10,140 | 99% | 98% | 93% | 14 | 8% | Bulgaria |
| 1,330 | 61% | 24% | 45% | 204 | 15% | Burkina Faso |
| – | 78% | 90% | 90% | 104 | 5% | Burma |
| 710 | 79% | 59% | 60% | 181 | 66% | Burundi |
| 2,920 | 41% | 74% | 99% | 82 | 33% | Cambodia |
| 2,370 | 66% | 68% | – | 149 | 26% | Cameroon |
| 34,610 | 100% | – | 99% | 6 | <2.5 | Canada |
| 5,980 | 80% | 81% | 90% | 34 | – | Cape Verde |
| 1,280 | 75% | 49% | – | 175 | 44% | Central African Republic |
| 1,230 | 42% | 26% | 61% | 209 | 35% | Chad |
| 11,270 | 95% | 96% | 90% | 9 | 4% | Chile |
| 7,740 | 77% | 91% | – | 24 | 12% | China |
| 7,620 | 93% | 93% | 87% | 21 | 13% | Colombia |
| 2,010 | 86% | – | 55% | 68 | 60% | Comoros |
| 870 | 58% | 85% | 44% | 126 | 33% | Congo |
| 720 | 46% | 67% | – | 205 | 74% | Congo, Dem. Rep. |
| – | – | – | – | – | – | Cook Islands |
| 10,770 | 97% | 95% | – | 12 | 5% | Costa Rica |
| 1,550 | 84% | 49% | 56% | 127 | 13% | Côte d'Ivoire |
| 13,680 | 100% | 98% | 87% | 6 | 7% | Croatia |
| – | 91% | 100% | 97% | 7 | <2.5% | Cuba |
| 21,490 | 100% | 97% | 99% | 4 | <2.5% | Cyprus |
| 21,470 | 100% | – | 92% | 4 | <2.5% | Czech Republic |

123

| Countries | Official capital | Land area 1,000 hectares 2008 | Population | | Migrants People born outside country (excl. refugees) as % of population 2005 | Life expectancy at birth 2005 |
|---|---|---|---|---|---|---|
| | | | 1,000s 2005 | Urban as % of total 2006 | | |
| Denmark | Copenhagen | 4,243 | 5,432 | 86% | 7.2% | 77.8 |
| Djibouti | Djibouti | 2,318 | 477 | 87% | 2.6% | 53.4 |
| Dominica | Roseau | 75 | 69 | 73% | 5.7% | 76.6 |
| Dominican Republic | Santo Domingo | 4,838 | 8,950 | 68% | 1.8% | 70.9 |
| East Timor | Dili | 1,487 | 1,041 | 27% | 0.6% | 56.7 |
| Ecuador | Quito | 27,684 | 13,364 | 63% | 0.9% | 74.7 |
| Egypt | Cairo | 99,545 | 77,506 | 43% | 0.2% | 70.5 |
| El Salvador | San Salvador | 2,072 | 6,705 | 60% | 0.3% | 71.3 |
| Equatorial Guinea | Malabo | 2,805 | 536 | 39% | 1.2% | 42.3 |
| Eritrea | Asmara | 10,100 | 4,562 | 20% | 0.3% | 54.9 |
| Estonia | Tallinn | 4,239 | 1,333 | 69% | 15.2% | 72.6 |
| Ethiopia | Addis Ababa | 100,000 | 69,114 | 16% | 0.7% | 42.7 |
| Fiji | Suva | 1,827 | 893 | 51% | 2.0% | 68.3 |
| Finland | Helsinki | 30,459 | 5,223 | 61% | 3.0% | 78.8 |
| France | Paris | 55,010 | 60,656 | 77% | 10.7% | 80.2 |
| Gabon | Libreville | 25,767 | 1,389 | 84% | 17.7% | 53.8 |
| Gambia | Banjul | 1,000 | 1,593 | 55% | 15.3% | 56.8 |
| Georgia | Tbilisi | 6,949 | 4,677 | 52% | 4.3% | 71.3 |
| Germany | Berlin | 34,877 | 82,431 | 75% | 12.3% | 78.9 |
| Ghana | Accra | 22,754 | 21,030 | 49% | 7.5% | 57.5 |
| Greece | Athens | 12,890 | 10,668 | 59% | 8.8% | 79.0 |
| Grenada | St George's | 34 | 90 | 31% | 10.5% | 73.0 |
| Guatemala | Guatemala City | 10,843 | 14,655 | 48% | 0.4% | 67.9 |
| Guinea | Conakry | 24,572 | 9,468 | 33% | 4.3% | 54.1 |
| Guinea-Bissau | Bissau | 2,812 | 1,416 | 30% | 1.2% | 45.1 |
| Guyana | Georgetown | 19,685 | 711 | 28% | 0.1% | 64.3 |
| Haiti | Port-au-Prince | 2,756 | 7,790 | 39% | 0.4% | 52.6 |
| Honduras | Tegucigalpa | 11,189 | 6,975 | 47% | 0.4% | 68.6 |
| Hungary | Budapest | 8,961 | 10,007 | 67% | 3.1% | 72.6 |
| Iceland | Reykjavik | 10,025 | 297 | 93% | 7.8% | 81.1 |
| India | New Delhi | 297,319 | 1,080,264 | 29% | 0.5% | 63.5 |
| Indonesia | Jakarta | 181,157 | 241,974 | 49% | 0.1% | 67.8 |
| Iran | Tehran | 162,855 | 68,018 | 67% | 2.8% | 71.1 |
| Iraq | Baghdad | 43,737 | 26,075 | 67% | 0.1% | 60.0 |
| Ireland | Dublin | 6,889 | 4,016 | 61% | 14.1% | 79.4 |
| Israel | Jerusalem | 2,164 | 6,277 | 92% | 39.6% | 79.7 |
| Italy | Rome | 29,411 | 58,103 | 68% | 4.3% | 80.3 |
| Jamaica | Kingston | 1,083 | 2,732 | 53% | 0.7% | 70.9 |
| Japan | Tokyo | 36,450 | 127,417 | 66% | 1.6% | 82.1 |
| Jordan | Amman | 8,824 | 5,760 | 83% | 39.0% | 72.0 |
| Kazakhstan | Astana | 269,970 | 15,186 | 58% | 16.9% | 66.2 |
| Kenya | Nairobi | 56,914 | 32,368 | 21% | 1.0% | 49.0 |
| Kiribati | Tarawa | 81 | 103 | 48% | 2.6% | 62.8 |
| Korea, North | Pyongyang | 12,041 | 22,912 | 62% | 0.2% | 63.9 |
| Korea, South | Seoul | 9,873 | 48,893 | 81% | 1.2% | 77.6 |
| Kuwait | Kuwait City | 1,782 | 2,336 | 98% | 62.1% | 77.5 |
| Kyrgyzstan | Bishkek | 19,180 | 5,146 | 36% | 5.5% | 68.3 |

# Indicators of Wellbeing

| Gross National Income GNI per capita 2005–06 current international $ | Water % with access to improved source 2004 | Literacy % of adult population who are literate 2005 | Education Net enrolment in primary school 2005 or latest available | Maternal mortality Deaths in childbirth per 100,000 live births 2006 | Undernourished people As % of population 2002–04 | Countries |
|---|---|---|---|---|---|---|
| 36,460 | 100% | – | 95% | 5 | <2.5% | Denmark |
| 2,540 | 73% | – | 33% | 130 | 24% | Djibouti |
| 6,490 | 97% | 88% | 84% | 15 | 8% | Dominica |
| 8,290 | 95% | 87% | 88% | 29 | 29% | Dominican Republic |
| – | 58% | 50% | 98% | 55 | 9% | East Timor |
| 4,400 | 94% | 91% | 98% | 24 | 6% | Ecuador |
| 4,690 | 98% | 71% | 94% | 35 | 4% | Egypt |
| 5,340 | 84% | 81% | 93% | 25 | 11% | El Salvador |
| 10,150 | 43% | 87% | 81% | 206 | – | Equatorial Guinea |
| 1,090 | 60% | – | 47% | 74 | 75% | Eritrea |
| 17,540 | 100% | 100% | 95% | 7 | <2.5% | Estonia |
| 1,190 | 22% | 36% | 61% | 123 | 46% | Ethiopia |
| 6,200 | 47% | – | 96% | 18 | 5% | Fiji |
| 35,150 | 100% | – | 98% | 4 | <2.5% | Finland |
| 33,740 | 100% | – | 99% | 4 | <2.5% | France |
| 5,310 | 88% | 84% | 77% | 91 | 5% | Gabon |
| 1,970 | 82% | – | 77% | 113 | 29% | Gambia |
| 3,690 | 82% | 100% | 93% | 32 | 9% | Georgia |
| 31,830 | 100% | – | 96% | 4 | <2.5% | Germany |
| 2,640 | 75% | 58% | 65% | 120 | 11% | Ghana |
| 24,560 | – | 96% | 99% | 4 | <2.5% | Greece |
| 7,810 | 95% | 96% | 84% | 20 | 7% | Grenada |
| 4,800 | 95% | 69% | 94% | 41 | 22% | Guatemala |
| 2,410 | 50% | 30% | 66% | 161 | 24% | Guinea |
| 970 | 59% | – | 45% | 200 | 39% | Guinea-Bissau |
| 4,680 | 83% | – | – | 62 | 8% | Guyana |
| 1,490 | 54% | – | – | 80 | 46% | Haiti |
| 3,540 | 87% | 80% | 91% | 27 | 23% | Honduras |
| 18,290 | 99% | – | 89% | 7 | <2.5% | Hungary |
| 36,560 | 100% | – | 99% | 3 | <2.5% | Iceland |
| 3,800 | 86% | 61% | – | 76 | 20% | India |
| 3,950 | 77% | 90% | 96% | 34 | 6% | Indonesia |
| 8,490 | 94% | 82% | 95% | 34 | 4% | Iran |
| – | – | – | 88% | – | – | Iraq |
| 35,900 | – | – | 96% | 5 | <2.5% | Ireland |
| 23,700 | 100% | 97% | 97% | 5 | <2.5% | Israel |
| 30,550 | – | 98% | 99% | 4 | <2.5% | Italy |
| 4,030 | 93% | 80% | 90% | 31 | 9% | Jamaica |
| 33,150 | 100% | – | 100% | 4 | <2.5% | Japan |
| 6,210 | 97% | 91% | 89% | 25 | 6% | Jordan |
| 7,780 | 86% | 100% | 91% | 29 | 6% | Kazakhstan |
| 1,300 | 61% | 74% | 79% | 121 | 31% | Kenya |
| 8,970 | – | – | 97% | 64 | – | Kiribati |
| – | – | – | – | 55 | – | Korea, North |
| 23,800 | 92% | – | 99% | 5 | <2.5% | Korea, South |
| 26,790 | – | 93% | 87% | 11 | 5% | Kuwait |
| 1,990 | 77% | 99% | 87% | 41 | 4% | Kyrgyzstan |

| Countries | Official capital | Land area 1,000 hectares 2008 | Population | | Migrants People born outside country (excl. refugees) as % of population 2005 | Life expectancy at birth 2005 |
| --- | --- | --- | --- | --- | --- | --- |
| | | | 1,000s 2005 | Urban as % of total 2006 | | |
| Laos | Vientiane | 23,080 | 6,217 | 21% | 0.4% | 61.9 |
| Latvia | Riga | 6,229 | 2,290 | 68% | 19.5% | 71.4 |
| Lebanon | Beirut | 1,023 | 3,826 | 87% | 18.4% | 72.5 |
| Lesotho | Maseru | 3,035 | 1,867 | 19% | 0.3% | 35.2 |
| Liberia | Monrovia | 9,632 | 3,482 | 59% | 1.5% | 42.5 |
| Libya | Tripoli | 175,954 | 5,766 | 85% | 10.5% | 74.4 |
| Lithuania | Vilnius | 6,268 | 3,597 | 67% | 4.8% | 71.3 |
| Luxembourg | Luxembourg | 259 | 469 | 83% | 37.4% | 79.2 |
| Macedonia | Skopje | 2,543 | 2,079 | 70% | 6.0% | 73.8 |
| Madagascar | Antananarivo | 58,154 | 18,040 | 27% | 0.3% | 55.8 |
| Malawi | Lilongwe | 9,408 | 12,159 | 18% | 2.2% | 40.5 |
| Malaysia | Kuala Lumpur | 32,855 | 23,953 | 68% | 6.5% | 73.7 |
| Maldives | Malé | 30 | 349 | 30% | 1.0% | 67.6 |
| Mali | Bamako | 122,019 | 12,292 | 31% | 0.3% | 48.6 |
| Malta | Valletta | 32 | 399 | 96% | 2.7% | 79.5 |
| Marshall Islands | Majuro | 18 | 59 | 67% | 2.7% | – |
| Mauritania | Nouakchott | 103,070 | 3,087 | 41% | 2.1% | 53.7 |
| Mauritius | Port Louis | 203 | 1,231 | 42% | 1.7% | 73.0 |
| Mexico | Mexico City | 194,395 | 106,203 | 76% | 0.6% | 75.4 |
| Micronesia, Fed. Sts. | Palikir | 70 | 108 | 22% | 3.2% | 68.1 |
| Moldova | Chisinau | 3,287 | 4,455 | 47% | 10.5% | 68.3 |
| Mongolia | Ulaan Baatar | 156,650 | 2,791 | 57% | 0.3% | 66.8 |
| Montenegro* | Podgorica | 1,381 | 678 | 52% | 4.9% | 74.1 |
| Morocco | Rabat | 44,630 | 32,726 | 59% | 0.4% | 70.4 |
| Mozambique | Maputo | 78,638 | 19,027 | 35% | 2.1% | 41.8 |
| Namibia | Windhoek | 82,329 | 1,976 | 36% | 7.1% | 46.9 |
| Nepal | Kathmandu | 14,300 | 27,677 | 16% | 3.0% | 62.7 |
| Netherlands | Amsterdam | 3,388 | 16,407 | 81% | 10.1% | 79.3 |
| New Zealand | Wellington | 26,771 | 4,035 | 86% | 15.9% | 79.6 |
| Nicaragua | Managua | 12,140 | 5,465 | 59% | 0.5% | 70.4 |
| Niger | Niamey | 126,670 | 11,666 | 17% | 0.9% | 44.9 |
| Nigeria | Abuja | 91,077 | 140,602 | 49% | 0.7% | 46.6 |
| Norway | Oslo | 30,428 | 4,593 | 78% | 7.4% | 80.0 |
| Oman | Muscat | 30,950 | 3,002 | 72% | 24.4% | 74.8 |
| Pakistan | Islamabad | 77,088 | 162,420 | 35% | 2.1% | 64.9 |
| Palestine Authority | – | 602 | 2,386 | 72% | 45.4% | 73.4 |
| Panama | Panama City | 7,443 | 3,039 | 72% | 3.2% | 75.2 |
| Papua New Guinea | Port Moresby | 45,286 | 5,545 | 14% | 0.4% | 56.4 |
| Paraguay | Asunción | 39,730 | 6,348 | 59% | 2.7% | 71.4 |
| Peru | Lima | 128,000 | 27,926 | 73% | 0.1% | 70.7 |
| Philippines | Manila | 29,817 | 87,857 | 63% | 0.5% | 71.0 |
| Poland | Warsaw | 30,633 | 38,635 | 62% | 1.8% | 75.0 |
| Portugal | Lisbon | 9,150 | 10,566 | 58% | 7.3% | 78.1 |
| Puerto Rico | San Juan | 887 | 3,917 | 98% | 10.6% | 77.6 |
| Qatar | Doha | 1,100 | 863 | 95% | 78.3% | 74.1 |
| Romania | Bucharest | 22,998 | 22,330 | 54% | 0.6% | 71.7 |
| Russia | Moscow | 1,638,139 | 143,155 | 73% | 8.4% | 65.5 |

* Data for Serbia and Montenegro on urban population, migrant population and school enrolment pre-date their separation in 2006 and apply to the country as a single entity.

# Indicators of Wellbeing 🌐

| Gross National Income GNI per capita 2005–06 current international $ | Water % with access to improved source 2004 | Literacy % of adult population who are literate 2005 | Education Net enrolment in primary school 2005 or latest available | Maternal mortality Deaths in childbirth per 100,000 live births 2006 | Undernourished people As % of population 2002–04 | Countries |
|---|---|---|---|---|---|---|
| 2,050 | 51% | 69% | 84% | 75 | 19% | Laos |
| 15,350 | 99% | 100% | 88% | 9 | 3% | Latvia |
| 5,460 | 100% | – | 92% | 30 | 3% | Lebanon |
| 4,340 | 79% | 82% | 87% | 132 | 13% | Lesotho |
| – | – | – | 66% | 235 | – | Liberia |
| – | – | 84% | – | 18 | <2.5% | Libya |
| 14,930 | – | 100% | 89% | 8 | <2.5% | Lithuania |
| – | 100% | – | 95% | 4 | <2.5% | Luxembourg |
| 7,610 | – | 96% | 92% | 17 | 5% | Macedonia |
| 960 | 50% | 71% | 92% | 115 | 38% | Madagascar |
| 720 | 73% | 64% | 95% | 120 | 35% | Malawi |
| 11,300 | 99% | 89% | 95% | 12 | 3% | Malaysia |
| – | 83% | 96% | 79% | 30 | 10% | Maldives |
| 1,130 | 50% | 24% | 51% | 217 | 29% | Mali |
| 18,020 | 100% | 88% | 86% | 6 | <2.5% | Malta |
| – | – | – | 90% | 56 | – | Marshall Islands |
| 2,600 | 53% | 51% | 72% | 125 | 10% | Mauritania |
| 13,510 | 100% | 84% | 95% | 14 | 5% | Mauritius |
| 11,410 | 97% | 92% | 98% | 35 | 5% | Mexico |
| 7,830 | – | – | – | 41 | – | Micronesia, Fed. Sts. |
| 2,880 | 92% | 99% | 86% | 19 | 11% | Moldova |
| 2,280 | 62% | 98% | 84% | 43 | 27% | Mongolia |
| – | – | – | 96% | 10 | – | Montenegro* |
| 5,000 | 81% | 52% | 86% | 37 | 6% | Morocco |
| 1,220 | 43% | 39% | 77% | 138 | 44% | Mozambique |
| 8,110 | 87% | 85% | 72% | 61 | 24% | Namibia |
| 1,630 | 90% | 49% | 79% | 59 | 17% | Nepal |
| 37,580 | 100% | – | 99% | 5 | <2.5% | Netherlands |
| 27,220 | – | – | 99% | 6 | <2.5% | New Zealand |
| 4,010 | 79% | 77% | 87% | 36 | 27% | Nicaragua |
| 830 | 46% | 29% | 40% | 253 | 32% | Niger |
| 1,050 | 48% | 69% | 68% | 191 | 9% | Nigeria |
| 43,820 | 100% | – | 98% | 4 | <2.5% | Norway |
| 14,570 | – | 81% | 76% | 12 | – | Oman |
| 2,500 | 91% | 50% | 68% | 97 | 24% | Pakistan |
| – | 92% | 92% | 80% | 22 | 16% | Palestine Authority |
| 7,680 | 90% | 92% | 98% | 23 | 23% | Panama |
| 2,410 | 39% | 57% | – | 73 | – | Papua New Guinea |
| 5,070 | 86% | 94% | 88% | 22 | 15% | Paraguay |
| 6,080 | 83% | 88% | 96% | 25 | 12% | Peru |
| 5,980 | 85% | 93% | 94% | 32 | 18% | Philippines |
| 14,830 | – | – | 96% | 7 | <2.5% | Poland |
| 21,580 | – | 94% | 98% | 5 | <2.5% | Portugal |
| – | – | – | – | – | – | Puerto Rico |
| – | 100% | 89% | 96% | 21 | – | Qatar |
| 9,820 | 57% | 97% | 93% | 18 | <2.5% | Romania |
| 11,630 | 97% | 99% | 92% | 16 | 3% | Russia |

| Countries | Official capital | Land area 1,000 hectares 2008 | Population 1,000s 2005 | Population Urban as % of total 2006 | Migrants People born outside country (excl. refugees) as % of population 2005 | Life expectancy at birth 2005 |
|---|---|---|---|---|---|---|
| Rwanda | Kigali | 2,467 | 8,099 | 20% | 1.3% | 44.1 |
| Samoa | Apia | 283 | 177 | 23% | 5.0% | 70.7 |
| São Tomé and Principe | São Tomé | 96 | 187 | 59% | 4.8% | 63.5 |
| Saudi Arabia | Riyadh | 214,969 | 26,418 | 81% | 25.9% | 72.6 |
| Senegal | Dakar | 19,253 | 11,127 | 42% | 2.8% | 56.5 |
| Serbia* | Belgrade | 7,747 | 10,159 | 52% | 4.9% | 72.8 |
| Seychelles | Victoria | 46 | 81 | 53% | 6.1% | 73.0 |
| Sierra Leone | Freetown | 7,162 | 6,018 | 41% | 2.2% | 41.4 |
| Singapore | Singapore | 69 | 4,426 | 100% | 42.6% | 79.7 |
| Slovakia | Bratislava | 4,810 | 5,431 | 56% | 2.3% | 73.9 |
| Slovenia | Ljubljana | 2,014 | 2,011 | 51% | 8.5% | 77.6 |
| Solomon Islands | Honiara | 2,799 | 538 | 17% | 0.7% | 62.9 |
| Somalia | Mogadishu | 62,734 | 8,592 | 36% | 3.4% | 47.7 |
| South Africa | Pretoria | 121,447 | 42,552 | 60% | 2.3% | 47.7 |
| Spain | Madrid | 49,919 | 40,341 | 77% | 11.1% | 80.6 |
| Sri Lanka | Colombo | 6,463 | 20,065 | 15% | 1.8% | 74.7 |
| St. Kitts and Nevis | Basseterre | – | 39 | 32% | 10.4% | 71.3 |
| St. Lucia | Castries | – | 166 | 28% | 5.4% | 74.2 |
| St. Vincent and Grenadines | Kingstown | – | 118 | 46% | 8.7% | 72.3 |
| Sudan | Khartoum | 237,600 | 40,187 | 42% | 1.8% | 56.7 |
| Suriname | Paramaribo | 15,600 | 438 | 74% | 1.2% | 69.7 |
| Swaziland | Mbabane | 1,720 | 1,174 | 24% | 4.4% | 41.5 |
| Sweden | Stockholm | 41,033 | 9,002 | 84% | 12.4% | 80.5 |
| Switzerland | Bern | 4,000 | 7,489 | 76% | 22.9% | 81.2 |
| Syria | Damascus | 18,378 | 18,449 | 51% | 5.2% | 73.8 |
| Tajikistan | Dushanbe | 13,996 | 7,164 | 25% | 4.7% | 64.0 |
| Tanzania | Dar es Salaam | 88,580 | 37,323 | 25% | 2.1% | 46.3 |
| Thailand | Bangkok | 51,089 | 65,444 | 33% | 1.6% | 70.9 |
| Togo | Lomé | 5,439 | 5,682 | 41% | 3.0% | 55.1 |
| Tonga | Nuku'alofa | 72 | 112 | 24% | 1.1% | 72.6 |
| Trinidad and Tobago | Port-of-Spain | 513 | 1,089 | 13% | 2.9% | 70.0 |
| Tunisia | Tunis | 15,536 | 10,075 | 66% | 0.4% | 73.5 |
| Turkey | Ankara | 76,963 | 69,661 | 68% | 1.8% | 71.3 |
| Turkmenistan | Ashgabat | 46,993 | 4,952 | 47% | 4.6% | 62.9 |
| Uganda | Kampala | 19,710 | 27,202 | 13% | 1.8% | 50.0 |
| Ukraine | Kyiv | 57,938 | 47,425 | 68% | 14.7% | 68.0 |
| United Arab Emirates | Abu Dhabi | 8,360 | 2,563 | 77% | 71.4% | 79.2 |
| United Kingdom | London | 24,193 | 60,441 | 90% | 9.1% | 78.9 |
| United States | Washington D.C. | 916,192 | 295,734 | 81% | 12.9% | 77.7 |
| Uruguay | Montevideo | 17,502 | 3,416 | 92% | 2.4% | 75.6 |
| Uzbekistan | Tashkent | 42,540 | 26,851 | 37% | 4.8% | 67.4 |
| Vanuatu | Port-Vila | 1,219 | 206 | 24% | 0.5% | 69.5 |
| Venezuela | Caracas | 88,205 | 25,375 | 94% | 3.8% | 74.2 |
| Vietnam | Hanoi | 31,007 | 83,770 | 27% | 0.0% | 70.7 |
| Yemen | Sanaá | 52,797 | 20,727 | 28% | 1.3% | 61.7 |
| Zambia | Lusaka | 74,339 | 10,614 | 35% | 2.4% | 38.4 |
| Zimbabwe | Harare | 38,685 | 12,747 | 36% | 3.9% | 37.3 |

* Data for Serbia and Montenegro on urban population, migrant population and school enrolment pre-date their separation in 2006 and apply to the country as a single entity.

# Indicators of Wellbeing

| Gross National Income GNI per capita 2005–06 current international $ | Water % with access to improved source 2004 | Literacy % of adult population who are literate 2005 | Education Net enrolment in primary school 2005 or latest available | Maternal mortality Deaths in childbirth per 100,000 live births 2006 | Undernourished people As % of population 2002–04 | Countries |
|---|---|---|---|---|---|---|
| 1,270 | 74% | 65% | 74% | 160 | 33% | Rwanda |
| 6,400 | 88% | 99% | 90% | 28 | 4% | Samoa |
| – | 79% | 85% | – | 96 | 10% | São Tomé and Principe |
| 15,550 | – | 83% | 78% | 25 | 4% | Saudi Arabia |
| 1,840 | 76% | 39% | 69% | 116 | 20% | Senegal |
| – | – | – | 96% | 8 | – | Serbia* |
| 16,560 | 88% | 92% | 99% | 13 | 9% | Seychelles |
| 850 | 57% | 35% | – | 270 | 51% | Sierra Leone |
| 31,710 | 100% | 93% | – | 3 | – | Singapore |
| 17,600 | 100% | – | 92% | 8 | 7% | Slovakia |
| 23,970 | – | 100% | 98% | 4 | 3% | Slovenia |
| 2,170 | 70% | 77% | 63% | 73 | 21% | Solomon Islands |
| – | – | – | – | 145 | – | Somalia |
| 11,710 | 88% | 82% | 87% | 69 | <2.5% | South Africa |
| 28,030 | 100% | 97% | 99% | 4 | <2.5% | Spain |
| 5,010 | 79% | 91% | 97% | 13 | 22% | Sri Lanka |
| 12,690 | 100% | 98% | 93% | 19 | 10% | St. Kitts and Nevis |
| 6,970 | 98% | 95% | – | 14 | 5% | St. Lucia |
| 7,010 | – | 88% | 90% | 20 | 10% | St. Vincent and Grenadines |
| 2,160 | 70% | 61% | 43% | 89 | 26% | Sudan |
| 8,120 | 92% | 90% | 94% | 39 | 8% | Suriname |
| 5,170 | 62% | 80% | 80% | 164 | 22% | Swaziland |
| 35,070 | 100% | – | 96% | 3 | <2.5% | Sweden |
| 40,930 | 100% | – | 93% | 5 | <2.5% | Switzerland |
| 3,930 | 93% | 81% | 95% | 14 | 4% | Syria |
| 1,410 | 59% | 100% | 97% | 68 | 56% | Tajikistan |
| 740 | 62% | 69% | 91% | 118 | 44% | Tanzania |
| 9,140 | 99% | 93% | – | 8 | 22% | Thailand |
| 1,490 | 52% | 53% | 78% | 108 | 24% | Togo |
| 8,580 | 100% | 99% | 95% | 24 | – | Tonga |
| 16,260 | 91% | 98% | 90% | 38 | 10% | Trinidad and Tobago |
| 8,490 | 93% | 74% | 97% | 23 | <2.5% | Tunisia |
| 9,060 | 96% | 87% | 89% | 26 | 3% | Turkey |
| – | 72% | 99% | – | 51 | 7% | Turkmenistan |
| 1,490 | 60% | 67% | – | 134 | 19% | Uganda |
| 7,520 | 96% | 99% | 83% | 24 | <2.5% | Ukraine |
| 23,990 | 100% | 89% | 71% | 8 | <2.5% | United Arab Emirates |
| 35,580 | 100% | – | 99% | 6 | <2.5% | United Kingdom |
| 44,260 | 100% | – | 92% | 8 | <2.5% | United States |
| 11,150 | 100% | 97% | 93% | 12 | <2.5% | Uruguay |
| 2,250 | 82% | – | – | 43 | 25% | Uzbekistan |
| 3,280 | 60% | 74% | 94% | 36 | 11% | Vanuatu |
| 7,440 | 83% | 93% | 91% | 21 | 18% | Venezuela |
| 3,300 | 85% | 90% | 88% | 17 | 16% | Vietnam |
| 920 | 67% | 54% | 75% | 100 | 38% | Yemen |
| 1,000 | 58% | 68% | 89% | 182 | 46% | Zambia |
| 2,030 | 81% | 89% | 82% | 105 | 47% | Zimbabwe |

129

| Countries | GDP Total US$ millions 2006 or latest available | Trade As % of GDP 2006 | | Investment Net inflow of FDI as % of GDP 2005 | Aid Amount received as % of GDP 2005 | Military expenditure 2006 | |
|---|---|---|---|---|---|---|---|
| | | goods | services | | | total | as % of GDP |
| Afghanistan | 8,399 | 39% | – | – | 37.9% | 143 | 1.7% |
| Albania | 9,098 | 42% | 34% | 3.1% | 3.7% | 141 | 1.5% |
| Algeria | 114,727 | 64% | – | 1.1% | 0.4% | 3,096 | 2.7% |
| Angola | 45,163 | 106% | 21% | –4.0% | 1.5% | 1,588 | 4.7% |
| Antigua and Barbuda | 998 | 63% | 76% | – | 0.9% | 5 | 5.5% |
| Argentina | 214,241 | 38% | 7% | 2.6% | 0.1% | 1,873 | 0.9% |
| Armenia | 6,387 | 50% | 12% | 5.3% | 3.9% | 184 | 2.9% |
| Australia | 780,531 | 34% | 8% | –4.7% | – | 17,208 | 2.4% |
| Austria | 322,001 | 86% | 24% | 3.0% | – | 2,630 | 0.8% |
| Azerbaijan | 19,851 | 54% | 25% | 12.7% | 1.9% | 658 | 3.3% |
| Bahamas | 5,502 | – | 60% | – | – | 40 | 0.7% |
| Bahrain | 16,041 | – | 20% | – | 1.0% | 532 | 3.4% |
| Bangladesh | 61,897 | 45% | 6% | 1.3% | 2.1% | 938 | 1.6% |
| Barbados | 3,430 | – | 69% | 2.0% | –0.1% | 25 | 0.7% |
| Belarus | 36,945 | 114% | 10% | 1.0% | 0.2% | 279 | 0.8% |
| Belgium | 394,033 | 186% | 29% | 8.6% | – | 4,428 | 1.1% |
| Belize | 1,214 | 77% | 41% | 11.4% | 1.3% | 18 | 1.5% |
| Benin | 4,775 | 33% | 12% | 0.5% | 8.2% | 47 | 1.0% |
| Bhutan | 942 | 72% | – | 0.1% | 11.1% | – | – |
| Bolivia | 11,162 | 60% | 12% | –2.9% | 6.4% | 156 | 1.4% |
| Bosnia and Herzegovina | 12,255 | 94% | 14% | 3.0% | 5.3% | 142 | 1.2% |
| Botswana | 10,598 | 75% | 16% | 2.7% | 0.7% | 289 | 3.0% |
| Brazil | 1,067,472 | 21% | 5% | 1.7% | 0.0% | 16,206 | 1.5% |
| Brunei | 11,562 | – | – | – | – | 328 | 2.8% |
| Bulgaria | 31,483 | 121% | 29% | 9.6% | 2.5% | 703 | 2.3% |
| Burkina Faso | 6,173 | 30% | 7% | 0.3% | 11.6% | 85 | 1.4% |
| Burma | – | – | – | – | – | 6,920 | 18.7% |
| Burundi | 903 | 59% | 18% | 0.1% | 47.0% | 49 | 5.1% |
| Cambodia | 7,258 | 121% | 28% | 6.1% | 9.0% | 123 | 1.7% |
| Cameroon | 18,323 | 38% | 15% | 0.1% | 2.5% | 257 | 1.4% |
| Canada | 1,271,593 | 60% | 10% | 3.1% | – | 14,958 | 1.2% |
| Cape Verde | 1,144 | 49% | 49% | 5.4% | 16.6% | 7 | 0.6% |
| Central African Republic | 1,494 | 22% | – | 0.4% | 7.0% | 16 | 1.0% |
| Chad | 6,541 | 76% | – | 12.0% | 7.8% | 59 | 0.9% |
| Chile | 145,843 | 67% | 11% | 5.6% | 0.1% | 4,677 | 3.2% |
| China | 2,644,681 | 66% | 7% | 3.5% | 0.1% | 121,872 | 1.3% |
| Colombia | 153,405 | 37% | 7% | 8.4% | 0.4% | 5,377 | 4.0% |
| Comoros | 403 | 30% | – | 0.3% | 6.6% | – | – |
| Congo | 7,385 | 116% | 30% | 12.1% | 32.5% | 84 | 1.2% |
| Congo, Dem. Rep. | 8,543 | 60% | – | 5.7% | 27.0% | 163 | 1.0% |
| Cook Islands | – | – | – | – | – | – | – |
| Costa Rica | 22,229 | 89% | 21% | 4.3% | 0.2% | 99 | 0.4% |
| Côte d'Ivoire | 17,551 | 80% | 18% | 1.7% | 0.8% | 266 | 1.5% |
| Croatia | 42,925 | 75% | 34% | 4.5% | 0.3% | 693 | 1.6% |
| Cuba | – | – | – | – | – | 1,660 | 4.0% |
| Cyprus | 18,371 | – | 58% | – | 0.4% | 240 | 1.3% |
| Czech Republic | 143,018 | 133% | 16% | – | 0.3% | 2,464 | 1.7% |

# Economy and Environment

| Energy Use Oil equivalent 2004 | | CO$_2$ Emissions Tonnes of CO$_2$ 2004 | | Water | | Countries |
|---|---|---|---|---|---|---|
| total tonnes | kg per capita | total | per capita | Cubic metres of annual renewable water available per capita 2007 | Cubic metres withdrawn per capita 2007 | |
| – | – | 0.7 | 0.0 | 2,015 | 1,014 | Afghanistan |
| 2 | 760 | 5.2 | 1.7 | 13,184 | 544 | Albania |
| 33 | 1,017 | 91.6 | 2.8 | 423 | 194 | Algeria |
| 9 | 613 | 19.8 | 1.3 | 10,909 | 26 | Angola |
| – | – | 0.4 | 5.1 | 619 | 78 | Antigua and Barbuda |
| 64 | 1,660 | 145.6 | 3.8 | 20,591 | 765 | Argentina |
| 2 | 704 | 3.7 | 1.2 | 3,511 | 960 | Armenia |
| 116 | 5,762 | 350.9 | 17.5 | 23,911 | 1,224 | Australia |
| 33 | 4,060 | 76.8 | 9.4 | 9,455 | 260 | Austria |
| 13 | 1,559 | 30.9 | 3.7 | 3,547 | 2,079 | Azerbaijan |
| – | – | 2.0 | 6.3 | 60 | – | Bahamas |
| 7 | 10,469 | 16.4 | 22.9 | 155 | 423 | Bahrain |
| 23 | 164 | 37.5 | 0.3 | 8,232 | 552 | Bangladesh |
| – | – | 1.4 | 5.3 | 295 | 297 | Barbados |
| 27 | 2,725 | 65.9 | 6.7 | 6,014 | 281 | Belarus |
| 58 | 5,536 | 119.2 | 11.4 | 1,751 | 916 | Belgium |
| – | – | 0.8 | 2.8 | 66,268 | 478 | Belize |
| 2 | 303 | 2.4 | 0.3 | 2,765 | 20 | Benin |
| – | – | 0.5 | 0.8 | 42,035 | 192 | Bhutan |
| 5 | 553 | 12.2 | 1.4 | 65,358 | 161 | Bolivia |
| 5 | 1,203 | 15.7 | 4.0 | 9,566 | – | Bosnia and Herzegovina |
| 2 | 1,055 | 4.4 | 2.5 | 8,215 | 110 | Botswana |
| 205 | 1,114 | 346.2 | 1.9 | 43,028 | 336 | Brazil |
| 3 | 7,370 | 8.9 | 24.4 | 21,795 | 296 | Brunei |
| 19 | 2,434 | 47.4 | 6.1 | 2,797 | 1,318 | Bulgaria |
| – | – | 1.1 | 0.1 | 890 | 62 | Burkina Faso |
| 14 | 283 | 10.2 | 0.2 | 20,313 | 680 | Burma |
| – | – | 0.2 | 0.0 | 442 | 44 | Burundi |
| – | – | 0.5 | 0.0 | 32,526 | 296 | Cambodia |
| 7 | 433 | 6.9 | 0.4 | 16,920 | 63 | Cameroon |
| 269 | 8,411 | 549.1 | 17.0 | 88,336 | 1,470 | Canada |
| – | – | 0.3 | 0.6 | 566 | 48 | Cape Verde |
| – | – | 0.3 | 0.1 | 34,787 | 5 | Central African Republic |
| – | – | 0.1 | 0.0 | 4,174 | 28 | Chad |
| 28 | 1,732 | 63.4 | 3.9 | 55,425 | 803 | Chile |
| 1,609 | 1,242 | 5,204.8 | 4.0 | 2,125 | 484 | China |
| 28 | 625 | 61.7 | 1.4 | 45,408 | 246 | Colombia |
| – | – | 0.1 | 0.1 | 1,427 | 13 | Comoros |
| 1 | 274 | 3.3 | 0.8 | 196,319 | 13 | Congo |
| 17 | 296 | 2.2 | 0.0 | 20,973 | 7 | Congo, Dem. Rep. |
| – | – | 0.0 | 1.4 | – | – | Cook Islands |
| 4 | 870 | 6.1 | 1.4 | 25,157 | 655 | Costa Rica |
| 7 | 388 | 6.4 | 0.4 | 4,315 | 57 | Côte d'Ivoire |
| 9 | 1,985 | 22.4 | 5.0 | 23,161 | – | Croatia |
| 11 | 950 | 25.8 | 2.3 | 3,368 | 728 | Cuba |
| 3 | 3,535 | 7.3 | 9.8 | 913 | 302 | Cyprus |
| 46 | 4,460 | 125.2 | 12.3 | 1,290 | 251 | Czech Republic |

131

| Countries | GDP Total US$ millions 2006 or latest available | Trade As % of GDP 2006 | | Investment Net inflow of FDI as % of GDP 2005 | Aid Amount received as % of GDP 2005 | Military expenditure 2006 | |
|---|---|---|---|---|---|---|---|
| | | goods | services | | | total | as % of GDP |
| Denmark | 275,366 | 65% | 35% | 2.0% | – | 3,876 | 1.4% |
| Djibouti | 769 | 44% | – | 3.2% | 10.1% | 17 | 2.3% |
| Dominica | 319 | 68% | 47% | 9.2% | 5.8% | – | – |
| Dominican Republic | 31,846 | 58% | 18% | 3.5% | 0.3% | 256 | 0.7% |
| East Timor | 356 | – | – | – | 26.7% | – | – |
| Ecuador | 41,402 | 58% | 9% | 4.5% | 0.6% | 653 | 1.9% |
| Egypt | 107,484 | 32% | 28% | 6.0% | 1.0% | 4,337 | 4.0% |
| El Salvador | 18,654 | 61% | 14% | 3.0% | 1.2% | 106 | 0.6% |
| Equatorial Guinea | 8,565 | 133% | – | 24.7% | 1.1% | 8 | 0.1% |
| Eritrea | 1,085 | 38% | 14% | 1.2% | 36.9% | – | – |
| Estonia | 16,410 | 135% | 36% | 21.8% | 1.2% | 238 | 1.4% |
| Ethiopia | 13,315 | 43% | 18% | 2.3% | 17.1% | 345 | 2.6% |
| Fiji | 3,138 | 89% | – | –0.1% | 2.4% | 43 | 1.5% |
| Finland | 210,652 | 69% | 17% | 2.1% | – | 2,750 | 1.3% |
| France | 2,248,091 | 46% | 10% | 3.3% | – | 54,003 | 2.4% |
| Gabon | 9,546 | 74% | 15% | 3.5% | 0.8% | 21 | 0.2% |
| Gambia | 511 | 50% | 27% | 11.3% | 13.0% | 2 | 0.3% |
| Georgia | 7,744 | 62% | 21% | 7.0% | 4.9% | 339 | 4.4% |
| Germany | 2,896,876 | 70% | 14% | 1.1% | – | 37,775 | 1.3% |
| Ghana | 12,906 | 74% | 22% | 1.0% | 10.6% | 83 | 0.7% |
| Greece | 308,449 | 34% | 21% | 0.3% | – | 7,286 | 2.4% |
| Grenada | 525 | 58% | 49% | 5.6% | 10.4% | – | – |
| Guatemala | 35,325 | 51% | 9% | 0.7% | 0.8% | 146 | 0.4% |
| Guinea | 3,317 | 54% | 9% | 3.1% | 5.5% | 36 | 1.2% |
| Guinea-Bissau | 304 | 61% | 19% | 3.3% | 27.4% | 13 | 4.0% |
| Guyana | 896 | 161% | 43% | 9.7% | 18.3% | – | – |
| Haiti | 4,975 | 47% | 13% | 0.2% | 11.7% | – | – |
| Honduras | 9,235 | 80% | 20% | 5.6% | 8.6% | 55 | 0.6% |
| Hungary | 112,920 | 133% | 23% | 5.8% | 0.3% | 1,323 | 1.2% |
| Iceland | 16,265 | 60% | 28% | 15.6% | – | 46 | 0.3% |
| India | 911,813 | 33% | 8% | 0.8% | 0.2% | 22,428 | 2.5% |
| Indonesia | 364,790 | 50% | 13% | 1.8% | 0.9% | 3,645 | 1.0% |
| Iran | 217,898 | 57% | 4% | 0.0% | 0.1% | 7,160 | 3.3% |
| Iraq | – | – | – | – | – | – | – |
| Ireland | 220,137 | 83% | 63% | –14.7% | – | 1,113 | 0.5% |
| Israel | 140,457 | – | 25% | 4.5% | 0.4% | 11,031 | 7.9% |
| Italy | 1,850,961 | 46% | 10% | 1.1% | – | 30,635 | 1.7% |
| Jamaica | 10,023 | 69% | 42% | 7.0% | 0.4% | 57 | 0.6% |
| Japan | 4,368,435 | 28% | 6% | 0.1% | – | 41,144 | 0.9% |
| Jordan | 14,101 | 117% | 38% | 12.1% | 4.8% | 1,115 | 7.9% |
| Kazakhstan | 81,003 | 79% | 15% | 3.5% | 0.4% | 648 | 0.8% |
| Kenya | 22,779 | 51% | 16% | 0.1% | 4.0% | 355 | 1.6% |
| Kiribati | 71 | 86% | – | – | 24.5% | – | – |
| Korea, North | – | – | – | – | – | – | – |
| Korea, South | 888,024 | 72% | 14% | 0.5% | 0.0% | 24,645 | 2.8% |
| Kuwait | 80,781 | – | 17% | 0.3% | 0.0% | 3,497 | 3.4% |
| Kyrgyzstan | 2,818 | 92% | 22% | 1.7% | 11.3% | 36 | 1.3% |

# Economy and Environment

| Energy Use Oil equivalent 2004 | | CO$_2$ Emissions Tonnes of CO$_2$ 2004 | | Water | | Countries |
|---|---|---|---|---|---|---|
| total tonnes | kg per capita | total | per capita | Cubic metres of annual renewable water available per capita 2007 | Cubic metres withdrawn per capita 2007 | |
| 20 | 3,716 | 52.6 | 9.7 | 1,099 | 237 | Denmark |
| – | – | 0.4 | 0.5 | 366 | 27 | Djibouti |
| – | – | 0.1 | 1.5 | – | 210 | Dominica |
| 8 | 821 | 19.5 | 2.2 | 2,295 | 393 | Dominican Republic |
| – | – | – | – | – | – | East Timor |
| 10 | 773 | 28.2 | 2.2 | 31,739 | 1,326 | Ecuador |
| 57 | 783 | 152.2 | 2.1 | 759 | 969 | Egypt |
| 4 | 664 | 6.4 | 0.9 | 3,546 | 198 | El Salvador |
| – | – | 8.9 | 18.0 | 49,336 | 229 | Equatorial Guinea |
| – | – | 0.8 | 0.2 | 1,338 | 131 | Eritrea |
| 5 | 3,835 | 17.9 | 13.3 | 9,696 | 120 | Estonia |
| 21 | 303 | 5.8 | 0.1 | 1,355 | 81 | Ethiopia |
| – | – | 1.1 | 1.3 | 33,159 | 84 | Fiji |
| 38 | 7,286 | 72.1 | 13.8 | 20,857 | 477 | Finland |
| 275 | 4,547 | 396.7 | 6.6 | 3,343 | 668 | France |
| 2 | 1,243 | 4.6 | 3.4 | 114,766 | 100 | Gabon |
| – | – | 0.3 | 0.2 | 5,019 | 22 | Gambia |
| 3 | 626 | 3.9 | 0.9 | 14,406 | 697 | Georgia |
| 348 | 4,218 | 856.6 | 10.0 | 1,862 | 571 | Germany |
| 8 | 386 | 6.9 | 0.3 | 2,314 | 48 | Ghana |
| 30 | 2,755 | 98.8 | 8.9 | 6,653 | 707 | Greece |
| – | – | 0.2 | 2.0 | – | 125 | Grenada |
| 8 | 616 | 11.2 | 0.9 | 8,410 | 166 | Guatemala |
| – | – | 1.5 | 0.2 | 23,042 | 182 | Guinea |
| – | – | 0.3 | 0.2 | 18,430 | 121 | Guinea-Bissau |
| – | – | 1.4 | 1.9 | 320,479 | 2,147 | Guyana |
| 2 | 262 | 1.7 | 0.2 | 1,599 | 119 | Haiti |
| 4 | 548 | 7.3 | 1.0 | 12,755 | 127 | Honduras |
| 26 | 2,608 | 58.9 | 5.8 | 10,353 | 770 | Hungary |
| 3 | 11,976 | 2.3 | 7.9 | 566,667 | 523 | Iceland |
| 573 | 531 | 1,199.0 | 1.0 | 1,670 | 615 | India |
| 174 | 800 | 368.0 | 1.7 | 12,441 | 381 | Indonesia |
| 146 | 2,166 | 407.6 | 6.1 | 1,931 | 1,071 | Iran |
| 30 | 1,083 | 84.4 | 3.3 | 2,490 | 1,742 | Iraq |
| 15 | 3,738 | 43.6 | 10.7 | 12,187 | 289 | Ireland |
| 21 | 3,049 | 63.8 | 9.4 | 240 | 324 | Israel |
| 184 | 3,171 | 482.2 | 8.0 | 3,289 | 772 | Italy |
| 4 | 1,541 | 10.9 | 4.1 | 3,520 | 156 | Jamaica |
| 533 | 4,173 | 1,304.2 | 10.0 | 3,351 | 694 | Japan |
| 7 | 1,232 | 19.4 | 3.6 | 148 | 191 | Jordan |
| 55 | 3,651 | 178.4 | 11.9 | 7,405 | 2,263 | Kazakhstan |
| 17 | 506 | 10.7 | 0.3 | 839 | 50 | Kenya |
| – | – | 0.0 | 0.3 | – | – | Kiribati |
| 20 | 910 | 73.1 | 3.3 | 3,403 | 400 | Korea, North |
| 213 | 4,431 | 507.0 | 11.0 | 1,448 | 392 | Korea, South |
| 25 | 10,212 | 70.5 | 28.6 | 7 | 184 | Kuwait |
| 3 | 546 | 6.0 | 1.2 | 3,821 | 1,989 | Kyrgyzstan |

133

| Countries | GDP Total US$ millions 2006 or latest available | Trade As % of GDP 2006 | | Investment Net inflow of FDI as % of GDP 2005 | Aid Amount received as % of GDP 2005 | Military expenditure 2006 | |
|---|---|---|---|---|---|---|---|
| | | goods | services | | | total | as % of GDP |
| Laos | 3,437 | 61% | 13% | 1.0% | 11.3% | 13 | 0.4% |
| Latvia | 20,116 | 87% | 23% | 4.6% | 1.2% | 279 | 1.4% |
| Lebanon | 22,722 | 55% | 86% | 12.0% | 1.2% | 589 | 2.8% |
| Lesotho | 1,494 | 149% | 10% | 6.3% | 3.9% | 33 | 2.3% |
| Liberia | 631 | 107% | – | 36.7% | 56.8% | – | – |
| Libya | 50,320 | 92% | 7% | – | 0.1% | 593 | 1.1% |
| Lithuania | 29,766 | 112% | 21% | 4.0% | 1.2% | 349 | 1.2% |
| Luxembourg | 41,469 | 118% | 198% | 301.3% | – | 254 | 0.6% |
| Macedonia | 6,217 | 99% | 17% | 1.7% | 4.0% | 134 | 2.2% |
| Madagascar | 5,499 | 40% | 22% | 0.6% | 18.7% | 298 | 5.2% |
| Malawi | 3,164 | 73% | 12% | 0.1% | 28.3% | 20 | 0.9% |
| Malaysia | 150,672 | 196% | 32% | 3.0% | 0.0% | 3,206 | 2.1% |
| Maldives | 927 | 127% | 67% | 1.3% | 9.2% | 56 | 6.1% |
| Mali | 5,866 | 50% | 16% | 3.0% | 13.6% | 132 | 2.2% |
| Malta | 6,375 | – | 50% | – | 0.1% | 46 | 0.7% |
| Marshall Islands | 155 | 92% | – | – | 31.4% | – | – |
| Mauritania | 2,663 | 74% | – | 6.3% | 10.0% | 18 | 0.6% |
| Mauritius | 6,347 | 90% | 45% | 0.6% | 0.5% | 18 | 0.3% |
| Mexico | 839,182 | 62% | 5% | 2.4% | 0.0% | 3,229 | 0.4% |
| Micronesia, Fed. Sts. | 245 | 65% | – | – | 41.6% | – | – |
| Moldova | 3,356 | 111% | 30% | 6.6% | 5.6% | 10 | 0.3% |
| Mongolia | 3,132 | 112% | 42% | 8.7% | 10.4% | 19 | 0.8% |
| Montenegro* | 2,491 | 99% | – | 5.6% | 4.4% | 54 | 2.4% |
| Morocco | 65,401 | 63% | 23% | 3.0% | 1.3% | 2,161 | 3.8% |
| Mozambique | 6,833 | 71% | 15% | 1.6% | 20.1% | 57 | 0.8% |
| Namibia | 6,566 | 86% | 15% | – | 2.0% | 197 | 3.0% |
| Nepal | 8,938 | 36% | 11% | 0.0% | 5.7% | 158 | 2.0% |
| Netherlands | 662,296 | 134% | 25% | 6.5% | – | 9,904 | 1.5% |
| New Zealand | 104,519 | 47% | 15% | 1.8% | – | 1,544 | 1.5% |
| Nicaragua | 5,301 | 75% | 15% | 4.9% | 15.4% | 35 | 0.7% |
| Niger | 3,663 | 38% | 12% | 0.4% | 15.2% | 38 | 1.1% |
| Nigeria | 115,338 | 65% | 12% | 2.1% | 7.6% | 768 | 0.7% |
| Norway | 334,942 | 60% | 21% | 1.1% | – | 5,015 | 1.5% |
| Oman | 30,835 | – | 14% | – | 0.2% | 3,276 | 9.0% |
| Pakistan | 126,836 | 36% | 10% | 2.0% | 1.5% | 4,156 | 3.2% |
| Palestine Authority | 4,059 | – | – | – | 25.0% | – | – |
| Panama | 17,097 | 34% | 33% | 6.6% | 0.1% | 171 | 1.0% |
| Papua New Guinea | 5,654 | 112% | 30% | 0.7% | 5.8% | 30 | 0.6% |
| Paraguay | 9,275 | 88% | 14% | 0.9% | 0.7% | 67 | 0.7% |
| Peru | 92,416 | 42% | 6% | 3.2% | 0.5% | 1,108 | 1.2% |
| Philippines | 117,562 | 85% | 10% | 1.2% | 0.5% | 909 | 0.8% |
| Poland | 338,733 | 69% | 11% | 3.2% | 0.6% | 6,235 | 1.8% |
| Portugal | 194,726 | 57% | 15% | 1.7% | – | 3,080 | 1.6% |
| Puerto Rico | – | – | – | – | – | – | – |
| Qatar | 42,463 | – | – | – | – | 2,335 | 4.5% |
| Romania | 121,609 | 69% | 11% | 6.7% | 1.3% | 2,324 | 1.9% |
| Russia | 986,940 | 47% | 8% | 2.0% | 0.2% | 70,000 | 4.1% |

134

* Data for Serbia and Montenegro that pre-date their separation in 2006 apply to the country as a single entity.

# Economy and Environment

| Energy Use Oil equivalent 2004 | | CO₂ Emissions Tonnes of CO₂ 2004 | | Water | | Countries |
|---|---|---|---|---|---|---|
| total tonnes | kg per capita | total | per capita | Cubic metres of annual renewable water available per capita 2007 | Cubic metres withdrawn per capita 2007 | |
| – | – | 1.4 | 0.2 | 53,859 | 541 | Laos |
| 5 | 1,988 | 7.1 | 3.1 | 15,521 | 125 | Latvia |
| 5 | 1,361 | 16.8 | 4.8 | 1,206 | 381 | Lebanon |
| – | – | 0.2 | 0.1 | 1,693 | 28 | Lesotho |
| – | – | 0.5 | 0.2 | 67,207 | 34 | Liberia |
| 18 | 3,169 | 49.8 | 8.7 | 99 | 883 | Libya |
| 9 | 2,666 | 13.0 | 3.8 | 7,317 | 78 | Lithuania |
| 5 | 10,481 | 11.7 | 25.8 | 6,499 | 108 | Luxembourg |
| 3 | 1,328 | 8.7 | 4.3 | 3,137 | – | Macedonia |
| – | – | 2.8 | 0.2 | 17,186 | 885 | Madagascar |
| – | – | 1.1 | 0.1 | 1,285 | 85 | Malawi |
| 57 | 2,279 | 149.2 | 6.0 | 22,104 | 376 | Malaysia |
| – | – | 0.7 | 2.3 | 87 | 17 | Maldives |
| – | – | 0.6 | 0.0 | 6,981 | 519 | Mali |
| 1 | 2,263 | 2.5 | 6.3 | 124 | 153 | Malta |
| – | – | – | – | – | – | Marshall Islands |
| – | – | 2.7 | 0.9 | 3,511 | 606 | Mauritania |
| – | – | 3.2 | 2.6 | 1,744 | 583 | Mauritius |
| 165 | 1,622 | 415.3 | 4.1 | 4,172 | 767 | Mexico |
| – | – | – | – | – | – | Micronesia, Fed. Sts. |
| 3 | 862 | 7.9 | 1.9 | 2,783 | 541 | Moldova |
| – | – | 8.6 | 3.4 | 12,837 | 172 | Mongolia |
| – | 56.7 | 7.0 | – | 19,870 | – | Montenegro⁺ |
| 11 | 384 | 38.5 | 1.3 | 895 | 419 | Morocco |
| 9 | 441 | 2.0 | 0.1 | 10,531 | 35 | Mozambique |
| 1 | 665 | 2.7 | 1.3 | 8,658 | 153 | Namibia |
| 9 | 341 | 3.1 | 0.1 | 7,447 | 414 | Nepal |
| 82 | 5,045 | 187.1 | 11.5 | 5,539 | 494 | Netherlands |
| 18 | 4,344 | 33.1 | 8.1 | 79,893 | 549 | New Zealand |
| 3 | 643 | 4.4 | 0.9 | 34,416 | 244 | Nicaragua |
| – | – | 1.2 | 0.1 | 2,257 | 190 | Niger |
| 99 | 717 | 85.1 | 0.7 | 2,085 | 66 | Nigeria |
| 28 | 6,024 | 42.4 | 9.2 | 81,886 | 485 | Norway |
| 12 | 4,667 | 31.9 | 12.6 | 369 | 488 | Oman |
| 74 | 489 | 125.2 | 0.8 | 1,353 | 1,130 | Pakistan |
| – | – | – | – | 203 | – | Palestine Authority |
| 3 | 801 | 5.9 | 1.8 | 44,266 | 268 | Panama |
| – | – | 2.4 | 0.4 | 131,011 | 14 | Papua New Guinea |
| 4 | 694 | 4.1 | 0.7 | 52,133 | 85 | Paraguay |
| 13 | 479 | 29.6 | 1.1 | 66,431 | 752 | Peru |
| 44 | 542 | 80.3 | 1.0 | 5,577 | 363 | Philippines |
| 92 | 2,403 | 304.0 | 8.0 | 1,601 | 419 | Poland |
| 27 | 2,528 | 65.1 | 6.2 | 6,485 | 1,121 | Portugal |
| – | – | – | – | 1,776 | – | Puerto Rico |
| 18 | 23,246 | 39.1 | 50.3 | 62 | 483 | Qatar |
| 39 | 1,778 | 96.1 | 4.4 | 9,837 | 1,035 | Romania |
| 642 | 4,460 | 1,575.3 | 11.0 | 31,764 | 532 | Russia |

135

| Countries | GDP Total US$ millions 2006 or latest available | Trade As % of GDP 2006 | | Investment Net inflow of FDI as % of GDP 2005 | Aid Amount received as % of GDP 2005 | Military expenditure 2006 | |
|---|---|---|---|---|---|---|---|
| | | goods | services | | | total | as % of GDP |
| Rwanda | 2,494 | 25% | 20% | 0.4% | 27.2% | 72 | 2.4% |
| Samoa | 424 | 55% | 41% | −0.9% | 11.5% | – | – |
| São Tomé and Principe | 123 | 60% | – | 6.2% | – | – | – |
| Saudi Arabia | 349,138 | – | 11% | – | 0.0% | 29,514 | 8.5% |
| Senegal | 9,186 | 56% | 18% | 0.7% | 8.5% | 149 | 1.6% |
| Serbia* | 31,989 | 62% | – | 5.6% | 4.4% | 812 | 2.5% |
| Seychelles | 775 | 158% | 86% | 11.4% | 2.8% | 14 | 2.0% |
| Sierra Leone | 1,450 | 42% | 14% | 4.8% | 29.0% | 24 | 1.7% |
| Singapore | 132,158 | 386% | 90% | 17.2% | 0.0% | 6,321 | 4.8% |
| Slovakia | 55,049 | 159% | 20% | 4.0% | 0.6% | 957 | 1.7% |
| Slovenia | 37,303 | 127% | 21% | 1.6% | 0.2% | 629 | 1.7% |
| Solomon Islands | 336 | 99% | – | −0.3% | 66.5% | – | – |
| Somalia | – | – | – | – | – | – | – |
| South Africa | 255,155 | 53% | 10% | 2.6% | 0.3% | 3,527 | 1.4% |
| Spain | 1,224,676 | 43% | 15% | 2.0% | – | 14,415 | 1.2% |
| Sri Lanka | 26,964 | 63% | 15% | 1.2% | 5.1% | 943 | 3.4% |
| St. Kitts and Nevis | 477 | 65% | 52% | 10.4% | 0.9% | – | – |
| St. Lucia | 899 | 73% | 67% | 13.1% | 1.4% | – | – |
| St. Vincent and Grenadines | 423 | 58% | 56% | 12.9% | 1.2% | – | – |
| Sudan | 37,442 | 34% | 7% | 8.3% | 7.0% | 524 | 1.5% |
| Suriname | 2,115 | 131% | 41% | – | 3.8% | 20 | 1.3% |
| Swaziland | 2,648 | 162% | 28% | −0.6% | 1.7% | – | – |
| Sweden | 383,799 | 71% | 22% | 3.0% | – | 5,780 | 1.5% |
| Switzerland | 380,412 | 76% | 21% | 4.2% | – | 3,473 | 0.9% |
| Syria | 33,407 | 53% | 19% | 1.5% | 0.3% | 1,739 | 5.1% |
| Tajikistan | 2,811 | 110% | 19% | 2.4% | 10.8% | 73 | 2.7% |
| Tanzania | 12,784 | 44% | 19% | 3.8% | 12.2% | 143 | 1.2% |
| Thailand | 206,338 | 126% | 27% | 2.6% | −0.1% | 2,275 | 1.1% |
| Togo | 2,206 | 83% | 19% | 0.1% | 4.1% | 34 | 1.6% |
| Tonga | 223 | 63% | – | 2.1% | 15.0% | – | – |
| Trinidad and Tobago | 18,136 | 89% | 10% | 6.8% | 0.0% | 52 | 0.3% |
| Tunisia | 30,298 | 87% | 22% | 2.5% | 1.4% | 435 | 1.4% |
| Turkey | 402,710 | 55% | 10% | 2.7% | 0.1% | 11,630 | 2.9% |
| Turkmenistan | 10,496 | 80% | – | 0.8% | 0.4% | 184 | 1.8% |
| Uganda | 9,419 | 39% | 15% | 2.9% | 14.0% | 192 | 1.9% |
| Ukraine | 106,469 | 79% | 20% | 9.1% | 0.5% | 1,723 | 1.6% |
| United Arab Emirates | 129,702 | – | – | – | 0.0% | 9,482 | 6.7% |
| United Kingdom | 2,376,984 | 45% | 17% | 7.2% | – | 55,444 | 2.3% |
| United States | 13,163,870 | 22% | 6% | 0.9% | – | 535,943 | 4.0% |
| Uruguay | 19,308 | 46% | 11% | 4.3% | 0.1% | 227 | 1.2% |
| Uzbekistan | 17,178 | 54% | – | 0.3% | 1.2% | 85 | 0.5% |
| Vanuatu | 388 | 50% | 49% | 3.6% | 11.5% | – | – |
| Venezuela | 181,862 | 51% | 4% | 2.0% | 0.0% | 2,588 | 1.4% |
| Vietnam | 60,999 | 138% | 18% | 3.7% | 3.7% | 3,439 | 5.6% |
| Yemen | 19,057 | 73% | 9% | −1.6% | 2.2% | 824 | 4.2% |
| Zambia | 10,734 | 61% | 14% | 3.6% | 13.9% | 245 | 2.4% |
| Zimbabwe | – | 80% | – | 3.0% | 11.4% | 156 | 2.8% |

* Data for Serbia and Montenegro that pre-date their separation in 2006 apply to the country as a single entity.

# Economy and Environment

| Energy Use Oil equivalent 2004 | | CO$_2$ Emissions Tonnes of CO$_2$ 2004 | | Water | | Countries |
|---|---|---|---|---|---|---|
| total tonnes | kg per capita | total | per capita | Cubic metres of annual renewable water available per capita 2007 | Cubic metres withdrawn per capita 2007 | |
| – | – | 0.6 | 0.1 | 551 | 18 | Rwanda |
| – | – | 0.2 | 0.8 | – | – | Samoa |
| – | – | 0.1 | 0.6 | 13,293 | 51 | São Tomé and Principe |
| 140 | 6,232 | 342.9 | 15.2 | 93 | 736 | Saudi Arabia |
| 3 | 242 | 5.1 | 0.4 | 3,225 | 225 | Senegal |
| – | – | 56.7 | 7.0 | 19,870 | – | Serbia* |
| – | – | 0.5 | 6.5 | – | 150 | Seychelles |
| – | – | 1.1 | 0.2 | 27,577 | 80 | Sierra Leone |
| 26 | 6,034 | 50.1 | 11.8 | 135 | 82 | Singapore |
| 18 | 3,407 | 39.8 | 7.4 | 9,276 | – | Slovakia |
| 7 | 3,591 | 16.3 | 8.2 | 16,219 | – | Slovenia |
| – | – | 0.2 | 0.4 | 89,044 | – | Solomon Islands |
| – | – | – | – | 1,620 | 307 | Somalia |
| 131 | 2,829 | 427.9 | 9.2 | 1,048 | 279 | South Africa |
| 142 | 3,331 | 355.1 | 8.3 | 2,557 | 870 | Spain |
| 9 | 485 | 13.1 | 0.7 | 2,372 | 666 | Sri Lanka |
| – | – | 0.1 | 2.7 | 546 | – | St. Kitts and Nevis |
| – | – | 0.4 | 2.3 | – | 109 | St. Lucia |
| – | – | 0.2 | 1.7 | – | 86 | St. Vincent and Grenadines |
| 18 | 497 | 10.8 | 0.3 | 1,707 | 1,135 | Sudan |
| – | – | 2.3 | 5.2 | 268,132 | 1,551 | Suriname |
| – | – | 1.0 | 0.9 | 4,400 | 975 | Swaziland |
| 54 | 5,998 | 56.1 | 6.2 | 19,131 | 335 | Sweden |
| 27 | 3,672 | 44.6 | 6.0 | 7,354 | 358 | Switzerland |
| 18 | 993 | 51.7 | 2.8 | 1,314 | 1,148 | Syria |
| 3 | 516 | 5.5 | 0.9 | 2,392 | 1,931 | Tajikistan |
| 19 | 500 | 4.5 | 0.1 | 2,291 | 143 | Tanzania |
| 97 | 1,524 | 238.5 | 3.7 | 6,280 | 1,400 | Thailand |
| 3 | 449 | 2.3 | 0.4 | 2,272 | 35 | Togo |
| – | – | 0.1 | 1.1 | – | – | Tonga |
| 11 | 8,675 | 21.8 | 16.8 | 2,925 | 239 | Trinidad and Tobago |
| 9 | 876 | 23.8 | 2.4 | 442 | 271 | Tunisia |
| 82 | 1,151 | 229.2 | 3.2 | 3,051 | 534 | Turkey |
| 16 | 3,265 | 39.5 | 8.3 | 4,979 | 5,140 | Turkmenistan |
| – | – | 2.1 | 0.1 | 2,133 | 12 | Uganda |
| 140 | 2,958 | 329.6 | 6.9 | 3,066 | 767 | Ukraine |
| 44 | 10,142 | 104.0 | 24.1 | 31 | 787 | United Arab Emirates |
| 234 | 3,906 | 551.3 | 9.0 | 2,449 | 161 | United Kingdom |
| 2,326 | 7,920 | 5,888.7 | 20.0 | 6,816 | 1,647 | United States |
| 3 | 867 | 6.0 | 1.7 | 39,612 | 929 | Uruguay |
| 54 | 2,088 | 131.9 | 5.1 | 1,842 | 2,269 | Uzbekistan |
| – | – | 0.1 | 0.4 | – | – | Vanuatu |
| 56 | 2,149 | 140.2 | 5.4 | 44,545 | 332 | Venezuela |
| 50 | 612 | 91.8 | 1.1 | 10,310 | 889 | Vietnam |
| 6 | 313 | 19.2 | 0.9 | 184 | 343 | Yemen |
| 7 | 605 | 2.4 | 0.2 | 8,726 | 163 | Zambia |
| 9 | 719 | 10.0 | 0.8 | 1,520 | 328 | Zimbabwe |

137

# Sources

For sources available on the internet, in most cases only the root address has been given. To view the source, it is recommended that the reader type the title of the page or document into Google or another search engine.

## Introduction

**Dependent population**
UN Population Division. World Population Prospects. The 2006 Revision. http://esa.un.org/unpp

**Causes of death**
WHO. World Health Report 2004. www.who.int

**Energy production**
International Energy Agency: World Energy Statistics 2007. www.iea.org

## Part One: Who We Are

### 18–19 Population
**People in the world**
Population cartogram created by: ODT, Inc. www.odtmaps.com using data from US State Department.

Annual percentage change: WDI online database.

**Population growth**
CIA Factbook. www.cia.gov

### 20–21 Life Expectancy
**Life expectancy**
**Changing expectancy**
**Health and wealth**
**World average life expectancy**
World Bank estimates from sources including census reports, UN Population Division's World Population Prospects, national statistic offices, household surveys conducted by national agencies, and Macro International. Downloaded from WDI online. Data for Afghanistan and Iraq from: State of the world's children. 2007. New York: UNICEF 2006.
GNI in purchasing power parity dollars from WDI Online.

**The average lifespan...**
Kinsella KG. Changes in life expectancy 1900–1990. The American Journal of Clinical Nutrition.1992;55:1196S-1202S. www.ajcn.org

### 22–23 Ethnicity and Diversity
Turner B. The statesman's yearbook 2008: the politics, cultures and economies of the world. London: Palgrave Macmillan; 2007.
MSN Encarta encyclopaedia. http://encarta.msn.com
US Central Intelligence Agency. The world factbook. www.cia.gov
Refugees International. www.refugeesinternational.org

### 24–25 Religious Beliefs
O'Brien J, Palmer M. The atlas of religion. London: Earthscan. Berkeley and Los Angeles: University of California Press; 2007
CIA. The World Factbook

### 26–27 Education
**Primary education**
**Secondary education**
**Tertiary education**
United Nations Educational, Scientific, and Cultural Organization (UNESCO) Institute for Statistics. Downloaded from World Development Indicators online database.

**Adult literacy**
**Bangladesh and India**
UNDP. Human Development Report 2007/08. Table 1.

**Sub-Saharan Africa**
**57% of children...**
UNDP. Human Development Report 2007/08. Table 30.

### 28–29 Urbanization
UN World Urbanization Prospects. Downloaded from WDI online.
**50% of people...**
State of the world's cities 2006/7. London: Earthscan for UN-Habitat; 2006.

### 30–31 Diversity of Cities
Global Cities: Exhibition at Tate Modern, London, June–August 2007 www.tate.org.uk
City Mayors Statistics www.citymayors.com
State of the world's cities 2006/7. London: Earthscan for UN-Habitat; 2006.
Encarta online encyclopaedia: http://encarta.msn.com

### 32–33 Global Movement
UN Department of Economic and Social Affairs. Population Division. International Migration 2006.

## Part Two: Wealth and Power

### 36–37 Gross National Income
All data downloaded from WDI online database.

### 38–39 Inequality
**Distribution of wealth**
Gini index: WDI online.
Unemployment: Human Development Report 2007/2008. Fighting climate change: Human solidarity in a divided world. New York: UNDP; 2007. Table 21.
**Russia** – New York Times. 2007 Nov 29, quoting Forbes Rich List and World Bank.
**South Africa** – Merill Lynch/Capgemini 11th World Wealth Report, quoted in: South Africa the Good News. 2 July 2007 July 2. www.sagoodnews.co.za
**USA** – Forbes Rich List 2008 and calculation based on Human Development Report 2007/2008. New York: UNDP; 2007. Table 4: Human and income poverty.

**Poor people in rich countries**
Human Development Report 2007/2008. Table 4.

**In the hands of the few**
Forbes Rich List 2008  www.forbes.com

**The wealth of the 100 richest people...**
www.forbes.com
World Bank.

### 40–41 Quality of Life
**Relative human development**
UNDP. Human development report 2007–08. Fighting climate change: Human solidarity in a divided world. New York: UNDP; 2007. Table 1: Human development index.

**Healthy water**
UNDP. Human Development Report 2006. Beyond scarcity: Power, poverty and the global water crisis. New York: UNDP; 2006.

**Poor sanitation...**
State of the world's cities 2006/7. London: Earthscan for UN-Habitat; 2006.

### 42–43 Transnationals
**Corporate wealth**
GNI (current US$) 2006 from WDI online database.
Forbes 2000 largest companies by assets. 2007 March. www.forbes.com/lists.

**The global mix**
United Nations Conference on Trade and Development (UNCTAD). World investment report 2007, Annex table A.I.5.

**1.8 million people...**
UNCTAD. World investment report 2007, Annex Table A.I.13.

**Global players**
UNCTAD. World investment report 2007. Annex A, Table A.I.16 and A.I.15. The top 100 TNCs and non-TNCs by the number of host countries.

### 44–45 Foreign Investment
Elliott, L. Oil money is coming – and there is little the West can do about it. The Guardian. 2008 March 1:40-41.

**Importance of inward investment**
WDI online.

**Attractiveness to investors**
United Nations Conference on Trade and Development (UNCTAD). Inward FDI Indices. www.unctad.org

### 46–47 Trade
**Importance of trade**
World Trade Organization and World Bank GDP estimates.
**Merchandise exports**
**Changing places**
WTO. International Trade Statistics 2008. Table II.2. World merchandise exports by major product group and region, 2006. www.wto.org
**World trade in merchandise grew...**
WTO 2008 op.cit. Table 1.6.

### 48–49 Communications
OECD Factbook 2007. Telephone access.
**Telephones**
**In Africa**
International Telecommunications Union (ITU) via WDI online.
OECD Factbook 2007. Telephone access.
**Where the money is made**
OECD. Communications Outlook 2007.
**Internet access**
International Telecommunications Union (ITU). Accessed via WDI online database.
**Most popular internet search engines**
**Searchers**
comScore via BBC News. Google dominates world search. 2007 October 11. http://news.bbc.co.uk
**Mobiles in Africa**
International Telecommunications Union (ITU).

### 50–51 Energy Trade
IEA. World Energy Outlook 2007. Executive Summary. www.iea.org
**Who holds the power?**
International Energy Agency and United Nations, Energy statistics yearbook. Downloaded from WDI online.
**USA** – US Department of Energy. Biomass. FAQs. www1.eere.energy.gov
**Germany, Ukraine** – BBC. Russian gas cut will not hit EU. 2005 Dec 30. http://news.bbc.co.uk
**Russia** – BBC. Russia plants flag under North Pole. 2007 Aug 2. http://news.bbc.co.uk
BBC. Russia ahead in Arctic gold rush. 2007 Aug 1. http://news.bbc.co.uk
**Japan** – International Energy Agency and United Nations, Energy statistics yearbook.
**China** – China Institute, University of Alberta. China's crude oil imports up 12.3 pct in 2007. www.uofaweb.ualberta.ca

### 52–53 Tourism
World Tourism Organization. Yearbook of tourism statistics, compendium of tourism statistics and data files, and IMF and World Bank exports estimates.

### 54–55 Debt and Aid
**Aid received**
**Debt servicing costs**
Development Assistance Committee of the Organisation for Economic Co-operation and Development, and World Bank GNI estimates. Downloaded from WDI online.
**Official development assistance**
**Falling short**
HDR 2007/08 Table 17. OECD-DAC country expenditures on aid
**Only 3% of money...**
www.aafrc.org
NCVO, CAF. Results of the 2006/07 Individual Giving Survey on charitable giving with special reports on gender and causes. www.ncvo-vol.org.uk

## Part Three: War and Peace
### 58–59 War in the 21st Century
Smith D. The atlas of war & peace. New York: Penguin and London: Earthscan; 2003.
Uppsala University, Uppsala Conflict Data Program. www.pcr.uu.se

### 60–61 Warlords and Militias
**Non-state wars**
**Number of non-state wars**
Uppsala University, Uppsala Conflict Data Program. www.pcr.uu.se
Press reports.
**Child soldiers**
Coalition to Stop the Use of Child Soldiers. Global report 2004. 222.child-soldiers.org, cited in The World Bank and Human Security Report Project. Miniatlas of human security. 2008.
**Campaigns of violence against civilian populations**
Uppsala Conflict Data Program, Uppsala University/Human Security Report Projects dataset, 2006.

### 62–63 Terrorism
BBC world news http://news.bbc.co.uk
Country reports by International Crisis Group. www.crisisgroup.org
Press reports.

### 64–65 Military Spending
**Military spending**
**Total military spending**
International Institute for Strategic Studies (IISS). The military balance 2008. London: Routledge; 2008. Table 37.
**Arms transfer agreements**
Grimmett RF. Conventional arms transfers to developing nations 1999–2006. Figure 1. Washington DC: Congressional Research Service http://opencrs.com/document/RL34187.
**Recipients of arms transfers**
Grimmett RF. op. cit. Tables 1C and 1E.

### 66–67 Armed Forces
**Armed forces**
International Institute for Strategic Studies (IISS). The military balance 2008. London: Routledge; 2008. Table 37.
**Conscription**
The military balance 2008.
US Central Intelligence Agency. The World Factbook. www.cia.gov
**Total number of active military personnel...**
The military balance 2008. Table 37.
**Warlords and militias**
The military balance 2008. Table 47.

### 68–69 Peacekeeping
UN Peacekeeping. www.un.org/Depts/dpko/dpko
Department of Political Affairs. www0.un.org/Depts/dpa/fieldmissions.html
IISS. The military balance 2008. London. IISS; 2008.

### 70–71 Casualties of War
**Battle deaths since World War II**
**Battle deaths in the 21st century**
UCDP/PRIO Armed Conflict dataset v.4-2007, 1946–2006. www.prio.no
**Deaths in Iraq**
Iraq Body Count. www.iraqbodycount.net/database
Iraq Coalition Casualties. www.icasualties.org
Burnham G, Lafta R, Doocy S, Roberts L. Mortality after the 2003 invasion of Iraq: a cross-sectional cluster sample survey. The Lancet; 2006 October 11.
Iraqi health minister estimates as many as 150,000 Iraqis killed by insurgents. International Herald Tribune. 2006 November 9.
Iraq poll 2007: in graphics. BBC News. 2007 March 19. http://news.bbc.co.uk
More than 1,000,000 Iraqis murdered. 2007 September. Opinion Research Business. www.opinion.co.uk
Update on Iraqi Casualty Data. Opinion Research Business, 2008 January. www.opinion.co.uk
**The deadliest conflicts**
Death tolls for the major wars and atrocities of the twentieth century. http://users.erols.com/mwhite28/warstat2.htm
**Persistent killers**
International Campaign to Ban Landmines. Landmine monitor report 2007: toward a mine-free world. www.icbl.org

### 72–73 Refugees
United Nations High Commissioner for Refugees. UNHCR statistical yearbook 2006. www.unhcr.org/statistics.html

United Nations Relief and Works Agency for Palestinian Refugees in the Near East. Map of UNRWA's Area of Operations. www.un.org/unrwa/refugees/images/map.jpg

US Committee for Refugees and Immigrants. World refugee survey 2007. www.refugees.org

### 74–75 Global Peace
Vision of Humanity: Global Peace Index. www.visionofhumanity.org

# Part Four: Rights and Respect

### 78–79 Political Systems
**Political systems**
Country reports of the International Crisis Group, Brussels. www.icg.org

Human Development Report 2007/2008. New York: United Nations Development Programme; 2007.

BBC News http://news.bbc.co.uk/1/hi/world

**Voter turnout**
International Idea. www.idea.int

### 80–81 Religious Freedom
O'Brien J, Palmer M. The atlas of religion. London: Earthscan, Los Angeles and Berkeley: University of California Press; 2007.

### 82–83 Press Freedom
**Freedom of the press**
**Press freedom**
**Only 18%...**
Freedom House. Freedom of the press 2008. www.freedomhouse.org

**Journalists murdered**
International Federation of Journalists. Journalists put to the sword in 2006. IFJ 2007. www.ifj.org

### 84–85 Human Rights Abuses
**Extreme abuse of human rights**
Amnesty International report 2008: The state of the world's human rights. London: Amnesty International; 2008.

Amnesty International. "Rendition" and secret detention: A global system of human rights violations. Questions and answers. London: Amnesty International; 2006.

Human Rights Watch country reports  www.hrw.org

Human Rights Watch World Report 2007 www.hrw.org

**Extraordinary rendition**
Council of Europe, Alleged secret detentions and unlawful inter-state transfers of detainees involving Council of Europe member states; Report by the Committee on Legal Affairs and Human Rights (Rapporteur: Mr Dick Marty). Doc. 10957. 2006 June 12. www.coe.int

Secret detentions and illegal transfers of detainees involving Council of Europe member states; Second report by the Committee on Legal Affairs and Human Rights (Rapporteur: Mr Dick Marty), Doc. 11302. rev, 2007 June 11. www.coe.int

**2001–08 Guantanamo**
GlobalSecurity.org 2008 May 02.

**Executions**
Death sentences and executions in 2007. AI Index: ACT 50/001/2008. London: Amnesty International Secretariat; 2008 April 15.

**Judicial killings**
Amnesty International USA, 1 January 2007. www.amnestyusa.org
World moves closer to abolition of the death penalty. Amnesty International USA. www.amnestyusa.org

Death penalty laws in your state. www.amnestyusa.org

### 86–87 Trafficking and Sex Tourism
**Trafficking**
**Trafficking exists...**
Child trafficking in Europe: a broad vision to put children first. United Nations Children's Fund Innocenti Research Centre; 2008. www.unicef-irc.org

Trafficking in human beings, especially women and children, in Africa. United Nations Children's Fund Innocenti Research Centre: 2005. www.unicef-irc.org

**Travelling Sex Offenders**
**Legislation**
Draft working paper on the prevention of sexual exploitation of children in travel and tourism. United Nations Children's Fund

Innocenti Research Centre; Forthcoming publication 2008.
Some countries are mainly reported to be origin of travelling sex offenders, while others are mainly reported as destinations. Some countries may be origin and destination at the same time. For others, information is not yet available.
**Caribbean trafficking routes**
**Guatemala**
**Mexico**
In modern bondage: sex trafficking in the Americas. International Human Rights Law Institute, DePaul University College of Law. 2002 October.

**Australia, Japan, New Zealand** – Prostitution of children and child-sex tourism. an analysis of domestic and international responses. National Centre for Missing and Exploited Children; 1999.

**Eastern Europe, Men known as "lover boys"...**
Child trafficking in Europe. op. cit.

**Brazil** –Mattar MY. The role of the government in combating trafficking in persons - a global human rights approach; 2003 October 29. www.protectionproject.org/commentary/ctp.htm

**Cambodia, Thailand** – Regional consultation for Asia and the Pacific on the protection of children from sexual exploitation in tourism. World Tourism Organization (UNWTO); 2003:82.

**Canada** – Global Monitoring Report on the status of action against commercial sexual exploitation of children. ECPAT; 2006:11.

**Lithuania** – Looking back, thinking forward: the fourth report on the implementation of the agenda for action adopted at the First World Congress against Commercial Sexual Exploitation of Children. Stockholm, Sweden, 1996. Stockholm: Swedish International Development Agency; 1999-2000.

**UK** – Sexual Offences Act 2003. Chapter 42, Section 114

**Over 1.2 million children...**
ILO: A Future Without Child Labour; 2002.

### 88–89 Children's Rights
**Birth registration**
UNICEF Statistics. Birth Registration. www.childinfo.org
**Children not in school**
**Where children are working**
**Although the number...**
Hagemann F, Diallo Y, Etienne A, Mehran F. Global child labour trends 2000 to 2004. ILO; 2006. www.ilo.org
See also: www.ilo.org/ipec/index.htm

### 90–91 Women's Rights
**Equal rights**
UNDP. Human development report 2007/2008. Fighting climate change: human solidarity in a divided world. New York: UNDP; 2007.

**National parliament**
UN Women's Indicators and Statistics Database, downloaded from WDI online.

**Only 35 countries have...**
Seager J. The atlas of women. Berkeley: University of California Press and London: Earthscan; 2009.

**In Norway it is a legal requirement...**
Fouche G, Treanor J. In Norway, a woman's place is in the boardroom. 2006 January 9. www.guardian.co.uk

**Women earners**
HDR 2007/2008. Table 31. Gender inequality in economic activity.

### 92–93 Gay Rights
**Legislation on homosexuality**
The Guardian 2007 April 14. pp.20–21, based on: Ottosson D. State-sponsored homophobia. A world survey of laws prohibiting same-sex activity between consenting adults. ILGA; 2007. www.ilga.org  Cross-checked and updated against:

Johnson R. Where is gay life legal? http://gaylife.about.com

Grossman CL. Gay civil union not as divisive as marriage. www.usatoday.com

LGBT adoption. en.wikipedia.org/wiki/LGBT_adoption

# Part Five Health of the People

### 96–97 Malnutrition
WHO. Micronutrient deficiencies. www.who.int

### Undernourished people
UNDP. Human development report 2007/2008. Fighting climate change: human solidarity in a divided world. New York: UNDP; 2007. Table 7.

Johns Hopkins Bloomberg School of Public Health. Tables on the global burden of Vitamin A deficiency. www.jhsph.edu

West KP. Extent of vitamin A deficiency among preschool children and women of reproductive age. Journal of Nutrition 2002;132:2857S-2866S.

http://iodinenetwork.net/Score_Card/Score_Card_2006.html

FAO. Crop prospects and food situation; 2008(1). Table A4. p.34-35. www.fao.org

### Poor nutrition in babies and children...
www.wfp.org/english

### Food price rises...
Food riots fear after rice price hits a high. The Observer. 2008 April 6. www.guardian.co.uk

## 98–99 Obesity
### America's spreading obesity
Centers for Disease Control. Obesity trends among US adults between 1985 and 2006. Based on data from the Division of Nutrition, Physical Activity and Obesity. Powerpoint slideshow. www.cdc.gov

### Overweight adults
WHO Global Infobase www.who.int

**England** – Jotangia D, Moody A, Stamatakis E, Wardle H. Obesity among children under 11. National Centre for Social Research, UCL; revised 2006. www.dh.gov.uk

**USA** – Centers for Disease Control.

**Australia** – Obesity a public catastrophe, say researchers. Irish Times. 2008 March 11.

### Increased risk of disease
CHD and stroke: WHO. World Health Report 2002. Geneva: WHO; 2004. 57-61.

Cancer: National Cancer Institute. Obesity and cancer: questions and answers. www.cancer.gov

Diabetes: Department of Health. Obesity general information. www.dh.gov.uk

## 100–01 Smoking
Why is tobacco a public health priority? www.who.int

McGreal.C. Nigeria takes on big tobacco over campaigns that target the young. The Guardian. 2008 Jan 15. p.23.

### Deaths
Ezzati M, Lopez A. Mortality and burden of disease attributable to smoking and oral tobacco use: global and regional estimates for 2000. In: Comparative risk assessment. Geneva: World Health Organization; 2000.

### Global cigarette consumption
Guindon GE., Boisclair D. Cigarette consumption dataset 1970–2004. Prepared for the American Cancer Society. 2005.

Proctor RN. personal communication to Mackay J, Eriksen M, Shafey O. The tobacco atlas, 2nd ed. Atlanta, Georgia: The American Cancer Society; 2006.

McGinn AP. The nicotine cartel. WorldWatch 1997;10(4):18–27.

### The number of young smokers...
GYTS Collaborating Group. Differences in worldwide tobacco use by gender: findings from the Global Youth Tobacco Survey. J Sch Health 2003;73:207–15.

### Smoking among adults
Mackay J. et al. The cancer atlas. Atlanta, Georgia: American Cancer Society; 2006.

### Tobacco causes 10%...
Why is tobacco a public health priority? www.who.int/tobacco/health_priority/en/index.html

**India** – Gajalakshmi V, Peto R, Kanaka TS & Jha P, Smoking and mortality from tuberculosis and other diseases in India: retrospective study of 43,000 adult male deaths and 35,000 controls. Lancet 2003;362:507–15.

### Although fewer women smoke...
Asia: Growing smoking epidemic among young women. WHO. 1999 Nov.

## 102–03 Cancer
Ferlay J, Bray F, Pisani P, Parkin DM. GLOBOCAN 2002: Cancer incidence, mortality and prevalence worldwide. IARC CancerBase No. 5. version 2.0, IARCPress, Lyon, 2004.

## 104–05 HIV/AIDS
UNAIDS/WHO. UNAIDS epidemic update 07. www.unaids.org/en

UNAIDS/WHO. 2006 Report on the global AIDS epidemic.

# Part Six: Health of the Planet
## 108–09 Biodiversity
### Mammals, birds, plants
International Union for Conservation of Nature and Natural Resources (IUCN). 2006. 2006 IUCN Red List of Threatened Species. Gland, Switzerland: IUCN. www.redlist.org

### Panamanian golden frog
BBC News. 'Last wave' for wild golden frog. 2008 Feb 2. http://news.bbc.co.uk

### Protected areas
United Nations Environment Programme - World Conservation Monitoring Centre (UNEP-WCMC). 2004. World Database on Protected Areas (WDPA). http://sea.unep-wcmc.org/wdpa

### Threatened species
2006 IUCN Red List of Threatened Species.

### Rainforest loss
FAO. Global forest resources assessment. Downloaded from WDI online. www.mongabay.com

## 110–11 Water Resources
Comprehensive Assessment of Water in Agriculture. Water for food, water for life. Colombo, Sri Lanka: International Water Management Institute; 2006.

### Water available
### Water used
### Regional water use
FAO Aquastat. www.fao.org

### 70% of food emergencies . . .
FAO. Water at a glance. www.fao.org

## 112–13 Waste
### Nuclear waste
OECD statistics. www.oecd.org/statsportal

### Nuclear power
Australian Uranium Association. Nuclear power in the world today. Nuclear issues briefing paper 7. 2007 Aug. www.uic.com.au

**Japanese nuclear waste** – Australian Uranium Association. Japanese waste and MOX shipments from Europe. Nuclear issues briefing paper 23. 2007 Aug. www.uic.com.au

**US nuclear waste** – Spent nuclear fuel. Table 3. Annual spent fuel discharges and burnup, 1968-2002. www.eia.doe.gov

### Household waste
OECD Statistics. www.oecd.org/statsportal

### Plastic bags
Lowy J. Plastic left holding the bag as environmental plague. 2004 July 21. Seattle Post-Intelligence. www.commondreams.org

CBC News. It's official. Manitoba gives plastic bags the boot. 2007 April 2. www.cbc.ca

Plastic bags. www.worldwatch.org

Lynch N. The Green Room. Plastic Bags. Banned in Italy. Taxed in Belgium. http://theonlygreenroom.blogspot.com

Doan A. Africa wages war on plastic bags. inhabitat. 2007 Dec 17. www.inhabitat.com

### Great Pacific Garbage Patch
Algalitha Marine Research Foundation. www.algalita.org

Marks K, Howden D. The world's rubbish dump: a garbage tip that stretches from Hawaii to Japan. The Independent. 2008 Feb 5. www.independent.co.uk

**Ireland** – Irish bag tax hailed a success. 2002 Aug 20. http://news.bbc.co.uk

**Flooding** – Kalpana Sharma. Mumbai after the rain: piecemeal policies. The Hindu. 2005 Sept 9. www.sabrang.com

**Southern Ocean** – Australian Antarctic Division. www.aad.gov.au/default.asp?casid=14824

### One third of the world's electronics...
Goldstein J. China's international recycling trade. 2007 Aug 29. http://china.usc.edu

China International Plastic Recycling Forum 2008. www.recycle-china.com.cn/maoyien

## 114–15 Energy Use
**Total energy use**
**Energy use per capita**
International Energy Agency (IEA). Downloaded from WDI online.
**China** – China Statistical Yearbook 2007.
**Greenhouse gas emissions**
WRI, Climate Analysis Indicators Tool (CAIT). http://cait.wri.org
**83% of energy...**
**4% of energy...**
International Energy Agency: World Energy Statistics 2007. www.iea.org
**The world's oil production**
**Cars**
Feldman S. Massive global car growth to crash into peak oil. Solve Climate. 2008 Jan 25. www.solveclimate.com
**Renewable power**
**Wind power**
Martinot E. Renewables. global status report 2006 update. Renewable Energy Policy Network for 21st Century. www.ren21.net

## 116–17 Climate Change
**Extreme events**
Emergency Events Database. Centre for Research on the Epidemiology of Disasters (CRED). Université Catholique de Louvain – Ecole de Santé Publique.

Disasters are defined as events in which at least one of the following occurs: 10 or more people are killed, 100 or more are affected, there is a declaration of a state of emergency or a call for international assistance.
**Risk of armed conflict**
Smith D and Vivekananda J. A climate of conflict. op. cit.
**Exposure to climate change**
IPCC. Cited in Smith D and Vivekananda J. A climate of conflict. The links between climate change, peace and war. International Alert; 2007.

## 118–19 Warning Signs
**Alaskan permafrost**
Arctic Climate Impact Assessment (ACIA). Impacts of a warming Arctic. Cambridge University Press: 2004.

Reuters. Warming climate disrupts Alaska natives' lives, quoting Gunter Weller, director of the University of Alaska Fairbanks' Center for Global Change and Arctic System Research, 2004. www.planetark.com/dailynewsstory.cfm/newsid/24761/story.htm
**Atlantic hurricanes**
National Oceanographic and Atmosphere Administration. US Department of Commerce. NOAA reviews record-setting 2005 Atlantic hurricane season. www.noaanews.noaa.gov
**Asian summer monsoon**
World Meteorological Organization (WMO), statement on the status of global climate, 2004.
**Canadian polar bears**
World Meteorological Organization (WMO). Statement on the status of the global climate in 2006. WMO-No. 1016. Geneva, Switzerland, 2007. www.wmo.ch
**Coral bleaching**
Wilkinson C et al, International Society for Reef Studies (ISRS), Ecological and socioeconomic impacts of 1998 coral mortality in the Indian Ocean: An ENSO impact and a warning of future change? Ambio 1999:28;188–96.
ISRS. statement on global coral bleaching in 1997–98. www.uncwil.edu/isrs
**Drought in Australia**
Walker G & King D. The hot topic. London: Bloomsbury; 2008.
Human development report 2007/2008: fighting climate change: human solidarity in a divided world. New York: Palgrave Macmillan for the United Nations Development Programme; 2007.
**Drought in Africa**
**Drought in China**
**Drought in Southern Brazil**
WMO 2007. op.cit.
**European butterfly ranges**
Parmesan C et al, Poleward shifts in geographical ranges of butterfly species associated with regional warming. Nature 1999;399:579-83.
**European heatwave**
International Federation of Red Cross and Red Crescent Societies. Heatwaves: the developed world's hidden disaster. www.ifrc.org
**Extinction**
Walker G & King D. 2008 op. cit.
Human development report 2007/2008. op. cit.
**Floods in Bolivia**
WMO 2007. op. cit.
**Floods in China**
ACT Appeal China: Assistance to flood-affected ASCN52. www.reliefweb.int
**Larsen B ice shelf**
Larsen B Ice Shelf Collapses in Antarctica. www.nsidc.org
Rignot E. Changes in ice dynamics and mass balance of the Antarctic ice sheet. Philosophical Transactions of the Royal Society A: Mathematical Physical and Engineering Sciences 2006:364;1637-55.
**Madagascan Lemurs**
Walker G & King D. 2008 op.cit.
**Malaria**
Human development report 2007/2008. op. cit.
**North American mosquitoes**
Bradshaw WE, Holzapfel CM. Genetic shift in photoperiodic response correlated to global warming. Proceedings of the National Academy of Sciences of the United States of America (PNAS) 2001. www.pnas.org
**Siberian melt**
S N Kirpotin et al, Sub-Arctic palsas as indicator of climatic changes, INTAS report 2005 from Tomsk State University, Tomsk, Russia; Institute of Soil Science and Agrochemistry of the Siberian branch of Russian Academy of Science, Novosibirsk, Russia; Yugorskiy State University, Khanty–Mansiysk, Russia; University of Utrecht, Utrecht, Netherlands.
**South Asian cyclone**
Burma's rejection of aid has led to death of thousands, says US. 2008 May 31. www.guardian.co.uk
**South Asian heatwave**
World Meteorological Organization (WMO), statement on the status of global climate, 2004. Time-lag
**South Atlantic hurricane**
Catarina hits Brazil. www.metoffice.com
**Time-lag**
**Tropical Andes**
Walker G & King D. 2008 op.cit.
Human development report 2007/2008. op. cit.

# Part Seven: Vital Statistics
## 122–29 Table 1: Indicators of Wellbeing
**Official capital** http://geography.about.com; www.infoplease.com; CIA World Factbook
**Land area** UN Food & Agriculture Organization.
**Population total** See source for map on pp18–19.
**Urban population** See source for map on pp28–29.
**Migrants** See source for map on pp32–33.
**Life expectancy** See source for map on pp20–21.
**Gross National Income, Maternal mortality** WDI online database.
**Water Access** UNDP Human Development Report 2007.
**Literacy, Education, Undernourished people** Human development report 2007.

## 130–37 Table 2: Economy and Environment
**GDP, Investment, Aid, Energy Use** WDI online.
**Trade** World Trade Organization and World Bank GDP estimates.
**Military expenditure** International Institute for Strategic Studies (IISS). The military balance 2008. London: Routledge; 2008.
**$CO_2$ emissions** World Resources Institute, Climate Analysis Indicators Tool (CAIT). http://cait.wri.org
**Water** FAO Aquastat. www.fao.org

# Index